Tom Hopkins knows what it takes to be in sales.

"*Hopkins' Guide to Greatness in Sales* defines the real meaning of success—balance, control, good health, financial freedom, and above all, more peace of mind. Who doesn't need this book?"
—Danielle Kennedy, *author of* Selling— The Danielle Kennedy Way

"One of the greatest motivational speakers on the American platform today. . . . It has encouraged me that this brilliant speaker and writer persuades his readers and listeners to employ the principles of positive thinking in their own lives."
—Dr. Norman Vincent Peale

"The ideas and skills Tom Hopkins shares are made real by the way he shows how to apply them to real-life situations. Which is the bottom line to effective teaching in any situation."
—Warren Sloop, Farmers Insurance Group

"Tom Hopkins' method of visual aid, written work, and instructor guidance is superior to anything I have seen or read pertinent to salesmanship."
—V. T. Hutchinson, Pitney Bowes

"Without a doubt, the Tom Hopkins program is the finest I have experienced. It *does* relate to any marketplace."
—Peter Schwartz, Gould, Inc.

"Tom Hopkins is a one-man motivational blitzkrieg and perhaps the most visible exponent of the sales-training movement."
—America West *magazine*

Other best-selling titles by Tom Hopkins

How to Master the Art of Selling

The Official Guide to Success

How to Master the Art of Listing Real Estate

How to Master the Art of Selling Real Estate

TOM HOPKINS' GUIDE TO GREATNESS IN SALES

How to Become a Complete Salesperson

**With a Foreword
by Zig Ziglar**

Edited by Warren Jamison

WARNER BOOKS

A Time Warner Company

Portions of this book have appeared as copyrighted cassette recordings and videotape.

Warner Books Edition
Copyright © 1992 by Tom Hopkins International, Inc.

This Warner Books edition is published by arrangement with Tom Hopkins International, Inc.

Warner Books, Inc., 1271 Avenue of the Americas, New York, NY 10020

W A Time Warner Company

Printed in the United States of America

First Warner Books Printing: July 1993

10 9 8 7 6 5 4 3 2

Hopkins, Tom.
    [Guide to greatness in sales]
    Tom Hopkins' Guide to greatness in sales : how to become a complete salesperson / Tom Hopkins. — Warner Books ed.
        p. cm.
    "This Warner Books edition is published by arrangement with Tom Hopkins International, Inc."—T.p. verso.
    ISBN 0-446-39370-3
    1. Selling—Vocational guidance. I. Title. II. Title: Guide to greatness in sales.
HF5438.25.H658 1993
658.8′5′02373—dc20   92-35511
                                                      CIP

Cover by Michèle Brinson
Cover photo by Kevin Cruff

Book design: H. Roberts

To my devoted wife, Debbie, whose love and understanding have allowed me to become a person able to influence the lives of many. Without her support, the achievement of many of my goals would not have transpired.

CONTENTS

THE WRONG REASONS:
Big Money • I Really Like Cars • My Own Boss • The
Gift of Gab • Selling Is Easy Work • Meeting New
People • No More Studying • Nobody Will Know When I
Goof Off • I Really Like People
THE RIGHT REASONS:
It's Fun • Your Skills Are Portable • In Demand • No
Income Ceilings • Low Capital Investment • It's
Challenging • Individual Initiative • It's Satisfying •
Unlimited Personal Growth

CHAPTER SIX
YOUR BOSS OR YOUR COMPANY *90*

Loyalty When Your Boss Gets Fired • Conspiracy's
Lure • When You Know Someone Is Stealing From the
Company

CHAPTER SEVEN
MAKING THE RIGHT STAY-OR-QUIT DECISION *102*

Appraising Your Current Situation • The Two Sides of Job
Changing • How to Get the Best Results When Facing the
Big Question (The Ben Franklin Decision-Making
Method) • A Soft Exit Avoids a Hard Fall

CHAPTER EIGHT
STRATEGIES FOR PUTTING YOURSELF
IN A STRONGER POSITION *110*

Get Rid of Self-Imposed Restrictions • Work for a
Company That Appreciates Salespeople • Be Prepared to
Be a Professional • Pull Ahead Faster Using the Law of
Effect • Protect Yourself From Becoming Ineffective •
Shoddy Appearance Can Kill You in Selling • Dressing
Yourself Right Out of Sales

CHAPTER NINE
TRANSITIONS AND CHANGES *125*

The Life-Threatening Difference Between Workaholics and
the Work-Driven • Minimizing the Impact of Bad Hours
and Heavy Travel • Transitions • The Art of Making Quick
Switches • Typhoon Time • Better Work-to-Free-Time
Transitions for Everyone • Change

FOREWORD

BY ZIG ZIGLAR
Renowned Motivational Trainer
and Author

Tom Hopkins' Guide to Greatness in Sales could well be entitled "The Development of a Complete Sales Individual." There are many valuable insights, tips, techniques, and procedures that will help the salesperson be more effective and productive as a salesperson. These things definitely enhance the career objectives which all professional salespeople have. However, the book goes much further than that. It's more than just a cliché that you have got to "be" before you can "do" and you have got to "do" before you can "have." This book helps you to "be" and teaches you how to "do," which makes it possible to "have."

Tom Hopkins deals with the salesperson as a person, then he teaches the techniques and procedures which enable the "person" to become a complete sales professional. This approach enables the salesperson to increase his productivity, which increases his standard of living, but it also increases his standard of life. It helps people move from being workaholics to peak performers—and there is a difference. Workaholics invariably perform out of fear and/or greed, while peak performers work out of love—love for what they're doing; love for a belief in their goods, products, or services; love for the people they're helping with their product; and love for what they're able to provide for their own families.

There is a significant benefit in dealing with the entire

person. An article in *USA Today* on January 8, 1990 points out that the number-one cause of the decline in productivity is marital difficulty at home; number two is alcohol abuse; and number three is drug usage. *Tom Hopkins' Guide to Greatness in Sales* deals with the individual in such a way that the personal, family, and business life will all be enhanced.

Tom Hopkins has done a beautiful job in writing the book in a clear, straightforward manner so that the reader is never left in doubt as to the specific steps to take. Most importantly, Tom communicates in print what he lives in his life, so that there's no inconsistency between what he does and what he says. His own enormous success as a salesperson and sales trainer gives the book credibility. This is what makes *Tom Hopkins' Guide to Greatness in Sales* a serious sales manual that can make the difference we all are seeking in our personal, family, and business lives. I encourage you to read, then re-read and commit to action the lessons Tom Hopkins shares from his own successful background.

INTRODUCTION

I have been developing and teaching sales training skills for salespeople for nearly thirty years. I'm proud to say that many of the people who have come to my seminars, read my books, listened to tapes, or watched the program on video have benefited tremendously. They have learned selling skills that launched or at least boosted their sales careers so that they were making a good living, not just getting by.

It's fortunate for me that many of my past students keep in touch with me. They share their stories of success and new ideas that I can pass on to others in the field of selling.

After listening to hundreds, perhaps thousands, of stories about the ups and downs of various selling careers, I realized that the selling skills I have taught for years are just one aspect of a successful career. There are many situations salespeople encounter not in front of customers that have positive or negative effects on overall careers. They are situations with managers, fellow salespeople, and loved ones.

I've advised countless salespeople when they've encountered tough times in sales that weren't directly related to challenges with customers. They were often due to challenges with getting a good sales job, changing companies, working effectively with managers and peers, emotionally handling success or change, even considering the possibility of moving into management. I must have heard salespeople say hundreds of times, "If I'd only known" after a situation has turned sour.

This book is for salespeople in all fields of selling who have been uncomfortable at least once or twice in their careers about non-selling situations they've found themselves in. It's also for anyone considering taking up a selling career. It will help you get a better idea of what you're getting into. It's full of situations and advice on the right, wrong, and potentially disastrous ways of handling them. I hope this book will help you avoid at least one unsettling situation in which you would be left saying, "If only I'd known."

It's my understanding that the ideal solution regarding gender pronouns has not yet been found, such as the development of a generic pronoun. Therefore, upon the advice of my publisher, we have used the traditional masculine pronoun in most sentences for simplicity sake. It is my sincere hope that anyone reading this book will be doing so to gain mastery over the events in their sales careers, and not to examine it for gender equality.

CHAPTER ONE

DON'T GO INTO SALES FOR THE WRONG REASONS

THE WRONG REASONS

"Big money can be made in sales."

Big money certainly is being made in sales, by the top professionals. But the high-earning salespeople all do it the old-fashioned way: They work for it. It takes time and effort to learn effective selling methods and to establish a solid customer base. In fact, selling is the highest-paid hard work and the lowest-paid easy work there is. If you're willing to work hard, sales can be very lucrative for you. If not, expect slim pickings.

"I really like cars, so I guess I'd make a good car salesperson."

Just because you like the product doesn't mean that you can sell it, or anything else for that matter. While it certainly helps if you enjoy selling the product or service you choose to represent, limiting your choice of selling fields to your hobbies can prevent you from investigating careers that might prove to be more lucrative. Be smart and investigate all the alternatives.

Weigh the decision carefully before you make your hobby your life. You could lose two ways: (1) by not being a good salesperson and (2) by losing your enthusiasm for your hobby. The key word here is enthusiasm. Obviously, it's good for salespeople to have enthusiasm and knowledge about their products, but the knowledge is not always as necessary as the enthusiasm. If all it took to be a top salesperson were product knowledge, the people who designed the product would make the best salespeople. Many beginning salespeople have found that enthusiasm for their product has carried them through until they gained some selling skills and product knowledge.

On the other hand, in many fields you're under a severe handicap unless you are involved with what you're selling. This is particularly true in the field of recreational equipment, where many of the buyers are novices and won't give an order to anyone they don't think knows the sport or activity better than they do. Avid skiers seek the advice of expert skiers in selecting their equipment; boat buyers want to know that the boat salesperson understands the challenges involved in yachting; pilots can sell airplanes more easily than nonfliers can. Anyone desiring success in sales must also have the ability to match his or her product presentation to the educational level of the customer. For example, a computer nut who knows all there is to know about the machine and its software package may alienate a customer who only wants to write letters and balance the checkbook.

Before making your decision to get into sales with a certain product or service, talk to two or three top salespeople in that field. Ask them as many questions as they're willing to answer about the field as they know it. Take into consideration, though, their enthusiasm for the product. They may be somewhat prejudiced about the product and try to oversell you on it. You do, however, want to interview them as experts in the field.

"I want to be my own boss."

When you go into any type of selling, you are more or less your own boss with regard to how you spend your working hours. However, you must also motivate yourself and do a lot of things you might not necessarily like to do. Your income will be a direct reflection of your ability to do what needs to be done. There is an old saying that "Successful people begin where failures leave off." Nowhere does this hold truer than in selling. Many people go into sales wanting to be their own boss and find out they're not really happy with the boss they get. They don't have the self-discipline to boss themselves. Of course you'll have more freedom as a salesperson than will people who sit behind a desk, or punch a time clock. But, ultimately, you'll still have an employer whose main concern is the volume of sales you can generate. If you have a strong enough desire to be your own boss, perhaps you should consider going into business for yourself.

"I have the gift of gab, so I'd make a good salesperson."

Over the years, I have hired many salespeople. I can tell you for a fact that I have passed on many more extroverts than introverts. In my experience it's been easier to teach an introvert to ask questions than to teach an extrovert to shut up. The selling process is a two-part sequence. One part is educating yourself. The second part is educating your customer. A top salesperson asks questions, the answers to which he is able to give, thus educating the customer. He then listens to the customer very intently to find out exactly what the customer wants and exactly how he can help the customer obtain it. This is very difficult for the nonstop talker or poor listener.

Top salespeople know they must listen twice as much as they talk. The fact of the matter is, most of the people you'll be trying to sell to would far rather hear their own voice than yours. A great personality is a positive benefit in selling, but as Dale Carnegie teaches us, it's much better to be an *interested* person than to try to be an *interesting* person. If you are more interested in being interesting than interested, sales is probably not going to be your field.

"Selling is easy work with good hours."

You don't have to go into many showrooms or display areas to find some salespeople standing around telling jokes to each other and in general making sure that for them, selling is the lowest-paid easy work they can find. You will find that the top 20 percent of income earners in sales are putting in much more than 40-hour weeks and doing something positive with every minute of that time. If you are going into sales to work easy hours and be your own boss, you need to learn that the boss probably works more hours than anybody else and normally has the job with him wherever he goes. If you intend to make money in selling, do something productive with all your time on the job: prospect by phone, study the product literature, practice your techniques, learn new sales methods. Time management is a must.

"Meeting new people all the time will be exciting."

This is a great attitude to take into sales, and most of the great salespeople love meeting new people. But when you're a salesperson, a lot of the people you want to meet don't want to meet you. And you have to prospect to find them; they don't just come running in. Recognize that you'll have to work at meeting those exciting people, and that will involve putting up with a lot of rejection. In my book *How to Master the Art of Selling*, I cover how to handle rejection in great detail. If you're serious about selling as a career, you'll want to learn self-motivational techniques as well as sales techniques.

"I can get a job in selling without any education— no more studying."

You can stop studying if you're satisfied to accept selling as the lowest-paid easy work you can find. However, a beginner's usual problems—lack of sales skills and product knowledge—can only be conquered by study and practice. If you truly want to become a high-income earner in sales, you must make selling a way of life. It can't be just a job. By this I mean you live, breathe, walk, and talk selling every minute of your waking hours. You make the study of selling your hobby. You watch other salespeople when you are in buying situations. You develop and practice new sales material with your family and friends and in other social settings. You sell your ideas to others when you're not selling your product or service. Your education in selling can never stop because products, people, ideas, and economies are constantly changing. You have to keep current to keep up. Education and sharing new ideas also help keep your enthusiasm at its peak. Unless you already possess formidable people skills and an expert's product knowledge, you have a great deal to learn.

On the up side, those who acquire and use the skills and knowledge necessary for sales success are assured of generous rewards.

In selling there are right and wrong ways to handle every situation you'll encounter. By learning from the top people, you'll start breaking your personal income records sooner.

"I'll be out in the field by myself; if I want to goof off now and then, nobody will know."

Correct; nobody will know or care when you take a little time off—if you're a big producer. Why should they? You've earned it.

The story is entirely different when you're not a big producer. In sales it's easy for management to know who's producing and who isn't; every sales report makes that crystal clear. Since this readily available bit of information determines who stays and who leaves, no one can hold a good sales position for long without having the self-discipline to be productive. For at least the first few years this means using every minute of the working day to its best advantage.

What you will achieve in your selling career is entirely up to you. What anyone else wants or expects isn't going to make much difference. What anyone else will or won't give you isn't going to make much difference either. The only thing that really matters is what you'll give yourself in the way of determination, drive, training, practice, and attitude.

Will you agree with me on that? I hope so, because the whole point of this book is that the skills, knowledge, and drive within you are what will make you great in selling and in life and that these qualities can be expanded and intensified—if you're willing to invest time, effort, and money in yourself.

Can there be any better investment than in yourself? Most of us know there isn't, but many of us don't act often enough, or decisively enough, on that belief.

You are your greatest asset. Put your time, effort, and money into training, grooming, and encouraging your greatest asset. I will be the first to admit that lifelong habits or patterns are hard to break, but break them you must if you want to grow beyond where you are today.

Keep in mind that if you want to be your own boss, you have to take the blame for failure as well as the recognition for success. So, if you are goofing off and don't have the intestinal fortitude it takes to get yourself going, you might find yourself going back to that old job and old boss you didn't like telling you what to do. Remember, if you can't tell yourself what to do, before long someone else will.

"I really like people."

That's both a right and wrong reason to go into selling. You must like people to succeed in sales; however, you must like all kinds of people. And, you must like "serving" people because that's what selling is all about. If you aren't willing to assume a somewhat subservient role in many selling situations, you won't last long in sales. Please don't make the mistake of going into sales with a dream that you'll like all the people you meet and that they'll like you. It won't happen. Sure, for the most part the people you meet will be nice enough. After all, they'll be dealing with you in a professional situation. However, there will also be those people who will try to take advantage of you, talk down to you, try to get you to lower the cost of your product and, yes, even sue you if you don't follow through on your promises. Liking and wanting to help people is very important, but remember that selling isn't a social game. How well you handle the people you sell to will be directly reflected in your pocketbook.

The best salespeople are those who are not afraid to confront an issue, to get to the heart of things and go forward from there. If you are so fainthearted that you dance all around being nice instead of getting to the point of the meeting, which is the sale, your career will never take off. Salespeople are paid well to be problem solvers for their clients. If you aren't strong enough to dig to the root of the problem, you'll never be able to solve it.

THE RIGHT REASONS

While I want to discourage anyone from going into sales for the wrong reasons, I also want to make it clear that there are many powerful advantages to a career in sales. Here are nine of them:

It's Fun

The first great thing about selling is that it's fun. Do you know how many people aren't having fun with what they're doing? Life was meant to be fun, and there's no reason not to have some of it while you're earning a nice income for your family.

Your Skills Are Portable

The selling and people skills you perfect over the years are readily adaptable in times of change. Sure, you'll lose your product knowledge if you're obliged to start over somewhere else, but your chief skills—that is, your experience, confidence, and knowledge of how to work with people—remain as valid with toothpaste as they are with computers.

This mobility means that you can adapt to downturns in the economy and the restructuring of industries much less painfully than can people in most other occupations. Skilled people, even skilled professionals, in crafts that become obsolete or overcrowded must retrain to survive. Unfortunately, retraining is costly and time-consuming, and there's always the risk that opportunities in the new trade will vanish before the retrainees have time to enter it.

By contrast, strong salespeople leaving a dying company,

industry, or region quickly become productive again in a new field or at a new location. They don't have to relearn their selling skills, they don't have to learn a new way to make money; they merely acquire some new product knowledge. Since products and services in most industries are constantly being advanced, skilled salespeople are used to constantly updating their product knowledge. It's an accepted fact in any selling job.

In Demand

Skilled salespeople are always in demand. In almost every company nearly all the time, the individual the company would really like to hire is a top-quality person to sell the product or service. Day in, day out, top management's most pressing need is to maintain or increase profits; with few exceptions, doing that requires more sales.

So, as a skilled salesperson it's your job to enable top management to conquer their worst difficulties. Without someone just like you going out and bringing in sales, nothing works. It's your initiative and your skill that keeps the wheels turning.

The demand for top-quality salespeople is almost impossible to fill. It's rare to find a company anywhere in the free world that isn't looking for more professional salespeople to market its products or services. The key word here is *professional*. If you're not sure what a professional salesperson is, keep reading. By the time you finish this book you'll have a very good idea. You'll also know the commonplace pitfalls you must avoid in order to become a true selling professional.

No Income Ceilings

You have the freedom to become as successful as you'd like to be. In our profession no one limits your income but you.

You may think the limit is the highest income anyone has made thus far in selling for your company. Does that mean it's not possible to earn more? Of course not. But it does mean that all the salespeople in your company who aren't earning the highest income aren't applying all the strategies and techniques of the top professionals.

Can you imagine your sales manager coming up to you and saying "You are doing a great job, but you are selling too much. You'll have to slow down?" Obviously, that's not a big problem in selling. If you become a top producer in a company and the money you earn still falls short of your expectations, this doesn't mean you've reached a ceiling on your earnings as a salesperson. It may just mean you have reached a ceiling on your earnings with this company. If you have raised yourself high enough in your sales career to reach an income ceiling with your company, I take my hat off to you. Being in this position may open some of the wonderful opportunities or potential problems we cover in Chapter Five.

Low Capital Investment

Selling offers high potential returns from a low capital investment. What does it cost to gain entry into this profession that has no income ceiling? Compare whatever you think that cost is to the investment required for one of the fast food franchises that have been so successful.

Owners of new fast food operations typically invest a quarter of a million dollars or more, work long hours, and pay themselves small salaries during their start-up years. They do all this in the hope that, after the first tough and often profitless year, they'll begin realizing a 20 percent return on the money they've invested.

You can launch yourself into a sales career for a tiny fraction of the franchiser's investment. Your major investment will be the time and effort you put into learning your product and honing your skills. By doing this, you will have greater earning power sooner. This enormous leverage on the small investment required to get into selling has always fascinated me. What an exciting prospect!

Selling Is Always a Challenge

Selling is a daily challenge. You can go into almost any business and have no hurdles to leap. That's never the case in selling, where every day you're confronted with new obstacles to overcome.

Make sure that you organize your mind and attitude so that selling's constant challenge refreshes you instead of wearing you down. Glory in the challenge. Our highly organized society provides few lucrative work activities in which what will happen each day isn't known before that day dawns. In sales, you're privileged to be involved in one of the precious few activities in which freedom and challenge aren't rarities, they're constant companions.

If you ask people doing rather mundane jobs what their number-one complaint is, it's the fact that they do a mindless job over and over and over again with no creative opportunities. In essence, boredom.

In sales, you never know what opportunities the day will open up. You never know what prizes will be offered that you can win—or what catastrophes may befall you. To the salesperson, every day is an adventure. Working at this profession, we can go from the heights of exhilaration to the depths of despair within forty-eight hours, and climb back to the heights again the next day. Isn't that exciting?

Tell me it is. Because if the challenge and uncertainty of selling turns you off, you'll never be happy selling. And if you're not happy in your work, you probably aren't going to be good at it.

Every morning, tell yourself that challenge is exciting, it's fun, and you look forward to it. Tell yourself that—and mean it. Psyche yourself up to enjoy challenge. Then go on the prowl for it, find it, and overcome it. If you want to be better than average, do that. If you aspire to greatness, you won't hesitate. The shortest route to high earnings goes straight through the challenges you'll encounter.

Individual Initiative

The reason I love selling is its freedom of expression. Ours is one of the few professions left in which you can be yourself and can, in essence, do what you like. This freedom you've won for yourself by successfully competing where resourcefulness and perseverance are demanded and highly valued. No activity is more vital to the economy's health than selling; no activity is more dependent on individual initiative than selling.

High Personal Satisfaction

The selling profession is very satisfying. You feel good when your client walks out with your product. It's a thrill to know you've helped people when you go home at night and can say, "I got another individual (or company) involved in what my company provides."

When an executive or official approves your purchase order, it's exciting and satisfying to know you've helped those people or that organization carry out their purposes. The people you serve benefit in direct proportion to your ability and skills. The better you are at sales, the more you benefit others—your clients, your family, and the nation's economy.

Unlimited Personal Growth

No one limits your growth but you. If you want to earn more, learn more. You'll work harder for a while; you'll work longer hours for a while, but in sales you'll be paid for your extra effort with enhanced earnings down the road.

Most people in this world have jobs and professions— mere existences, many of them feel—that can't fulfill their potential. The scope of their labor is confined to narrow limits; their toil hinders rather than fosters their growth; they dislike everything about their employment except the sense of security its familiarity has bred in them. So, instead of venturing into what they don't know and might love, they allow themselves to be trapped by what they do know and strongly dislike.

The professional salesperson recognizes no limits to his or her growth except those limits that are self-imposed. They know that they can always reach out for more. They know they will grow in direct proportion to their competence. And they have little fear of the unknown because overcoming the unknown is their daily work. That's the ninth great thing about being a professional salesperson: it stimulates your personal growth enormously.

CHAPTER TWO

HOW NOT TO DIE AT YOUR JOB INTERVIEW

Your first challenge in sales will be to sell a company on the idea of hiring you as one of their salespeople. In other words, you can't get into selling if you can't sell something you know better than anyone else in the world: yourself.

A WINNING STRATEGY FOR THE JOB-HUNTING INTERVIEW

Six Preparatory Steps and Fourteen Tough Questions You Must Be Ready to Answer Effectively

First of all, accept the idea that interviewing for a sales job ranks with the most important selling opportunities you'll ever have: if you don't get the job, all the sales you would have made for that particular company, plus all commission you would have earned (we called it a commission here because that's what it's commonly called, however, trained, professional salespeople call the income they earn the *fee for service*) and all the experience you would have gained, go down the drain with one fast gurgle. So the job-seeking interview is the last place you want to wing it by going in unprepared. Not only should you prepare thoroughly, you should also psyche yourself up so you'll give that interviewer the best you're capable of delivering.

Here are six specific moves you can make to ensure that you'll give your best possible interview. (Additional how-to details for all steps appear after Step 6.)

1. Investigate the company you've gotten the interview with. If you know who will be interviewing you, try to find out something about them as well. If you're being interviewed for a job with a rather small company, the business owner may be doing the hiring. If you're looking at a position with a large corporation, you will most likely be interviewed by someone in personnel. If the corporation is extremely large, you might be interviewed by several people. The important thing is to make yourself as knowledgeable as you can about that firm and person.

2. Gather your résumé, letters of recommendation, and other documentation (diplomas, transcripts, licenses) well ahead of time. Make copies; leave the originals in a safe place, because you'll need them again. Interviewers are notorious paper losers.

3. Anticipate the questions you'll be asked and be prepared with your best answers beforehand. Snap answers, answers given off the top of your head, sometimes make you seem arrogant, sarcastic, or stupid; they can conflict with something else you've said, making it obvious that at one time or the other you may be making yourself up to be something you're not. Snap answers often emphasize negative things about you, and they rarely deliver all the positive power you could pack into a well-thought-out response. You wouldn't give a snap answer to a customer when discussing your product, so don't do it when you're selling yourself. Taking time to gather your thoughts, even if they're for answers you have already prepared, shows that you are giving it serious consideration, instead of being a hotshot ready with a quick reply. If you are nervous during the interview, when asked a question, try to remember to silently count to five before answering a question. Snap answers often show a lack of salesmanship that could cost you the job. Well-thought-out answers show concern for the other party. A review of fourteen questions you might encounter in a sales-position-seeking interview is given below, beginning on page 22.

4. Give careful thought to your clothing and grooming. If the job is to market farm equipment, you might want to dress a little differently than if it's to sell luxury automobiles. Start for the interview early enough so that you'll arrive on time without a hectic last-minute rush that will shatter your composure. Making a positive first impression is so important.

5. Wait for the interviewer to offer information about salary, commission, territory, expense account, and company benefits. Limit your questions to those that involve what you'll do for the company, not what you'll get from the company. In most interviewing situations, the interviewer will give you this information without your having to ask.

6. Psyche yourself to be relaxed and confident, and to take a strong role in the interview without overpowering the interviewers and making them want to fight you. Also psyche up against interrupting the interviewers, and against babbling or volunteering unfavorable information about yourself. Ask permission to take brief notes during the interview. And please make them brief. Don't whip out your lap-top computer and try to take down every word that's said. And, never, I repeat never, attempt to tape record an interview. If something comes to mind while the interviewer is talking, jot it down on a small note pad and be sure you get it covered before you leave. I recommend you take notes throughout the entire interview so you will have your facts straight rather than trying to remember them later.

PREPARATION

How well you prepare for an interview relative to how well the next-best-qualified candidate prepares will probably decide whether you're offered the job or get a limp handshake and the old "We'll-keep-your-name-on-file" brush-off. Will the interviewers forgive you for coming in unprepared? More likely, they'll figure you'd try to wing it when selling their product or service, and they'll hire someone who took the opportunity seriously.

Thoroughly Investigate the Company and the Interviewer You'll Be Seeing.

Make yourself as knowledgeable about that firm and person as you can. Unless you're interviewing with a small or new firm, you can probably learn a lot about the company in a good public library. Check the trade directories and magazines in their field.

If your library doesn't have the company's latest annual report, try to get one from its corporate headquarters. The annual report will give you a pool of valuable information—not only the direction it's going and the areas it plans to enter, but also the names of its officers and directors and many other useful details. You may cinch the job by making a comment that shows you're familiar with the company's plans and operations. If you can't find this information, contact a salesperson currently working for the company. I strongly recommend you talk with one of their better salespeople. If you talk with someone who may be on his way out of the company, he won't have much good news to share with you. A good salesperson loves to talk about the positives of his company. Try to arrange a meeting with a top salesperson, one who has built a solid foundation with the company. This person will answer many of your questions. In fact, this person may help you make a decision about whether or not you really want a job with this particular company. He may even give you questions you should ask the interviewer. If you do want the job, you may want to make a list of questions to ask just to verify what this salesperson has told you.

Gather Letters of Recommendation and All Your Other Documentation (Diplomas, Transcripts, Licenses) Well Ahead of Time.

If you're applying for your first full-time job, make up a résumé of the after-school and summer jobs you've held. If there weren't enough to fill a page, include your paper route, and the juice stand you operated as a little kid—if you really did. It all shows enterprise and energy.

Aside from your work experience, document where you went to school and the grades you earned. Include any special courses you've taken. Go in with an impressive stack of diplomas and transcripts. Chances are the interviewer will only glance at the pile, but they'll make a good impression just by being there. If you've held several jobs, have letters of recommendation, if possible, from each one. The best way to ensure that you'll be able to get a letter of recommendation is to earn it with loyal, honest, and effective work at each job. However, no matter how good your record is with a company, in many cases you'll have to be persistent to get a letter of recommendation written. If it's left to an overworked person—likely in today's hectic business environment—you may have better luck by filling in the blanks on the following letter template. Then ask your former bosses to make any changes they desire before having a secretary type it up on their letterhead.

TEMPLATE FOR A LETTER OF RECOMMENDATION

To Whom It May Concern:
_____ (your name) was employed by this organization from _____ (your hire date) to _____ (your termination date) in the capacity of (your position or job title).

Mr./Mrs./Miss _____ (your last name) proved to be efficient, honest, and reliable. During his/her employment, the subject was (promoted, awarded, named employee of the month, received raises) (give details of any good stuff).

The subject's sales performance was (choose one) consistently/frequently among the top (third) of our sales force. His/her relations with customers were (choose one) satisfactory/excellent/completely trouble-free.

(Each time you use this template, select a different paragraph from the four given below:)

The subject was an outstanding employee. We were sorry to lose him/her.

Allow me to recommend the subject for any position that he/she applies for.

I have no hesitation in recommending the subject to you for any position in which you may be considering employing him/her.

I have no hesitation in recommending the subject to you for the position of (the job you're trying to get) with your company.

Sincerely,
(name and title)

By typing this template with your name in the blanks and taking it to a copy shop, you can easily provide all the aids to getting letters of recommendation that you might need.

When you present it to one of your ex-bosses, emphasize that you'd like to have them use their own words as much as they find convenient.

What References Can Do for You—And to You

Today many companies have a policy against giving out any information about a former employee except salary data and the dates of employment and termination. Enough companies have been sued for giving out harmful, but honest information that giving sparse information has become common business practice. It would seem that this trend would make the written reference letters more effective and this may be true of most jobs. But here we're concerned only with a selling position.

Certainly collect any good reference letters you can whenever you leave a job, sales related or not. Ask for them immediately upon getting or giving notice that you'll be changing employment. But be aware that the feelings you leave behind are far more important than any letter you might be given. Avoid temptation and steer clear of getting involved in anything while you're working for a company that will leave your former bosses feeling that you've taken advantage of your situation with them or been less than honest. Be aboveboard and completely ethical when you leave; take nothing that belongs to the company—especially customers, mailing lists, software, and trade secrets. Such things have a way of being revealed after you leave.

Don't assume that you'll get a good reference from your former employers. Keep in touch with them; remind them that you've been aboveboard with them. Especially if your employment was for a short period or a lot of time has elapsed, they may have forgotten you or confused you with someone else. Keep in mind that being forgotten is in itself a poor reference, so stop by and renew your acquaintance with your old bosses before they get a reference-checking phone call about someone they can't remember.

If you had a less than happy parting from one of your old jobs, perhaps now enough time has passed that you can take a stab at repairing the damage.

Smart Interviewers Dig Deep

Smart interviewers (the kind you're most likely to encounter when applying for a really good job) won't settle for the references on your list. They know that many employers are reluctant to give out adverse information about any former employee, so they'll try to reach some of your former customers, who can be as frank as they like over the phone without any realistic worry about being sued.

Remember throughout your career that the best way to avoid bad references is not to deserve them.

Another method used by some companies is to check your credit report. What shows up there will give them a hint as to your overall stability. Also, it will tell them if you have any felony convictions, such as drunk driving.

Choose Your Interviewing Wardrobe Carefully.

When applying for a sales position, dress like a successful salesperson. No sneakers and jeans—unless that's what you'd be expected to wear while you're selling for that particular company. Don't go in dressed like the chairman of the board, but don't dress like a construction worker either. If you dress the way most of the company's salespeople dress, it will be a lot easier for the interviewer to see you performing that job.

Make certain you are comfortable in the clothing you choose to wear to your interview. If you are uncomfortable, your attention will be distracted from the interviewer. If you're uncomfortable enough that you fidget during your appointment, you may distract the interviewer as well. Neither of those scenarios bodes well for your getting the job.

Women have more leeway in what they can wear to an employment interview and still get the job; they also have more ways to go wrong in their choice of outfit. But the same basic rule still applies: dress the way that company's salespeople dress. If you arrive looking like you're going to a cocktail party, they may find it hard to believe you'll become a steady producer.

Do your most careful job of personal grooming before the selling-job interview. A few strands of hair that wave with every puff of air can be very distracting to interviewers—and they'll feel that your lack of awareness will distract customers if they hire you.

The day before, carefully check the clothes you'll wear. Make sure there are no loose threads hanging or buttons about to pop off that would give you an unkempt appearance. And just before you go in for the interview, give yourself another quick check in a mirror.

Anticipate the Questions You'll Be Asked and Decide on Your Best Answers Beforehand.

Don't wait until the interviewer hits you with a series of totally unexpected questions, because your off-the-cuff answers might hurt you badly; in any case they probably won't be your best possible job-getting replies. Try to imagine what questions the interviewer will ask, so that you can devise your strongest answers beforehand. Doing this ahead of time allows you to work out exactly how you'll minimize the negatives and emphasize the positives in the many aspects of work, life, and personality that may be covered.

What do interviewers try to find out?

They'll be looking for tip-offs to your energy level, how well you get along with people, whether you can be trusted, how effective you'll be as a salesperson, whether they can reasonably expect you to stay with them long enough to make the company money and make themselves look good, and, probably but not always, how much you know about their industry. They will certainly attempt to determine whether you have any habits or addictions that will prevent you from doing a terrific job for them, and they may try to gain an insight into the quality of your family life as well.

Skilled interviewers can toss any one of the following fourteen questions over the desk so smoothly you might think they're just making conversation. They're not; they're artfully sniffing out indications as to what their best hire/don't-hire decision would be.

I'll have to give you the basic questions because the variations are endless. The ones you'll hear will be phrased differently, but, stripped down to their essentials, this is what's being asked:

1. "How do you spend your spare time?"

The question searches for clues as to what makes you tick, your energy level, your intellectual level, how solid your family life is, whether you have hobbies and pursuits that would interfere with your performance on the job. Come up with an answer that's true and doesn't paint you as a perpetually dog-tired couch potato or a brainless deadhead.

I would like to think I don't have to mention that your answers should be true, but I feel I must. You see, if your answer isn't honest, it will be inconsistent with other things they'll learn about you; they'll know you've lied and they won't hire you.

2. "Why do you want to work for this company?"

This ought to be an easy one because you should have good reasons for wanting to work for any company where you go to the trouble of applying for a job. Come up with some solid reasons other than that you think you can make lots of money working for them. Make some comments about how much you're impressed with their reputation, design, and engineering—if you really are. Mix in some reasons that have to do with your personal situation—perhaps that they're close to your home; you like the amount of travel you'd be doing for them; from what you've heard about their training program, you feel it's just what you need.

Plan what you'll say ahead of time—you might even want to practice out loud—so that you'll sound like the sort of salesperson they'd like to have representing them.

3. "Where do you want to be professionally, personally, and financially, in 1, 5, 10, and 20 years?"

No matter how you answer this one, even if you mumble, stumble, or clam up, you'll reveal a lot about yourself. Make sure that what you reveal strengthens the interviewer's urge to hire you.

Think this question through—in fact, it's a good one to ask yourself every month. Make sure your goals are realistic and don't conflict—for example, if you say that you want to be the company's top salesperson in a year's time, make a lot of progress toward an MBA, and run a few marathons, the interviewer is likely to feel that you're being wildly unrealistic. That knocks your credibility.

4. "Why did you choose a career in sales?"

This question shouldn't take any salesperson by surprise, but it often does. It's a favorite with many skilled interviewers, who find that the answers it evokes are highly revealing about the applicant's true goals, personality, and overall prospects for success with their company.

If you reply with some of the wrong reasons given in Chapter One, you'll probably blow your chances with that particular company. Think through a short, truthful, convincing response that emphasizes the right reasons for being in sales (which I also gave you in Chapter One), and add some positive reasons of your own.

5. "Are you a team player?"

You'll rarely hear this question in those exact words; generally it's pretty well disguised. Nevertheless it boils down to those five words, and your answer should go straight to the heart of the matter.

While it's true that salespeople do their most important work alone, they still must be good team players to reach their full potential. Say that you understand this, that you know your ability to get along with other people in the company—and your willingness to do so—are important considerations.

Your answer will be stronger if you include an anecdote, a little story about yourself that illustrates what a good team player you are.

6. "Why should I consider you for this sales position?"

Here's the original "Show-me-your-selling-talents" question. It's often phrased like this: "What can you do for our company?" They may also put it this way: "What makes you the best person for this job?" Or, "What are your qualifications?"

For this one, prepare what Danielle Kennedy, a top sales trainer, calls a "winning script." Jot down the main points you want to cover, and run through the script enough times to smooth it out and get it down so pat that you can say it with conviction without sounding like you've memorized it.

Here are some things any dedicated salesperson can bring to any legitimate company: enthusiasm, honesty, the determination to acquire in-depth knowledge of the product or service, and loyalty. Don't just list these qualities. Expand on all of them in your own words and work them up into a forceful, brief but convincing discussion.

7. "What are your personal strengths?"

Your answer here must mesh with the one you gave or would give to the previous one because it covers much of the same ground. Another "winning script" may be required here so that you can answer either one forcefully without repeating yourself.

8. "What are your personal weaknesses?"

This one is a favorite with many interviewers because so many applicants blow themselves out of the water when they answer it. Once they get started on their weaknesses, some people just can't stop.

However, with some careful thought you can turn this one to your advantage—and thereby demonstrate to the interviewers that you could do the same with problems that plague their product or service. For example, you might feel that you sometimes spend too much time making sure you have minor details right—and the interviewer can infer that you'd turn in mistake-free orders that would make the internal job of filling the orders by the staff much easier.

9. "How well did you get along with your previous bosses?"

Few questions sink more job seekers than this one. Skillful interviewers ask it in a way that invites you to unload, and they'll nod their heads sympathetically while you drop stones on your feet by telling them what miserable jerks all your bosses were. Plan carefully how you'll deal with this one, and follow your plan to the letter in the interview. Remember that the harder you try to get your side of any story across, the worse you make the whole incident sound.

If you had a serious run-in with a previous boss, how can you handle it truthfully without destroying your chances? Say something like, "My last boss was a very effective person who has my complete respect. But we had a personality clash that might have been my fault as much as anyone else's. However, I learned a lot from that experience and I'm certainly not going down that road again." Keep this old saying in mind: "He who excuses, accuses." Avoid long drawn-out excuses and get on to more positive things in your background as quickly as possible.

10. "Do you consider yourself to be a follower or a leader?"

The interviewer hopes to get you to reveal more about your self-image. If you're applying for an entry-level sales position in a gigantic corporation, they'll probably want to hear that you're a follower. For a senior sales position in a smaller firm, they'll probably want to hear that you're a leader. Put a positive face on how you feel about yourself and tell it like it is.

11. "Are you energetic?"

Find some way to emphasize your high energy level without sounding like a fitness fanatic—unless you're applying for a job selling fitness products or services.

12. "What do you expect to get from this firm?"

While your answer to this one shouldn't conflict with your response to the question about your personal goals, you'll miss an important opportunity to sell yourself by merely repeating your aims. Also say something intelligent and sincere about what you can learn about sales from selling their product or service, and the good you can do bringing their benefits to more people.

13. "What would make you unhappy with this job?"

This certainly isn't the time to say that you hate to prospect if success at the job you're applying for requires prospecting (as many sales jobs do). And don't sludge up the place by reciting your pet peeves about management and coworkers.

Take this as an opportunity to convert a negative trap into a positive selling point for yourself with something like, "I'd be unhappy if the company abandoned its commitment to quality and innovative design."

14. "Why do you want to leave your present job?" or "Why did you leave your last job?"

This is another opportunity to drop rocks on your toes. Don't respond to this question by detailing the faults and failures of your last boss and company. No matter how bad they may have been, the interviewer will feel that if the people or company you're criticizing were there to defend themselves, a very different picture would emerge. Don't get into it, because if you do, it merely shows that you can't convert a negative into a positive.

There must be some positive things about your leaving your last job, even if you lost a good one. You can admit to feeling a lack of challenge in your previous sales job, to feeling that it was too structured or not structured enough. You can also admit that you want to get involved in the exciting, faster growing, and more challenging field served by the company you're talking to.

Testing

Some companies use very sophisticated testing methods before hiring new people. You may be asked to take any number of psychological, personality, or skill tests. Some companies have developed their own ways of finding out the same type of information simply by offering you selling scenarios and evaluating your method of handling each situation.

Answer Awkward Questions Instead of Ducking Them

In ordinary conversation, we can avoid answering unwelcome questions by saying, "It's none of your business," or more subtly by simply talking about the matter without giving any clear information. However, in the hiring interview either response will hurt your chances.

Interviewers aren't fooled when you dodge a legitimate question even though they apparently let you get away with it. Don't think it's a victory when you seem to have evaded a question. Some interviewers will think, "Aha, something's wrong here. I'll check it out another way." More likely, they'll trash your application because checking on what you're concealing is too much trouble.

Other interviewers, sensing that you have something to conceal, will press hard for the answers you're most reluctant to give. Many interviewers believe that what applicants won't tell them is far more important than the information they readily offer.

Wait for the Interviewers to Offer Information About Training, Salary, Commission, Territory, Expense Account, and Company Benefits.

The person doing the interviewing is mainly interested in what you'll do for the company, so limit your questions to those that explore that matter. For example, ask (if the answers aren't obvious) about the people you'll be selling to, how much pricing leeway you'll be given, what reports the company requires, and anything else having to do with what you'll do for the company. Wait to ask about what you'll get from the company until after they've offered you the job. I recommend that you prepare a list of questions that you will need to have answered before you would agree to take the position. When you ask them, be sure to write down the answers. For example, if the position is one involving outside sales, do they give you a car allowance or a company car, or are you on your own? Are you required to generate all of your own leads or does the company provide leads? How much advertising is done to generate business? What type of training is offered and how long is the training period? In your first interview you should learn what's expected, and decide whether that company's expectations fit your needs and goals. Ask for a manual of policies and guidelines and read it thoroughly.

Psyche Yourself Up Against Babbling, Against Volunteering Negative Information About Yourself, and Against Interrupting the Interviewers.

It's a common saying among interviewers that applicants will tell the most amazing things about themselves if given the chance. Applicants don't often come right out with, "I'm a grudge-holder," or "I'm quarrelsome." Instead they'll tell little stories about themselves—about how they got even with a coworker, or how they told somebody off. The bad reference you give yourself is the worst kind you can get.

Most job applicants are tense; it's a natural reaction to an interview that can determine one's future. Unfortunately, many applicants relieve their tension by babbling instead of giving well-thought-out answers that stick to the point. Commonly they'll tell damning things about themselves they'd never reveal in a less stressful situation. Skilled interviewers know they can eliminate lots of applicants simply by listening in a friendly way that encourages the applicants to ramble—it's a lot easier than hammering away on the phone for hours checking references.

Go in Prepared to Sell Yourself Strongly

How well you sell yourself is the interviewer's best clue as to how well you'd sell his product or service. As in any sales situation, it's possible to lose by being too pushy. On the other hand, you're applying for a sales position, not for a membership in the Milquetoast Society. When interviewing for a sales job, being a bit too aggressive is safer than being too timid. Be tactful, exercise your diplomatic skills, but be forceful and confident almost to the point of dominating the interview. The interviewer will probably be visualizing you sitting in front of a customer. If he sees a weak, indecisive person, he'll think the customer will see the same thing.

CAN YOU MAKE ENOUGH MONEY AT XYZ CORPORATION TO CRACK YOUR EXPENSE NUT?

First you need to figure out how big a nut you have to crack. Use your checkbook and previous budgets to figure out your basic requirements. But don't only look back.

If you'll be jumping to outside sales from a nonselling or an inside selling job, your expenses will increase, maybe substantially; so look ahead and estimate them.

If you've been driving to work at a nearby office or plant and now will be on the road every day, your auto expense will go up dramatically. Call your auto insurance agent and find out what being rated as an outside salesperson will do to your insurance premiums. Talk to salespeople to help you estimate how many miles you can expect to rack up in your new job and then figure what it will cost. Your estimates may cause you to reevaluate your attitude toward taking a job with a company that doesn't offer help on auto expense.

Another important point: "Is my car good enough?" If your car is older and not reliable, you may have to get a newer model that would be reliable enough to meet the demands of your new job.

You may also have added expense for client lunches and entertainment. If the job you want involves overnight travel, consider the cost of lodging, phone calls on the road, and meals away from home. Do you have credit cards now? If not, you'd better get some. Nearly all sales jobs will require the use of credit cards at one time or another.

Discuss your estimates with salespeople in the company you're planning to join and make sure they're realistic. Once you're confident you have a good understanding of how much you'll need to make in an outside sales position, compare that to the compensation structure at a particular company before you take a job there. Don't go into a heads-I-don't win, tails-I-lose situation.

SIMPLIFYING THE COMPLEXITIES OF COMMISSION

The compensation of salespeople has steadily evolved toward more complex systems due to computerization and the growing sophistication of sales managers. However, by stripping away all the confusing terminology and elaborate formulas, it all comes down to just five basic commission plans:

1. Distributors' profits
2. Straight commission
3. Modified straight commission
4. Straight salary
5. Salary plus commission

Any of these plans may offer bonuses for exceeding certain sales levels, or for bringing in certain types of business.

When the Company Would Require You to Carry an Inventory of Its Products

Be aware that a few unethical companies don't really expect you to sell much of their product; they make most of their money selling to prospective salespeople. So be extremely cautious when you're considering the possibility of shelling out your own money for inventory.

Don't limit your investigation to the references the company offers because it may be a setup between two or three fast-buck artists working together. On your own, find people who are selling that company's product and get the unpolished truth about how good a proposition it is. If you can't independently verify that it's a good opportunity, hang onto your money.

Even with good, independent reports, start with samples only. Make sure you're not only making sales but that your customers are satisfied with the delivered product before you consider committing to a large inventory.

Another point to consider: will you be selling on credit? If so, you will have collection losses, and collection expenses on the accounts you do collect. This can be ruinous. For example, if your discount is 25 percent and you fail to collect one sale in four, your margin is zero, meaning that all your expenses are a loss.

Straight Commission

In most cases, under this system you furnish your own car and pay all your own expenses. The way it's supposed to work, you get your travel, auto, and other selling expenses back from the commissions you earn, and have enough left over for an excellent income. There's no guarantee, however. If you don't earn any commissions at all, you are still out whatever you've spent on selling and living expenses while you're earning no money. The risk is highest with straight commission, but the payoff is generally much greater than in the lower-risk sales jobs.

Straight commission varies from one field to another. Some independent sales reps operate out of their homes or their own offices on straight commission; they may sell for one manufacturer exclusively or represent several suppliers. Generally the independent reps carry little or no inventory and receive no expense money from their manufacturers.

Straight commission prevails in the resale home segment of the real estate industry. In this field, the employer (called a broker) usually furnishes the salesperson (called an agent or associate) with a desk and a phone and provides signs and a varying amount of support in the way of advertising and prestige. Nevertheless, the salesperson's auto and other expenses can be substantial.

The straight-commission system is self-regulating: nonproducers aren't fired, they're forced out by lack of income. For that reason straight-commission selling may be the easiest interview to pass because the employer won't be investing salary and expenses in you. The real test is whether you have the resources to stick it out until your commissions equal your living and job expenses. Unless you're willing and able to invest savings that are equal to at least six months of selling and living expenses, you can't afford to take a straight-commission job unless you know the field well enough to make a go of it in a shorter time.

Modified Straight Commission

Some employers find they can't expand or maintain their sales forces unless they give new salespeople some financial help to get started. This help often takes the form of a draw, that is, commission money paid before it's earned. The draw has to be paid back out of future commissions. In comparing job opportunities, don't confuse draw with a salary that doesn't have to be paid back. When draw is called a guarantee, it doesn't have to be paid back—but make sure you understand all the fine print in your employment contract before you take this for granted.

Some modified-straight-commission plans provide monthly allowances to help with auto and other expenses.

Straight Salary

You're not likely to encounter a straight-salary situation because most companies know they get more sales for less money with the constant incentive that commissions provide. However in some fields sales are large, take five or more years to close, and involve many people. In these cases, commission may not be offered.

Salary Plus Commission

The idea here is to get the best of two worlds: the security of a base salary for the salesperson plus the incentive of the commission system. A salary generally means the commission rate will be set lower than in a straight commission arrangement—but the yearly income potential may be about as good.

In many salary-plus-commission plans, a quota must be met before the salesperson is eligible for more than the base salary.

Income Capping

Some companies limit how much income salespeople can earn. This is called income capping. For most companies, the top level of income is very high—high enough to be a very good income, but low enough that the salesperson never makes more than the company does. Some companies, especially those relatively new in business, will offer very high percentages of commissions to their salespeople to get good people and to inspire them to do well. Then, many companies find that after a period of time, some salespeople are doing so well that they're earning more than the owner of the company. While many top salespeople prefer to have no income ceilings placed on their earnings, good salespeople will understand that they will not have this wonderful product to continue selling if the company doesn't make more money than they do. It may seem a bit egotistical to ask about income capping at a job interview for a sales position when you haven't been in sales a long time. However, if you have a proven track record of success with other companies, you'll want to know if this company applies any income capping before you agree to work for them.

CHAPTER THREE

THE SALESPERSON'S WORLD

The selling game mirrors professional tennis in several basic ways. In tennis, as in selling, the players are divided into the top producers, the middle group, and the bottom group. The same few individuals win all the big tournaments and take home most of the money. These champions can retire rich at an early age if they like. It's the same in sales.

A larger group of people regularly win the smaller tournaments or reach the quarter-finals of big ones. These people make a very good living, as do the middle group in selling.

And then comes an even larger group: the serious but losing pro tennis players, the bottom people who never hit a big payday because they never reach the quarter-finals anywhere.

Surprisingly few of this group, either in tennis or in selling, ever go all out to learn all they can about their chosen profession. While no precise data is available, as a rule, individually the bottom group devotes less time to practicing their skills than do members of the top group. Or, they spend so much time practicing their skills at this one aspect of their lives that they totally ignore the rest of their lives and get grossly out of balance as people. Distresses or failures in their personal lives begin to dominate their thoughts, and all the work they've done practicing their skills goes out the window with lack of concentration. As a result, the bottom group burns a lot of its energy fighting discouragement.

In selling, the bottom group is the bunch behind the doughnuts, the hang-around-the-office types. They may be the nay-sayers or the goof-offs. Again, as a rule, you will find the low-end people making excuses instead of money. These people insist on playing their games by ear. They won't bother with the practice, drill, and rehearsal that are so vital in selling; they have no time for the seminars, tapes, and books that could add to their skills and inspire them to greater success; they don't prepare or plan. Generally, they feel that the higher people either have a "gift of gab" or get all the breaks.

UNDERSTANDING THE GAME YOU'RE PLAYING

To be successful in selling, it helps to look at daily activities as a game to be played. But by "game" I'm not talking about a childish activity conducted to pass the time of day. To me, "game" signifies an important action governed by precise rules that determine who wins and gets the prizes and the acclaim, and who loses and gets nothing. The game concept keeps me aware of several important considerations: Once you're on the playing field, it takes as much time and effort to lose as it does to win. Also, there are rules that must be followed. Score is being kept. And the effectiveness of my overall performance determines whether I'll be a winner or a loser.

Equally important, the game concept helps me hold things in perspective. It keeps me from forgetting that even if I lose, water will still boil at 212 degrees Fahrenheit, birds will still sing in the meadows, and tomorrow won't fail to bring me new opportunities.

WHOSE GAME IS IT?

To some extent, it's always the company's game. They make the rules, set their goals, and create your general opportunity. But as you follow their rules and help them achieve their goals, you need to set your own goals and create your own specific opportunities.

If you want to play their game to win, that is, to make the most money possible, you must do several things:

- Learn who the players are. This includes both management players and fellow members of your sales team.
- Learn what the written rules (company policies) are, and how to use them to your best advantage.
- Learn how to profit from the unwritten rules—the gray areas.
- Learn what the score is, and who keeps it.

Those are the basic things you do first. Then you learn how to play your position with the consummate skill of a champion.

Once you achieve champion status in your organization, then you have the right to speak up about the rules. Perhaps you feel some of them should be changed, or occasionally bent to the benefit of all parties involved. Management will probably appreciate your input, coming as it does from a top producer, since it's sure to be presented with the tact and persuasive skill that made you a champion.

You see, no one in management wants to listen to a bottom producer tell them the problems with the rules. You have to earn the right to be taken seriously.

WHO ARE THE PLAYERS?

Who calls the shots in the game you're playing? Is it the sales manager, or the vice president of sales? Who do you really have to make happy—not just to hang in there, but to get a crack at the best opportunities that game provides?

Your boss has great power over your future, but never forget that if you make lots of customers happy by giving great service and having them buy from you, part of that power automatically shifts to you. However, you are still a player on the company team. Even if you feel you have some power as a top producer, you need to weigh very carefully whether or not you want to throw that power around.

How can you play smarter and stay within the rules? You must learn when to approach the company about bending the rules. It must always be to their advantage as well as yours. Selling is and always will be a team effort. You can't just twist everything to suit yourself and expect to have a long, successful career in sales. You must realize that because you are a top producer, everyone is watching you. They want to see how you handle this position you worked so hard to earn. If you get too cocky and take advantage of it, you could hurt the whole team and lose their respect. I don't care how much anyone says they just let that stuff roll off their backs, selling is a team effort and you need that team for support. If you honestly feel you can do it without them, try to find yourself a company that appreciates mavericks rather than risking the ruin of your current team.

The other members of your sales team can have a tremendous impact on the game you play. There are several personality types of salespeople I've found through my career and through the observances of others. Each type you encounter will have an effect on you. How powerful that effect is, is up to you. I'll tell you about seven of those types of salespeople and how to handle them for your peak performance.

1. Albert Analytical—Albert receives as much, if not more, joy from analyzing and keeping the statistics on his sales career current than he does from actually making sales. He'll have charts, graphs, goals, and checklists. He's usually very well organized and up to date on compensation levels and incentive programs. However, he may not always keep as well informed on product knowledge.

Albert is proud of all of his analytical work and will be happy to show it to you, sharing demographic information and organizational skills. Be cautious, though, not to get too caught up in analysis of your own sales during "sales-making" hours. The in-depth analysis is great, but very time-consuming. Unless Albert also happens to be the top producer at your company, let him know you appreciate his abilities, but dedicate your best hours to the people to whom you can sell your product or service.

2. Hiding Harry—Harry can be found at most companies. He's an okay salesperson, but he doesn't strive to excel. He sells enough to keep his job. If, by chance, he makes a big sale this month, you can bet he'll sell less next month, to stay on an even keel of earning income. His self-image just won't let him earn more than a certain average income. Harry spends a good bit of valuable selling time reading, at the movies, getting his car fixed, or doing other nonproductive work. If your goal is to be a top salesperson at your company, don't become buddies with Harry. He'd like nothing more than to have someone else to spend time with—anyone other than customers.

3. Charlene Champion—Charlene is usually a top producer in the company. She'll hardly ever be in the office unless it's to set up appointments by phone or to handle customer problems. If you watch carefully, you'll notice she has fewer problem clients than most salespeople. That's because she gives the kind of service clients expect, not allowing problems to develop. Or, she handles them so well and so quickly that they're over before they can become office gossip. Charlene will always speak up positively about the company. She's definitely a positive force. She's happy to share her success stories, new techniques, and sales strategies with others during non-sales hours. Charlene is a good person to get to know. However, don't expect her to adopt you. She'll always be positive and supportive, but she'll also be very busy taking care of her clients.

4. Eddie Eager—Eddie is the new kid in the company. This will be you at some time or another. He's excited about the potential he has with his new company. He wants to be everybody's friend and eventually the top producer. Praise him for his excitement. As a good team player, offer assistance without bogging down your existing work schedule. A good dose of Eddie's enthusiasm serves to reignite a productive, but not so enthusiastic, attitude about your career.

5. Nancy Negative—People like Nancy don't usually last long at any one place of business. She may be intelligent and competent, but she just can't keep from knocking another employee, the manager, the product, or the company as a whole in some shape or form. She's an instigator, trying to rally others around her for support. Unless Nancy has the ear of someone higher up in your company, steer clear of her. If she does have a certain amount of influence in your company, be pleasant enough, but don't become buddies with her. If management decides suddenly that she has to go, some of her supporters might be swept out the door with her.

6. Bob Barracuda—Bob is very often in the top 5 percent of producers. He likes being there—above the masses. He hopes to become a manager some day and doesn't want anyone or anything to get in the way of his goal. He may try to intimidate the rest of the sales staff by undermining their faith in their own abilities. You'll have to learn to let his comments run off you like water off a duck's back. Otherwise, you'll have doubts about your abilities as a sales professional.

7. Roberta Rebel—Practically every sales force has a rebel who keeps things stirred up by opposing management at every opportunity. Rebels tend to be fascinating people who need a lot of admirers. They often go out of their way to welcome newcomers and offer their friendship. If you like your new position, avoid getting closely associated with the rebel unless you're clearly headed for top production. The reason is that rebels don't last unless they're top producers. In other words, they've earned an immunity from managerial retaliation for their harassments. But don't count on the top producing rebel's immunity rubbing off on you if management thinks you're supporting the rebel against them.

Most rebels are lifelong misfits. They pretend to oppose a current injustice, but in reality they are refighting hopeless emotional battles they lost years ago, perhaps in childhood.

Many times these rebels get to be so obnoxious that, no matter how great their sales are, they still get fired. Or they quit over some trifle. In either case, being closely associated with them can leave a stain on your reputation that will last long after they're gone.

* * *

Face it, we all have a certain amount of self-doubt about our abilities until we learn, try, and test new and better ways of doing things. Don't allow anyone else to infect your mind with problems generated by their own self-doubts. In other words, don't take advice from anyone more messed up than you are.

Other important players, whose impact you need to consider, may be in the picture too. Make it your business to find out if anyone, whether an inside executive or an outside person, wields more influence and power behind the scenes than the casual observer would suspect. You're a long way from being a casual observer when you reach the top in sales in a company. You have a heavy investment in your continued association with that firm.

If important shots in your company are being called from the shadows, this situation poses both dangers and opportunities. A key part of the art of staying on top is learning how to minimize the negatives and maximize the positives in your relationships with everyone who has power in your company. Do this regardless of whether each individual's real power matches his place, if any, on the company's organizational chart.

How do you find these things out? Ask discreetly and observe attentively. Most of all, think through the ramifications of whatever you learn. It's important not to get caught up in company politics. If you concentrate mainly on serving your customers and making sales, you'll be much better off. Politics steal too much of your time and energy.

WHAT ARE THE WRITTEN RULES?

Not all companies lay down written guidelines and rules. Even where they exist, they're often out of date or so generalized that they aren't functional in the daily scramble. But there may be unwritten policies and guidelines, and it's your responsibility to yourself to dig them out if they are not offered upon hiring.

Maybe you already have. But are you getting all the mileage out of those rules that you can? Ask yourself, "Do I understand exactly what the company expects of me and what they want?" If not, find out.

If they plan on you knocking yourself out to earn $24,000 a year and you need $48,000, there's big trouble down the road.

WHAT'S THE SCORE—AND WHO KEEPS IT?

Take the situation where you need twice the income the company expects you to earn. Are you more worried about what they want done, or are you thinking more about what you want? Living up to what they want might not be in your best interests. It may be in your best interests to find a company where you will be given the support to stretch beyond your current limits.

Again this requires thinking. If the game is selling widgets, find out exactly how many widgets you should sell to be considered to be doing the job well. Get it in writing.

WHAT ARE THE UNWRITTEN RULES?

Chances are you'll be obliged to work with accounting people on credit approval and with warehouse people on deliveries. Perhaps you must also work with estimating, design, manufacturing, and other departments to get your inquiries turned into orders and your orders made to specifications and shipped on time.

How these various departments come into the game, and what you must do to keep them on your team, is something you've got to know. Most accounting types think salespeople don't know how to handle dollars and cents. The shipping people don't think you know how to properly fill out paperwork. Learn exactly what they need to do their job well and learn to give it to them as quickly and efficiently as possible. In doing this, you'll lessen the number of mistakes and delays in filling your orders, thus making for greater customer satisfaction. One more thing: Always take time to show your appreciation to the members of accounting and shipping for a job well done. Let them know how important they are in servicing the needs of your customers.

You want to be actively playing three main games to the best of your ability all the time. First, there's your customers' game. Second, there's the company's game as judged from management's standpoint. And finally, there's your own game. There's never just one game going on. To keep on winning big you have to play all three vigorously.

PROBLEMS AND OPPORTUNITIES

You can't afford to take a shortsighted view of your selling career. All sorts of problems and opportunities revolve around your customers and your product.

Putting Your All into a Fading Market

It's vital to do some serious thinking and planning about your career rather than just barging in, figuring that whatever you like to sell is here to stay. What if it doesn't stay? As a general rule, nothing does.

There are exceptions. Two important ones are real estate sales and stock brokerage. Those two fields are as permanent as the capitalist system in this country. They're also prone to dream-shattering downswings that strike suddenly.

If you sell any line of manufactured products, the market for what you're selling can evaporate with painful speed.

It's only a few years since electric typewriters looked like a product that was here to stay. The first word processors gave their market a hard knock, and then the personal computer came along. Suddenly it was all over for electric typewriters.

Today's swift thrust of product development zaps product after product. Every time it does, a lot of salespeople who thought it could never happen to them are taken by surprise, knocked off the top, and forced to start over somewhere else.

When new products and technologies burst into the marketplace they often rack up explosive gains. For a time anyone who has the product can sell it—whether or not they know how to make a good presentation or close a sale. Demand is so great that customers insist on buying.

If you get in early enough on a hot item or new product, you can have an easy ride for several weeks, months, or even years until the initial demand is satisfied. Then look out.

Examples abound: television sets, hand-held calculators, personal computers. Go back further and you can include just about every appliance found around the house today. At one time refrigerators and vacuum cleaners were hot items sold door to door. These appliances have been slow replacement markets for a long time now, but in their day each of them boomed because nobody had them.

Suddenly the market for each of these items was saturated, market share nosedived, and the industry involved went though a painful shakeout. Thousands of salespeople, who had planned to spend their working careers selling those widgets, found themselves scrambling for a new connection.

On trendy items, reality strikes like a tornado. But in fields in which demand is more solidly based and growth has been steadier over a period of years, downturns usually come as slow downward slides rather than as sudden avalanches. Both are bound to happen at some point or another in most industries.

However, the slow downward slide has the enormous advantage of allowing you ample time to adjust to the new realities in your market—if you're alert enough to see the trend. If you stubbornly ignore the trend, you'll eventually find a sudden decision forced on you.

Slow or sudden, when you move from a first-purchase market into a replacement market on any product, the downturn will last until new technology obsoletes the products now being used. This often happens after a few months in electronics. However, in fields in which the underlying technology is older, this obsoleting process can take decades. And it may never happen.

Study your product line. Are you and your industry working mostly with first-time buyers or mostly with replacement buyers?

If sales in your field are primarily initial purchases, a hard bump is coming. For many people and companies, that hard bump will be a knockout punch. Don't delay giving this matter deep thought. When you do, keep in mind that it's always later than you think.

Sometimes the repair people can give you early warning. If there's a sudden increase in repair business on a product, it can indicate that the market for new products is heading for a sharp change.

And keep in touch with the research and development people for your product. You can get a lot of this information by reading the trade publications in your field. Better yet, make friends in your company's R & D department. If you do that, develop a reputation for having a closed mouth. Otherwise, you may get your R & D friend in trouble and shut off your supply of inside information at the same time.

When Your Company Doesn't Run at the Front of the Pack

If your product is widgets and eight other widget companies are staying on the cutting edge of product innovation but your company isn't, you may suddenly find that nobody wants your widgets anymore.

This can happen even though the overall market for widgets remains strong. Maybe your company doesn't have the funds for the research and the retooling it takes to come up with widgets that are ahead of the market.

What do you do at that point as a salesperson?

Do you sit around and grumble about it with the other salespeople, do you go out and try to get a sales position with a competing widget company, or do you sit down and talk with management before you make a decision? Choose the third option: Sit down and talk with management first. If they can't give you a clear answer, you'll know it's time to consider making a change. It could be that they have a new product waiting in the wings and are waiting for the best time to announce it. Maybe they would rather put you in another department temporarily until the new product is ready, rather than lose you. You won't know unless you ask.

Ethical Questions About Your Product or Service

You might have something in your line that you don't feel good about. You may need to go to your sales manager and say, "I've got a real problem on this item. I wouldn't use it myself, and I don't like to sell it. How can I overcome this feeling?"

Often a better approach is to find salespeople who are hot on the item you're cold on. Get them to tell you why they feel that product is great and how they're selling it.

A lot of people sell things they can't or wouldn't use themselves. It's not an ideal situation, but most of us live most of our lives in less than ideal situations. For example, suppose you're in office equipment and you have several lines. Many of your customers want heavily advertised Brand "A" because they've heard it's the best.

You also carry Brand "X," and you know it's a better product for the same money. But the company wants you to push Brand "A." Maybe they have quotas to meet to keep this popular product line, or maybe its discount is better. Whatever their practical business reasons for pushing Brand "A" might be, when you weigh that position against the customer's best interest, selling Brand "A" makes you uncomfortable. What do you do?

First of all, you need to reeducate yourself. Between two successful product lines, you can't really know which is the best in all future situations for all your customers. Factors you might overlook may be very important to some of your customers. For example: Some customers may want to exactly match the furniture they buy today with additional items they might buy ten years from now. They feel confident Brand "A" will be there to supply them; Brand "X" they have their doubts about.

The problem here lies in trying to find a single answer that will fit every case. Every customer's situation is unique. Keep in mind that all your customers know their own individual situations better than you do. Give them the facts and let them decide.

However, the product you're uncomfortable about selling may pose more serious difficulties: It may directly conflict with your moral values.

You may be able to sell around the problem, that is, sell so much of the stuff you're enthusiastic about that nobody cares whether you sell the bothersome item.

If you can't sell around the item or quiet your moral reservations about it, you may want to consider reappraising your situation. Always be true to yourself.

Your Product or Service

Is it right for you?

Skiers sell ski gear better than nonskiers do. Computer fanatics sell computer hardware and software; computer illiterates can't. Slim, fit people do well selling health club memberships; overweight, out-of-condition people usually get their egos pounded if they try.

Do you have an evangelistic belief in your product or service?

Before he became a chiropractor, a young man I know injured himself on a motorcycle. He was a medical student at the time. After the accident he couldn't stand straight and suffered constant pain. Conventional medical treatment didn't help. In desperation he went to a chiropractor, whose treatments soon eliminated the problem.

This experience impressed the young man so much that he switched to chiropractic study. Later he used the chiropractic method to cure an arthritic problem that had plagued his father for many years. As a result of these experiences and his ongoing success with many patients, today this young man sells his chiropractic services with evangelical zeal.

If you sell sand and gravel to ready-mix companies or pesticides to bug exterminators, you'll probably find it hard to work up that kind of enthusiastic determination. Nevertheless, if you believe your gravel or pesticides are the best to be had, and that your company's products, service, and reliability are also the best, you can psyche yourself up to sell with evangelical zeal. You owe it to your customers and to yourself to do just that.

Office Problems and Opportunities

Office problems and opportunities revolve around your boss, and the people in the other departments you must work with.

Wishing for an Empathetic Boss

There's no excuse for needing empathy from your boss. He or she is there to do a job. You're there to do a job. You're both professionals.

Other Departments

Every department in the company has its own goals, difficulties, and priorities. Meeting its own deadlines, aims, and priorities is enormously more important to that department than meeting yours. In many cases, and all too often for good reason, non-sales departments feel their greatest problems are certain salespeople.

How are you viewed by the line departments? Do they see you as one of the most aggravating problems they must fight, or as someone they really enjoy working with?

Many salespeople never give these matters a moment's thought, believing that accountants, warehouse workers, manufacturing people, and all the other support departments are paid to serve their needs. By disregarding the feelings, priorities, and problems of the organization's internal workers, salespeople plant a lust for revenge in their hearts.

If you operate that way, and it's all too easy to fall into the habit, you're badly mistaken. This mode of operation can result in mysterious screwups in your orders that you'll be forced to waste precious time trying to rectify.

Chances are you'll never know the what or why of these mysterious screwups. The inside people who quietly exacted their revenge for slights suffered at your hands will do so in ways that can't be traced to them.

The mission of the line departments is to make a profit for the company, and to serve all the company's customers, not just yours. They're certainly not there for your personal convenience.

So if you're seen as a troublesome salesperson in any of the departments you must work with, it will hurt you in more ways than you can imagine. Crying wolf too much, playing the prima donna, going over people's heads with unnecessary complaints—these are but a few of the ways you can turn a line department against you. If that happens, your orders won't be filled in a reasonable time. Make more of a nuisance of yourself and instead of pushing your orders to the top of the heap, you may push them clean off the pile.

Keep in mind that as a salesperson you enjoy advantages and perks the people in accounting and manufacturing never see. You probably make more money. You might drive a company car and have an expense account. You don't punch a time clock. You call your own shots to an extent the staffers can only dream about.

In brief, you're envied. Consider whether this means that you're obligated—toward those less privileged than you—to behave with greater restraint, responsibility, and thoughtfulness than the average clock-puncher needs to display.

If you want to stay on top, you'll give careful consideration to making restraint, responsibility, and thoughtfulness your working rule with everybody, especially with your organization's inside people. After all, how good a salesperson can you be if you can't sell the other members of your team on working with you?

REALISTIC EXPECTATIONS

Onward, upward, downward, or outward? As a salesperson, you have four ways to go:

1. Stay where you are, keep getting better known and more skillful, and make more money every year. Whether or not you can do this depends equally on two things: (a) that you haven't locked yourself into a fading market, and (b) that you continue to improve your skills, knowledge, and contacts as the years pass. Far too many salespeople who stay put simply repeat their first year's selling experience every year until they retire. This usually means that their incomes never increase faster than the inflation rate.

2. Accept the promotion to management that could lead either to a higher administrative position or to dissatisfaction and disappointment. If you don't think you know much about management, you're probably right. If you aren't sure if you want to get into management, take some time to educate yourself about management-level positions. Rarely are people taught to be sales managers. They are most often promoted because their selling skills are very good and upper management hopes some of them will rub off on the other salespeople. Before making this risky leap, invest in psychological testing to determine whether you have the personality and value structure that makes for success in management. Whatever you spend for such testing will be only a fraction of the cost of making a major career mistake. Find out what type of training you'll receive to make you a successful manager. Is this a sink or swim management program or is there help?

3. Burn out, slump, or otherwise lose income-generating power. While defeating these dismal developments is the overall subject of this book, the next two chapters zero in on how to beat burnout and snap back from sales slumps.

4. Change jobs. Often looked on as a quick and easy fix for more basic problems, changing jobs is an important career decision and should be carefully considered. Before committing yourself to a job change, make sure you aren't making it for trivial emotional reasons rather than for logical career-building reasons.

Salespeople often quit their jobs to take another sales job, to get out of sales, or to start and run their own businesses. While I'm not a specialist in the art of starting your own business, I've done it. I left my sales management job in Simi Valley, California and founded my own business in Scottsdale, Arizona. Starting your own business is an enormous topic that's mostly outside the scope of this book. However, aspects that apply to salespeople wanting to stay on top are discussed in Chapter Eleven.

IF YOU'VE BEEN WARNED ABOUT POOR SALES

If you are on top of things, keeping records of your sales, ratios, and other data, the warning should come as no shock to you. First of all, don't waste time and energy burning about how the warning is given. After all, there's no easy way to tell someone his performance isn't satisfactory. No matter how the warning was phrased, be happy you were warned instead of being fired without warning.

Then sit down and analyze your actions. Do it privately so you can be totally, brutally honest with yourself. Ask yourself these ten questions:

SECTION 1:

Rate your answers from 10 (always) to 0 (never)

1. Have I been doing the most productive thing every minute of my working day?
2. During the preceding weekend, do I plan my entire work week in general?
3. The night before, do I plan every working day in detail?
4. Do I use test closes in my presentation to determine if my client is warming to my proposition?
5. Do I know at least five closes I can use before walking away from a possible sale?
6. Do I psyche myself up before going into a selling situation?

SECTION 2:

Rate your answers from 10 (frequently) to 0 (never)

7. Have I used my spare time to expand my knowledge about my product or service?
8. Do I work effectively at phone prospecting?
9. Have I rehearsed my presentation?
10. Have I updated my written goals?

ANALYZING THE RESULTS

Now add up the ratings you've given yourself. Your total for all ten questions has to be between 0 and 100.

0 to 29: No wonder you're having problems. The good news is that you'll find it easy to score great gains simply by reversing your action on the above ten questions.

30 to 70: Now you have a list of your weaknesses and strengths. Without allowing your strengths to backslide, start working on your weak points, as indicated by your low ratings.

71 to 100: If your total on these ten questions is more than 70 and you've been warned about your poor sales performance when the overall market for your company's products is satisfactory, only two explanations are likely: your product isn't competitive, or you aren't being realistic in your self-appraisal.

Try the questions again. This time pull off the rose-colored glasses and be tough on yourself. It's a hard world out there.

When you're satisfied that you've been constructive and positive in your self-assessment, develop a plan for raising your ratings on every question. One way is to find out whose sales are up. Ask the top people for help and advice. Find out what they're doing differently. You'll find a wealth of additional ideas for raising your potential in my two earlier books, *How to Master the Art of Selling* and *The Official Guide to Success*.

Concentrate first on bringing up your lowest rating. Then move on to the next lowest rating and work your way through to the top.

But what if you're convinced the problem isn't you, that it's your company's lack of competitiveness?

Before jumping ship because you suspect your company lacks competitiveness, determine whether other salespeople there are doing much better than you with the product. If someone else is doing well, the problem can't be with the product. Sit down with the highest producer and find out what they're doing that's different. If no one else is doing better, go to your sales manager for help before making a new connection.

If It Looks Like You'll Be Asked to Leave

If it looks like you'll be let go because your sales are down, ask if you can be given an opportunity to resign. This will help you save face and possibly leave your record with that company looking a little better than if you were fired. It's simple to do. Just have a talk with your sales manager. Let him or her know you are aware that you're skating on thin ice with this company. Ask for assistance to do better, but if they feel you're beyond help, or cannot wait for you to turn your production around, ask to be given the latitude to resign. Before you ask this question, be aware that you cannot draw unemployment if you resign. Do you think you can get another job quickly or will you need help from the unemployment office until you can find something? In other words, is unemployment compensation worth having the stigma of getting fired?

If You Do Get Fired, What Should Your Attitude Be?

Make sure you fully understand why you were fired. Ask if you aren't sure. Realistically, though, you'll never be told the real reason if there's any possibility—in reality or in someone's overactive imagination—that telling you the truth could fuel a lawsuit.

Begin your rebuilding process with a session of constructive self-criticism. The key word here is constructive. Avoid being too hard on yourself. It can't be all bad. Begin by making a list of all the qualities and abilities you have that are right for a career in selling. Add in the training and skills you've adopted lately. Remind yourself of success stories of past sales situations.

It would be rare to get fired for poor sales and not see it coming. If you are in the lower producing portion of the sales force, you should be going to your sales manager or a top producer regularly for assistance. Don't try to hide the fact that you need help, because your manager knows better. He or she is looking at the sales figures every day.

Make sure you analyze your performance thoroughly enough to recognize the negative attitudes that got you fired. The purpose is to avoid carrying those negative attitudes into your new job, and to avoid setting yourself up for a quick replay of the same old scenario.

Should You Knock the Company That Fired You?

The instinctive reaction is to hit back. Yet doing that makes you look even worse. Most people know companies are looking too hard for good sales producers and don't fire them without serious consideration. If you don't knock the company or the person who fired you, you can save face in several ways.

Ask the company for a letter of reference as to your punctuality, desire to work hard, and positive attitude. Ask that it be placed in your permanent file.

If you're being fired for lack of production, explain to

them that their product might not be the right one for you to sell. Ask them to put that in the letter.

You're probably not the first salesperson to leave because "your heart's not in it" for that product. Chances are it's happened to them frequently.

Let them know that you won't be saying anything negative about them or their product, and that you would expect the same level of professionalism from them in not knocking you.

Let them know you won't be happy with anything negative that might be said about your term of employment with them. If they won't give you a letter, ask them at least not to give out unfavorable references about you. Ask that an instruction to this effect be put in your file. This is where it becomes important that you conduct yourself professionally. It might pay off well at this time if you weren't a member of a clique.

When you start your next job, the chances are no one will know you were fired from your last one unless you tell them yourself. Don't tell anyone that. And don't knock your old employer, because that's almost the same thing as saying you were fired. Instead of knocking them, praise your previous employer whenever you have an opportunity to do so.

The best possible way to save face is to start your new job with enthusiasm, excitement, and determination, and then go on to make a big success of it.

JOB JUMPING

If you change employers too frequently you'll be looked on as a jumper. Ideally you'd stay at least two years with each company you work for. I'm not saying you should stay if you are truly unhappy, but don't be too quick to jump. The problem with many salespeople is that they're looking for that get-rich-quick sales job and can always find what they think are greener pastures. Ninety-nine percent of the time those dreams don't become reality. It takes a commitment of time and dedication to build a customer base that will get you to a point of making high earnings and keep you there.

Have a good reason for making every move, and always make each one in a way that makes you look good. That is to say, don't burn bridges behind you. Never make an enemy unnecessarily. It's a small world.

And make sure to say something nice when you leave. It's the most cost-effective investment you can make in your future—and you can always afford it.

RÉSUMÉS

Think about your résumé as you build your career and especially when you consider changing jobs. Before you quit, it's a good idea to update your résumé to show the change you're considering. How does your résumé look now? Has your stay in your present job been so short that it will cast a bad light over your whole career?

The Impact of Reference Checking

Keep in mind that as a general rule the best employers are the best reference checkers. In the first place, they can afford to be, because the best people want to work for them. Secondly, they are well managed, and one of the hallmarks of a well-managed company is the intense effort it puts into recruitment.

However, it's far more difficult to check references than it used to be. Today almost a third of libel and slander judgments are handed down in suits against employers for something said about a former employee—almost always in response to a reference check.

At the insistence of their legal staffs, most major companies today limit their references to the dates of employment and the job title. However, you can't be sure a previous employer will stonewall a reference checker. If someone in the company with which you're seeking a job knows someone in your old company, they'll quietly get the real story.

In any case, this trend toward limiting information given out to reference checkers serves to emphasize the importance of avoiding rapid job changes, which can be verified. Frequent job changes are a danger signal to most employers; they're taken to indicate problems in your attitude or performance.

Unaccounted-For Time

If you have a lot of time on your résumé that's not accounted for, a prospective employer may think the worst. But sometimes you can leave one job off your résumé without damage, especially if you held the omitted job several years back. However, excluding your current position from your résumé is very likely to hurt your chances of getting the job you want.

Personnel departments see a lot of résumés that account for time in one of the following ways:

Consultant. Many prospective employers will ignore this entry, assuming that during the time in question you couldn't find the job you wanted. Others will suspect that you're concealing a work experience you don't want investigated. If you really were a consultant, provide a list of former clients and other people who will verify that fact.

Employer went out of business. Try to keep in touch with the former owners or supervisors so you can give current phone numbers and addresses for employment verification.

Self-employed. Check with your former suppliers and customers, and use the best of them as references.

Putting a Strong Résumé Together

Before you begin, I suggest going to your local library or bookstore. They will have the most current books available on writing successful résumés. Do your research carefully. Then determine what information you need to gather and get started. If you aren't comfortable in preparing the résumé yourself or don't have someone to help you, try going to a shop that specializes in résumés. You'll probably find one listed in the local Yellow Pages.

This service should be willing to keep your résumé filed electronically on a floppy disk or on a hard drive. This will allow you to update it without retyping the whole thing.

Adopt a simple format and put down the details of each job you've held in the same order. State the facts simply. Weed out unnecessary words and details—when you give dates, for example, provide the years only unless there's a compelling reason to add the days and months. People grasp 1992 more quickly than November 19, 1992. Your résumé will project greater confidence and authority if it's not peppered with useless trivia.

Take the time to make sure your grammar and spelling are impeccable. Don't throw your first draft at prospective employers; keep reworking your résumé until you can't improve it anymore.

Keep your résumé up to date all the time. Don't wait until the need for an up-to-date résumé strikes, because when that happens you'll probably be very busy. Time will be even more precious than usual.

So keep on updating your résumé. Be sure to include training classes and seminars. Also mention any community service organizations you belong to that might provide valuable contacts for a future employer.

CHANGING YOUR JOB IF YOU'RE TRULY UNHAPPY WITH IT

Free yourself from anger and any desire for revenge. This is the most important consideration in breaking off any connection. All too many people quit jobs for real or imagined slights and then waste energy trying to hit back.

They knock their former employers every chance they get; sometimes they take jobs with competitors to pass on trade secrets. Generally, the most they accomplish is to bounce a bullet off their former employer's armor. Only rarely will a departing employee be able to do important and lasting damage that will match the damage they inflict on themselves.

And don't forget the legal ramifications of passing trade secrets. If you let a big cat out of the bag, your former employer may leave no stone unturned to make you pay. Even if they don't win a judgment, your legal expenses could be staggering.

If you're talking to other companies during time your present employer is paying you for, you're being dishonest. This fact won't escape the best companies that you approach for a job. So, don't do it.

In most situations, you're far better off taking the high road, especially if your performance has been good and your relationship with your employer is a positive one.

Take some time to think through your reasons for being dissatisfied, that is, the reasons you can tell your employer without giving offense. If you find yourself worried about handling the situation, perhaps you're not being honest with yourself about why you really want to leave this company. Once you have decided and if there will be no hard feelings, ask your boss for a private meeting. At that meeting present your plans openly. There's no reason to be emotional; it's business—you're making a well-thought-out career move. Let him or her know that you are concerned with the welfare of your customers and will help make their transition to another representative as smooth as possible. State that you'll continue to be productive while you're looking for another connection.

Reassure your employer that you won't knock the company or carry trade secrets to competitors. Tell him that you'll schedule as many job interviews as possible on your own time. Offer to keep your planned resignation secret from the other employees for as long as possible.

In brief, demonstrate a strong desire to minimize the employer's loss of face and inconvenience occasioned by your departure. And, of course, make sure your performance lives up to your promises.

While at first glance this approach might appear too generous by far, in reality it's greatly to your advantage. This way of handling things almost guarantees that you'll get the best reference they can give you. What your present employer says about you could be the key to your being offered the position you want.

Even in these days of caution about slander and libel, the careful reference checkers who control the best positions still look for applicants whose previous employers praise them enthusiastically. Lack of praise, although it's not slander, can have the same effect as a negative report if it turns you into a runner-up for the job you want.

One caution though: Many businesses make it a practice to immediately terminate the employment of anyone who even hints that they are considering leaving the company. You should know what your company's policy is on this matter before asking for that meeting with your manager. And, it's wise to be emotionally and financially prepared to be unemployed at the end of the meeting if that be the case.

How to Get the Best Possible Next Job

1. Initiate the move yourself instead of waiting for the axe to fall.

2. Plan your move carefully, but keep your plans to yourself. If you can't keep a secret this important to your future, how can you expect secrecy from anyone else?

3. Check the help wanted ads in national newspapers such as *USA Today* and the *Wall Street Journal* as well as in your local papers.

4. Many of the best jobs are never advertised; they're filled through networking. This is another good reason to keep in contact with as many people as possible.

5. Many companies prefer to work with employment placement services (often called headhunters) when filling jobs. Generally the employers pay the fees, so you can explore this route to your next job almost without any cost at all. You'll find employment agencies listed in your local Yellow Pages; some specialize in salespeople.

6. Three kinds of responses are frequently made to an ad:

  a. A phone call
  b. A letter with résumé
  c. Appearing in person

You can show aggressiveness and enthusiasm by phoning for information, following up with a quick letter addressed to the right person, and then, after allowing time for the letter to be received, calling to request an interview.

7. Avoid firing off more applications than you can carefully research. You can generate so much paper and phone work with inferior opportunities that your best opportunity gets lost in the shuffle.

8. While you're working at your present job, keep in close enough touch with your previous employers to ensure that they'll remember who you are and what a great job you did.

9. Send a typewritten letter with your résumé. Here are some specific tips on writing a stronger letter:

  a. Center the job title you're seeking in capitals above your salutation.
  b. Don't begin with "Gentlemen," or "Dear Sirs." A woman will probably be the first one who reads your letter—and you don't necessarily want her to be the last one who sees it. Also avoid "To Whom It May Concern." It's old-time. Use "Good Morning" as your salutation. So they read the letter in the P.M. How upset can they get about that?
  c. Mirror their ad in your letter by reflecting their wants. For example, if they say they need a dynamic, nonsmoking self-starter, weave those words and concepts into your explanation of what you can do for them. The idea is to produce a letter that will read like it's from someone who fits their wants almost perfectly, so that you'll get your foot in their door.

    However, if you use their ad word-for-word they'll know what you're doing, and they'll probably distrust what you've written. Instead of their precise words, reflect the qualities they want as clearly as you truthfully can.

d. After the salutation, get right to the point. Keep the body of your letter brief. Don't say the obvious. In particular, don't tell them how you happened to see their ad. Who cares?

e. Be enthusiastic and aggressive but avoid arrogance. Don't tell them you're very qualified for their job; they'll be the judges of that. Instead, tell them you're a hard worker and an enthusiastic quick study.

f. The self-evident next step—if you're being considered—is an interview. They know that. Avoid urging the obvious on them. But maybe you're a long distance away. If you're willing to fly in for an interview, say so.

g. Staple your résumé to your letter. Want ads can generate hundreds of replies, and it's easy for your letter and résumé to get separated.

CHAPTER FOUR

ROADBLOCKS TO SUCCESS

Few people reach the top in sales, unless they're internally motivated self-starters. Even fewer stay there long unless they are able to recharge their ability to motivate themselves.

DEPENDING ON SUPERVISION

If your motivation to succeed in sales is dependent on a supervisor—or on anyone at all except yourself—you're outer-directed. This means that in the selling game you're like a nonswimmer floating in the middle of a lake on an inner tube. When the inner tube blows, you drown.

Let's say you're depending on someone to pump you up—or kick your backside when you really need a jolting. Sooner or later that person simply won't do it. Maybe they've been fired, maybe they're sick, maybe they're too occupied with things they consider more important than your selling performance. And maybe they just want you to grow up.

The reason doesn't matter because the effect is the same. Without the outer direction you've always used for motivation, you'll lose drive, confidence, and purpose. Your sales performance will nose-dive. If your motivator is permanently out of your life, you're probably in for a long, severe slump. It may well last until, as a last resort, you develop the ability to direct yourself.

Inner-directed people—that is, people who derive their motivation from their own minds rather than from any source outside their skins—never have a slump caused by a supervisor's inattention, failure, or absence. And they rarely have the deep, long-lasting slumps that outer-directed people are so prone to, either. Because they are inner-directed, they know how to control their emotions and change direction when what they're doing isn't achieving the results they desire.

If you've been depending on someone to wind you up and get you running, make it your first business to become inner-directed. How? By developing your self-motivation skills. Until you learn how to drive yourself, you're a flyer who can't land a plane. If your pilot passes out, your future isn't promising. In most cases, people who aren't motivated really have a problem with goals.

WHAT TURNS YOUR TURBO ON?

While you're studying the motivations that cause people to buy your product or service, also study the motivations that could make your motor run faster. In other words, figure out exactly what excites you, what keys you up, what pulls you forward.

The trick to staying on top is to stay motivated. To do that, you've got to know what turns your own turbo on. What excites your father, thrills your Uncle Ted, or makes your boss dance on the counter won't necessarily do it for you. Know yourself.

Actors might draw on the experience of their grandmother dying when they need to portray sadness, on how they felt on their first date when they need to depict uncertainty. They can do this because they know themselves and, through themselves, all of mankind.

In much the same way, a few astute salespeople intensify their sales presentations by drawing on powerful emotional memories of a personal nature. They do this internally. Their customers are never aware that the enthusiasm with which they sell springs from events long past, rather than from the immediate situation.

Channeling yesterday's positive personal feelings into today's sales challenge is of great value. If you can do that, you can easily acquire another closely associated skill that's immensely more valuable: the ability to understand what feelings motivate you. When you know that, your success is assured because you'll be able to harness the enormous power of emotion to achieve your goals. Unfortunately, negative feelings also come into play here. That's why you must learn how to handle them.

The experience of Jake Adams illustrates how this works. Jake was in the habit of taking a shortcut across the graveyard to get home. Coming across the graveyard one rainy night, he fell into a freshly dug grave.

Jake landed in soft mud, picked himself up, and tried to climb out. But the sides of the grave were slippery from the rain and he kept sliding back. He was soon covered with mud from head to foot and exhausted.

"Well, I've got to make the best of it here until help comes in the morning," Jake told himself at last, giving up. He settled down in a corner and finally dozed off.

An hour later loud curses woke Jake up. Someone else had fallen into the grave and was grunting and swearing, vainly trying to get out.

From his corner Jake shouted over the rain, "It's no use. You can't get out."

Jake heard only a terrified squawk before a crack of lightning revealed the newcomer scrambling out of the grave. He had the motivation Jake lacked.

That kind of fire in your stomach can inspire you to do great things. Spend whatever time it takes to find out what turns you on. Then use that fire to get what you want out of life.

CLIQUES

Cliques can be very much like a silent but deadly virus to a salesperson's career. You don't always see it coming and before you know it, you're classified by the rest of the office as being in a certain group, with certain beliefs about the company, the product, and how things should be run. Needless to say, this is not always good.

Someone will always want to divide up the office into opposing cliques: the "in" people (me and my friends) and the "out" people (everybody else, usually thought of as "all the creeps around here"). It might be the salespeople against management, accounting, or the shipping department. It could be the underdogs against the top producers, or the swingers against the squares. This ancient tactic of divide and control is an emotional, almost instinctive, reaction many people have to the pressures of working with others. It would be nice if we could say there are a certain types of people causing these problems, but they can be caused by big-headed top producers or by low producers on their way out trying to take others with them. Some people just like to agitate things. Joe Average has nothing special in his life and wants to belong to a clique to feel important, to gain a sense of security. The result is always the same: interoffice turmoil and negativity.

What Do Cliques Do?

Cliques favor their members at the expense of outsiders, and in subtle and not-so-subtle ways try to make nonmembers feel inferior, unwanted, and ineffective. These tactics often succeed.

This means that an office clique is capable of stealing far more from you than some thief can snatch. The mugger only gets your wallet or purse, but the office clique can steal part of your livelihood and your self-image if you let it.

Where management is weak, a clique may determine who gets the best assignments, promotions, territories, and other benefits. Under capable management, however, cliques have little or no power.

Why Cliques Form

Cliques flourish in a climate of insecurity. Whenever a small group feels threatened by the results of its members' own negative attitudes and poor performances, the members are likely to try to form alliances to protect themselves. Sometimes one person is the clique's driving force from the beginning; sometimes the leader emerges later.

Top producers seldom organize a clique. They are normally too busy to even know this type of thing is going on. It's true that some top producers are very insecure people, but they cope with their fears by generating more sales.

If cliques wield power where you work, find out who the leaders are and study their motives. You'll generally find they're trying to justify their own poor sales performance or another lack in their lives by attacking the company or other employees. These people can be very persuasive as they argue that the company's advertising is a cruel joke, its pricing policies are unrealistic, and its products look sick compared to the competition's. When you can't deny that the problem exists, consider approaching the clique with a positive way of handling its gripes.

Newcomers' Difficulties in Avoiding Cliques

Two of the most universal and powerful needs that human beings feel are the desire to be accepted, and the desire for comfort. New circumstances—joining a new company, for example—knock away some accustomed sources of comfort and acceptance. This can make us emotionally vulnerable.

When coming into a new group to work, one of your most important defensive tasks is to figure out what kind of people are in the office, and what kind of group they are trying to put you into.

Say that as a new salesperson you join an insurance agency in which thirty people are selling insurance. Generally someone there wants you to get on his or her side. Maybe Mary and Bill have their little group that they want you to join. If so, what does that group represent?

When going into a new situation, everybody wants to be

comfortable. And, like the youngster who changes schools in fifth grade, they want to be comfortable now, not next week or next month.

The problem is that newcomers don't always get in with the best people. If they're lucky they might get in with a group that looks at things in a positive light. But newcomers tend to be so hungry for friends and acceptance that they'll go with the first people to show some friendliness.

On a new job, if you don't make it into the positive group right away, you're in danger of falling in with the wrong people—the complainers, the negative-minded, the goof-offs. Losers are always the easiest people to gain acceptance from. They don't expect much of themselves, so they don't expect much of you.

How do you avoid falling in with the wrong people? The best defense demands some emotional toughness. You have to be able to stand being alone until you have time to see what's what.

In the meantime, be cordial but reserved with everybody. Avoid getting involved too closely with any one person or group until you've had a chance to survey the entire office.

If you jump at the first close relationship that's offered, you're likely to get in with a bunch of people who are on their way out of the company. If this happens, when they go they're liable to take you with them.

You can spot such a group easily because right away you'll start hearing about how rotten the company is; how dumb, insensitive, and unreasonable the boss is; how unbeatable the competition is. Unfortunately, this happens to too many new salespeople.

If it happens to you, your success with that company probably hinges on whether you have the courage to say, "Hey, wait a minute. I haven't been here a week yet. Let me make up my mind for myself."

If saying something like that means someone or several people might not like you anymore, you must have enough emotional maturity and self-confidence to handle the situation. Otherwise it's questionable whether you have the mental toughness to succeed in selling.

After all, as a salesperson, you've chosen to operate on your own. And, as a salesperson, you'll succeed or fail with customers in the field, not with the bunch of nay-sayers camped around the coffee pot in the office.

When newcomers are lucky enough to have some of the top people take them under their wing, they'll hear things like, "This is a terrific company. Things are going great. You couldn't have come to a better place."

Getting in with positive people is a sensational break for anyone who gets it. But things don't always happen that way. Usually complainers are the quickest ones to buddy up with new people. They always need someone new to listen to their bitterness and excuses for not cutting it themselves. Complainers have a huge emotional stake in seeing a newcomer fail. Why? Because if a newcomer can do well, it's painfully clear that the complainers have only themselves to blame for their failure. They want to blame the company, the boss, the product—anything or anyone except the real cause: their own shortcomings.

RESISTING PEER PRESSURE

If you find yourself tempted to waste your time or feel peer pressure to do so, here's a way to focus your energy on making productive use of every minute.

Decide how much you want to make after taxes per week, add what it takes to cover taxes, and then divide that amount by the number of hours you plan to work each week. The result is your projected hourly rate. Divide by 60 to get your projected rate per minute.

The next time you're tempted to stand around your place of business telling jokes, ask yourself whether anybody will pay you that projected rate for killing time. When you know your projected rate per minute, you can quickly calculate how much it will cost you to shoot the breeze for ten or twenty valuable minutes.

And it's true, you don't punch in. But in sales you don't punch out at a set time either. Your hours are flexible, meaning that much of your sales work is done before or after the customers' offices open and close. That's why selling ranks among the highest-paid hard work and the lowest-paid easy work you can do.

The Us-Against-Them Battles You Don't Have to Fight

Time and effort put into supporting one clique against another goes right down the drain because it doesn't help you make sales. Far better to put that time and effort into figuring out ways to steer clear of cliques.

In a badly clique-ridden company, it will be difficult to avoid the realities. You're sure to come under heavy pressure to choose sides.

Before you put much time into a clique-corrupted company, consider taking your talents elsewhere. You don't have to stay. The best companies reward talent regardless of whether or not you pay homage to the right clique. In fact, where management is strong, your progress will be faster and more sure if you don't join a clique.

Management's Stake in Controlling Cliques

Companies are organized with the intention that all power and influence will be held by management. More precisely, it will be held by the people management hires, promotes, or anoints with power—that is to say, everybody who works for the company in a supervisory or managerial capacity. This means that cliques can gain power and influence only by taking it away from management.

In other words, cliques pose a direct threat to management's ability to direct the company's profitability and growth. Not surprisingly, managements tend to distrust cliques. Anyone who plays an active part in one will likely be viewed as a potential conspirator who is not to be trusted or rewarded any more than necessary.

Farsighted managers lose no opportunity to weaken or break up cliques among the people they supervise. When they have a promotion to make or a better territory to assign, the wise manager will give it to someone who steers clear of cliques.

Likewise, when they have the chance to reassign some-one to the company equivalent of Siberia, they'll send a clique leader. If that's too risky, they'll send a lower-ranked member of the clique. A manager who is timid about opposing a certain clique will often banish its newest member.

Whether you join a clique deliberately or drift into one unconsciously, the effect is the same in management's eyes. Your loyalty is suspect because part of it belongs to the clique. In other words, you're part of an anti-management group. Don't be surprised if you're treated that way.

If You're Already in a Clique, How Do You Get Out?

Many salespeople find themselves drawn into cliques without realizing what's involved. It's not as if there's a sign posted that says "Clique Initiation" and you receive a set of rules and an agenda for each clique.

Cliques make it easy for desirable new members to join—it happens without formality. The rewards are immediate, the penalties invisible—at first. Allowing yourself to be drawn into a clique often is the course of least resistance.

However, the penalties of belonging to cliques are clearly visible to those who are acquainted with the purposes of cliques. If you now realize that you are in a clique, how do you get out?

It's surprisingly simple: (1) Tell the clique members that you want to do better, and follow up with aggressive action to improve your sales performance. (2) Support the company's position whenever you can, and say good things about it every chance you get.

Like magic, you'll be out of the clique because now you're making everybody in it very uncomfortable. You won't be accepted by them anymore.

CONTESTS

Most companies provide stimulation for their salespeople in the form of sales contests. Some companies go so far as to have some sort of contest going on at all times. Others may use contests only when introducing new products or when management feels sales need a boost. If contests are set up properly there will be the same amount of challenge and opportunity for each salesperson.

Contests are great. Wise managers will establish prizes based on knowing what the "hot buttons" are for their salespeople. If the group is turned on by trips, there will usually be some sort of trip in the prize list. If the group gets more excited about extra cash, at least one of the rewards or options will be to take cash.

The emotional excitement created by contests is highly beneficial to both the salespeople and management. Salespeople who wouldn't ordinarily go out of their way to meet a tough prospect will do just that during a contest. Others who don't usually go for sales training will brush up on their basics as soon as a contest is announced.

I suggest that as soon as a contest is announced, you get all the details you possibly can about it. Make sure you understand all the rules of how it will work and what is expected of you. If it involves only one product, take a little extra time to reread any product literature available on that item. Get to know the product inside and out. Find out what you can about the customers who are currently satisfied with that product. By doing a little research, you'll probably be able to find similarities in the customer type that benefits most from that particular product. Then, go out and find more of those people!

If you aren't already in this habit, during a contest is the best time to begin listening to motivational and sales training tapes in your car. Every tidbit of information you can pick up can bring you one step closer to winning that prize that turned you on so much when the contest was announced.

If, during the contest, you feel your enthusiasm beginning to wane, get several pictures of the prize you're after and put them all around you. Put one inside your planner. Hang one above your desk. Put one on your bathroom mirror. Keep one in your car. Pretty soon you'll be able to not only see that prize, but feel it, smell it, and taste it, because it will be yours!

Contest Pitfalls

Some salespeople take contests so seriously that they forget they are on a team. They become totally self-centered about their selling and get paranoid about sharing positive experiences. These people are very insecure and somewhat immature. The key is to remember always that above all else, you are on a team. You all work for the same company. So, if you're one of those paranoid people, grow up and learn to be happy for others who are striving along the same lines you are. If the level of competition gets so high that the stress is too much to bear, go talk to your sales manager about it. Perhaps contests are not the right motivation for you. They're not for everyone.

Another pitfall of contests is that many salespeople work so hard during them that the following month, they have nothing left to give. Or, they do so well in the contest that they feel they can slide in the next month's production level. You should want to participate and do as much as you can during a contest, but not to the extent of having one great month followed by a bad month.

Level out your production. It can be very hard on some people emotionally to win the contest this month, and then find themselves worrying about cash the next month.

When Contests Just Aren't Your Thing

You have to know what's good for you psychologically, what's good for your physical and mental health. How much of this contest hype and hoopla can you handle?

But you don't want to be the type of person who says, "Nuts to this contest. I don't care about it."

You want to be a team player, but your game goes on every month, not just every third month or whenever the sales manager runs a contest. You want to be good every month, not just in a contest month.

If you can do a little more, or a lot more, in a contest month, that's fine. But not if it's going to burn you out and cause your sales to fall off the following month. Burnout means you have nothing left, emotionally or physically. Then it's slump time.

If you find out that contests aren't your thing, don't ruin it for the other salespeople by adopting a negative attitude. Don't make excuses. Just do the best you can, and if you don't win, so what. You can be the top producer in the company and never win a contest. Remember the old story of "The Tortoise and the Hare."

Some of the other top producers may hit big during contest months and slide off during the other months. Maybe you're in there producing steadily, at the same high level of performance month after month. It may fit your personality better to hit steadily like that. Just make sure that management understands your position of not fighting the contests, but not letting them destroy your effectiveness either. You can participate, but it might be that you don't change anything you're doing. If you don't change anything, you might still win once in a while.

Everybody is different. Take time to learn what situations bring out your best performances. Then follow the practices that will create those situations. If you consistently follow what makes you function best, in the long run your overall performance will be far above that of people who allow outside influences to push them into things that don't fit their personalities and physical limitations. You may find out that contests give you hives, or keep you from sleeping at nights. If so, they're not for you. But it's no big deal.

However, some people need stimulus from outside to perform. The point is, accept your own limitations but don't spoil things for anyone else. Go along with the contest, applaud whoever wins it. Contests are generally good for the company, so give it your vocal support even if you don't feel you can go all out to win it.

You may want to go to management and explain your position. "I'm going to be in there every month plugging for the company. You know that my production is steady, it's building, and I want to make more money. But there's something about contests that I just can't stand. Maybe it's something out of my childhood—I don't know—but contests drive me crazy."

Most managers will understand that position. Most of them will say something like, "It's okay. We know you're a self-starter, and we count on your production. But some of the people around here have dead batteries. They just can't get going unless we jump start them."

One of these days a contest might come along that does get your adrenaline pumping. The prize that gets you going might be two weeks in Tahiti, a month "down under," a wind-surfer—or a sizable hunk of hard cash.

How Do You Recover From a Bruising Sales Contest?

Some of the sales that would normally come in after the contest ends get accelerated so they'll count in the contest. Effective salespeople always give high priority to any sale that might be closed quickly, of course. It happens naturally, almost automatically.

In non-contest months, effective salespeople also spend considerable time hammering away at future-sales-building tactics. Top producers do this with consistent efficiency. However, during contests, some serious contestants have to let cold-calling and other long-term sales-building efforts slide while they concentrate on sales that can be closed before the contest ends. This causes a slump in sales performance after the contest ends because what's coming down the pipeline is considerably less than usual. Here are some ways to recover quickly from a contest:

Before the Contest Starts

- If you know a contest will be beginning next month, increase your cold-calling and other long-range sales-building efforts this month.
- Plan ahead. Prepare a detailed schedule for your first weeks after the contest. Schedule exactly who you'll see and what you'll do to make a fast, fresh start.

- Set new non-contest goals. Do this before the contest even starts, so you'll be working toward inspiring, achievable personal goals as you compete in the contest.
- Arrange your own reward. As soon as you hear about the contest, plan a special reward for yourself for turning in a strong first month after the contest.

After the Contest Ends

Companies often provide special pricing or financing during contest periods. When the contest ends, back to the regular pricing and financing you go.

Clearly, this development will make it harder to turn in a strong after-contest sales performance. But what is the real problem here? Is it the customers' feelings about the change—or your own?

You might have been happily selling all year long on 6 percent financing. The rate drops to 3 percent for contest month. Then the contest ends and you're back to 6 percent financing again. But now that 6 percent rate seems huge; you can't even talk about it with a customer without wincing—and your sales suffer.

Don't ignore this problem. Make a special effort to imprint the rightness of the regular rates or prices on your mind and emotions, so that you can quote them without the slightest hint of reluctance or apology.

- Motivate yourself. Don't wait around for someone else to get you up and running. Do it yourself.
- Get out into the field aggressively. Do it fast. Resist the urge to hang around the office jawing about the contest.
- Concentrate on your most effective sales-building tactics as shown by your records—cold-calling, lead follow-up, whatever. To a certain extent, you're starting over, so keep in mind that you have to work efficiently. Otherwise, your income will suffer.

CHAPTER FIVE

YOUR EGO, YOUR COMPANY, AND YOUR PERFORMANCE

REACTING TO ACHIEVEMENT

Once you begin to achieve success in your sales position, others will start to take notice of you. Of course, you'll receive recognition from your sales manager for a job well done. However, you could also catch the attention of upper management. Ego-wise, it's pretty terrific when busy executives with impressive titles start talking to you about how fantastic you're doing. Your fellow salespeople will be watching you as well. How will you react to all of this new attention?

There are four basic ways salespeople react to new levels of achievement and its attendant notoriety. Some salespeople are basically humble people who won't like being showered with the attention warranted by their achievement. They'll say little or nothing when congratulated and will wish as hard as they can that they could turn into wallpaper and no longer be noticed. It's okay to be modest, but your future successes are seeded in part by how you learn to handle today's success. So you're out of your comfort zone accepting praise and recognition. If it's your desire to stay in sales and do well in sales, you have to learn to handle the praise and recognition that comes with the territory. It's great to be humble, but not so humble that you don't allow yourself to accept the well-deserved praise of others and acknowledge to yourself that you've earned what you were working for. Let the effect of this new achievement take its course and increase your level of self-confidence. After all, self-confidence increases competence and competence increases sales.

Force yourself, if you have to, to step forward and accept the recognition with grace. Take a lesson from others you've seen accept recognition and awards, even if it's from the Academy Awards.

We've all seen actors and actresses, directors and writers get up on stage in front of millions of people and make complete fools of themselves. You don't want to do that, do you? Of course not. So, watch carefully those whose acceptances make you feel good and make you respect them. Study them and learn to do it with their style. Use their words if you have to. One word of caution, though: Don't try to use the words of someone else in your company. Let them think you're more creative than that, even if you borrow your words from someone outside the company.

Another type of salesperson will accept the recognition earned by an achievement, but will downplay it by saying, "It could have been better." Or, "I could have beaten that record if only . . ." These people are so driven to achieve a level down the road that is unrealistic that they never allow themselves to be happy with the present moment of glory. If you're one of those people, to you I say, "Stop and smell the roses." If you can't take a moment to sit back and bask in the exhilaration of achieving some great sales feat, you'll drive yourself into an early grave with stress and eventual burnout. We cover both of these topics in great detail in later chapters. For now, please realize that if you're always looking to some point in the future to be happy, you'll be missing a lot of great things that are happening all around you today.

It's great to have goals, and I highly recommend that you have your next level of goals in mind, if not already set, before you reach your current level. But, never forget to allow yourself time to accept and enjoy the rewards of each goal you achieve. If there's no time for enjoyment, why strive so hard for the goal?

A third type of salesperson is one I hope you never become because it only leads to unhappiness and ruin. That's the salesperson who becomes an egomaniac when he receives the lauds and praise that come with achievement. If you begin thinking of yourself as being a sales wizard and the hottest shot this company has ever seen, do you think the praise will last long? Probably not. It's okay to pat yourself on the back for making a tough sale or winning a contest, but don't take too long to get back to reality. You see, if you start to believe you're so good at selling that you don't have to work at it anymore, pretty soon you'll find yourself not working at it anymore. You'll be looking for another position.

The fourth type of salesperson is the ideal. It's what I'd love to see you become. When you are a top producer, accept the honor with grace. Thank all the people in the company who have helped you achieve that status. Give credit where credit is due. Be willing to share your experiences. If a new strategy or technique worked with your product, be willing to demonstrate it to the rest of the sales staff—when they ask. If they don't ask and you try to give them your best stuff, many average salespeople will let their egos get in the way. They won't want to accept help because it will be admitting they're not as good as you. No one ever wants to admit they're less than anyone, so be careful how you offer assistance. You might want to just share an idea in a casual manner while having coffee in the office. Don't try to establish the "Joe Champion School of Sales Techniques." Others on your team who are really serious about their selling careers will usually come to you one-on-one and ask for ideas or help. Give them all the help you can without putting a big dent in the time you spend with clients. After all, you won't be able to stay on top if you don't get out there and serve the clients well.

Always try to keep in mind that any recognition you earn in your sales career is a compliment you receive for serving the customers better than most salespeople do. The key phrase here is "serving the customers." I have taught for many years that in sales your income is a direct reflection of your ability to serve your clients. Never forget that. Don't let your ego get so blown out of proportion that it interferes with the level of service you give. I'm reminded of a message someone sent me to share with my students a few years back. It's called the Salesperson's Prayer. It goes like this: "Lord, protect me from my own ego."

You must always have, at the minimum, as much interest in your clients as you do in yourself. If your attitude gets too good for your customers, then pretty soon you're not going to have any. Beware of falling into the habit of calling your customers derogatory names such as "flakes" or "turkeys," or saying that doing business with them is "like shooting ducks in a barrel." If you allow yourself to do that, it will become twice as difficult to treat them well. The people you serve deserve your respect. They deserve to be called and thought of as clients or customers. I teach my students that in order to keep their egos in check, they should always think of clients and customers as "the people I serve."

YOUR FAME AROUND THE OFFICE

If your sales are rising steeply, there's another aspect you need to consider: How will your coworkers handle all the attention you're getting? It's been said that friends can stand anything except your success. More than a thousand years ago, envy was identified as the fourth deadly sin. It's vicious—and almost universal. If your personal friends will have trouble handling your success, how will the gang at the office cope with it?

A lot of how they handle your success will depend on how you handle the success of others. Think about it for a moment. I know this sounds a lot like "The Golden Rule," but if you treat others with admiration and respect for their successes, they'll probably treat you that way when you succeed. You can count on at least some of them—and maybe even most of them—not handling it well. Since you can't control their attitude, you'll have to cope with this problem by controlling your own attitude.

How will the office gang's envy be expressed? Subtly, because they can't admit, even to themselves, that they don't like you anymore just because you're doing better than they. But you may feel their disapproval, their coldness, their jealousy. Of course, the more mature members of your team will be the first to congratulate you and wish you continued success. However, it's unfortunate, but the working world isn't filled with mature, competent individuals. It takes all types of people to make up the world and, unfortunately, only one type is ideal. The other, less than ideal, personalities have to be recognized and dealt with as well.

What can you do with the people who aren't happy about your success and recognition? The key is to rid yourself of the idea that you must have their approval. If you crave the approval of the people around you, you're doomed to their level of mediocrity. Unconsciously, you'll limit your sales efforts so as not to upset your coworkers, which means pointing your career in the same direction as theirs. For most of the salespeople in the world, that direction is not very high up the ladder of achievement.

You have to make a choice. Are you willing to sacrifice your future for a warmer "Hi" in the morning from your fellow salespeople? Probably not. The best way to handle those people is to remain as positive and friendly as you've always been. Don't react outwardly to any jibes or comments they make. Take it all with a smile. It'll kill 'em. Eventually, the sport of knocking the top producer will lose its interest and they'll leave you alone.

If you are not the top producer, rather than joining the negative people in the office in condemning the top people, you should watch those high producers closely and learn from them so you can reach the heights they've attained.

MANAGING YOUR MANAGER

If you're lucky, as a new salesperson, you'll be hired by a very supportive, helpful manager. The supportive manager enjoys taking a certain amount of raw talent and training and molding it into successful sales material. This wise manager will also hire experienced, previously successful sales veterans to balance out his or her sales staff.

I wasn't so lucky in my first sales position. The support I got from my first sales manager consisted of a few slaps on the back and thumbs-up signs. Every now and then I'd hear a "Go get 'em, tiger!" Believe me, having a manager like that is like having no manager at all. But, as I covered in Chapter Four, you can't rely on your sales manager for all of your motivation. No manager will ever be all things to all salespeople.

On the whole, managers understand that their main job is selling salespeople on selling. This requires a myriad of methods, including helping the salesperson set goals, establishing quotas, and helping the salesperson analyze his selling skills so that he can get the help he needs to constantly improve. A warm smile, public praise, and private criticism are all essential to the effective sales manager. However, most salespeople fail to comprehend the level of stress the sales manager faces on a daily basis. His stress level is high simply because he's in a middle management position. The sales manager doesn't make the rules. He doesn't decide what the bottom line has to be and how that relates to sales. The sales manager gets orders from above and massages the figures around to fit the sales staff, then assigns quotas. And, believe me, that part of the job alone can be as difficult as hammering square pegs into round holes. Rarely do salespeople agree that their quotas are fair. But, it's the sales manager's job to help you stretch yourself to at least try to reach the goal.

LAYING THE GROUNDWORK

If you're hired by one person to work for another person, make sure you meet your boss-to-be. It is within your rights to meet the person you'll be working with, especially if someone else is doing the hiring. This will give you a chance to find out if there are ill feelings between those people. If you sense trouble, either square things away with your future manager or don't take the job.

If you're sincerely interested in the job, you might as well confront the situation and let the sparks fly where they will, because it's your job and your future. You don't want to get fired. You want to submit whatever recommendations you can for improving the situation, and if that doesn't work, leave before you invest much time in a hopeless cause.

An emotionally unstable boss can cause you a lot of grief over a long period of time—unless you move promptly to prevent it happening. Unstable bosses can hurt your attitude, not only toward selling and other people but, worse yet, they can inflict long-lasting damage to your attitude toward yourself.

There are plenty of managers who don't deal off the top of the deck, especially in companies in which managers are not allowed to hire their own people. Sometimes this is because they hire in their own image and their personalities are so bad that the results are disastrous. Some sales managers only want to have one type of salesperson on their staff, preferably someone who represents a clone of themselves. Or, they want to have a full staff of champion, top producers. Unfortunately, that's a dream that just can't come true. Not everyone can be on the top. And, no one personality type of salesperson will be able to relate to the various types of clients. So, when you're hired in a new sales position, ask to sit down with the manager as soon as possible. Ask a lot of questions and persist to get the answers before you have your heart and soul embedded in a company and product you love, only to find out there's a manager you just cannot work under.

"Exactly what is it that you expect from me?" This is a good question to ask your new boss. "What do you want me to do?" Take notes of his reply. Normally, in well-run companies, they sit down with you and go through the procedures you're expected to follow.

They'll tell you, "Here's what I want you to do. Here are the kind of people you should contact. Then you should do this, and that. I'm going to review your performance with you in this area."

If the company is not doing these things, be smart enough to help them by asking the right questions. You may have to sit down with your manager and determine what you need to do.

You want to be able to say something like, "Okay, Pat. You're telling me that if I call on ten customers a day, and I do this . . ." and this—a whole list of things . . . "you're going to be happy with what I'm doing. And I can report to you every week."

Your new boss will say, "Oh, yeah, that would be great."

"Thanks. I'll do all those things. I appreciate your giving me a chance to get all this straight."

If they're not giving new salespeople that kind of send-off, it's probably because they're overworked. Nevertheless, properly indoctrinating new salespeople is a vital task of sales management that your boss should be doing. If he or she isn't, take the initiative and get the answers you need in order to be a truly productive salesperson. You should have found out about available training, sales meetings, and review periods when you were interviewing. Don't hesitate to bring those things up if your sales manager is not seeing that you get what you were promised.

This way there's no doubt in your mind, or in your manager's mind, when you come back and say, "Okay, I've done all the things we talked about but I'm having a problem."

The way in which each sales manager handles the stresses and responsibilities of the job varies tremendously with experience and personality. It's helpful to describe a few types of sales managers you may encounter in your selling career and consider how to work most effectively with them.

TYPES OF MANAGERS

1. I already mentioned the NONINVOLVED manager I had when I began my selling career. His late-morning arrivals made it difficult for an outside sales force to meet with him. It was tough to get him to sit down and talk when I was facing challenges in my selling experiences. When you'd tell him you were having some problems, he'd give you a little motivational talk, but nothing concrete. If it weren't for the top people in the office who needed little or no direction to do well, the company never would have met its sales quotas. This type of manager may or may not believe in training. If he does believe in it, he'll invest in a couple of books or sets of tapes and have his secretary hand them out, but he won't become directly involved in training. If you are new in sales and find yourself working for this type of manager, try to find a top producer to work with you and give you the specific help you need to get your career off to a good start. If you can't find that support early on, your career will most likely flounder until you do. You may need to consider making a change. You might be able to transfer into another division of that company that will have a stronger, more supportive manager. If not, don't waste your time. Find another company to work for that does give strong support to its sales staff.

2. The next sales manager is the COACH. I hope you find one of these during your sales career. They're excellent for new salespeople. The coach has a lot of motivational meetings. He includes training and expects you to learn it and apply it. He wins your respect and you develop a desire to please him by doing your best for him. The door to his office will always be open for you. Be sure you share your successes as well as your failures with this coach. This type of person thrives on seeing the team perform well. A minor drawback is that sometimes this type of manager is so concerned with the overall team performance that he fails to treat each person as an individual. He treats everyone on the team equally, which is good and bad. There's no show of favoritism. However, if you are having a tough time and need a little extra help be cautious about your approach to the coach. Some coaches have been known to consider signs of weakness as reasons to look for a stronger replacement.

3. The CONTROLLER is the sales manager who finds it necessary to issue memos, change policies, and require additional paperwork and reports to be filled out as often as possible. This manager feels he won't have full control over

the sales staff until he has every piece of information in writing. This is good from a company standpoint. However, it's not very motivating to the sales staff. A lot of what we do in selling is emotional, and if your sales manager cannot or does not relate to you on a personal, emotional level, you'll probably find it difficult to stay motivated. I suggest you follow this manager's rules and regulations, but let him know that you also need some one-on-one time to discuss your particular situation with the company and your customers. Since he's so detail-minded he'll most likely set up a specific appointment for you even though he might not be available just when you need him.

While it's highly unlikely you'll ever get a manager who is perfect in every aspect of sales management, if you work with someone who is darn near perfect, it's highly likely that he'll be promoted to an even more powerful position within the company. That's why I stress so often the importance of depending primarily on yourself to find the direction and motivation you need in sales.

WHEN YOU LOVE YOUR COMPANY, BUT NOT YOUR MANAGER

If ever you find yourself in a position in which you love the company and the product you are selling, but you are having some challenges with your sales manager, stay cool. Fighting the sales manager is rarely a way to make him change. The first thing you should do is avoid any confrontations. Make a public show of enthusiastically accepting his proclamations, but privately go your own way. If you are a top producer, this will be pretty easily done.

If the challenges you face with the manager arise suddenly, take into consideration that there may have been a directive from above or some personal problem behind it. I suggest you play the waiting game to see how long the problem lasts. When the change is uncharacteristic of the manager's past behavior, chances are things will settle back into a more comfortable groove within 30 days.

Should things not settle down, try talking with the manager one-on-one and tactfully let him know the negative effect the changes are having on your production and/or attitude. Reassure him that you are a team player and that you enjoy working for the company. Maybe there's a reason behind the changes that is not obvious to you but that would explain a lot of things. If you are a good producer and the manager wants to keep you on board, he will help in any way he can.

If you get nowhere with the manager and don't want to change jobs, consider going over the manager's head. Please note: Consider this move very cautiously. Never, never go to upper management unless it's a stay-or-quit decision. When you go, go with a cool head and a list of facts. Prepare yourself as if it's your most important sales presentation, because if you're not prepared, it will backfire and you could find yourself very quickly on the street, looking for new employment.

Sometimes upper-level managers send out memos of changes and don't get enough feedback to make them realize the negative effect the changes are having on salespeople until they see it on the bottom line. If, for some reason, your manager doesn't effectively relay information back to them, it could cost the company and the sales staff a lot of money. Never go into a meeting of this sort knocking your sales manager. Just lay the problem out on the table and ask for help in finding a solution. Never point fingers! It doesn't do anyone any good and often causes hard feelings.

WHEN YOU GET A NEW SALES MANAGER

If you get a new manager, try to arrange a meeting with him before he comes to you. Get to know him. Let him know where you stand with the company and that you want to continue to do well. Let him know what your goals are—lay positive groundwork. And for heaven's sake, take good notes during this first meeting as in all meetings.

If you have a personality conflict going early, or the boss just seems to hate you, I urge you to clarify the situation immediately. To lessen your challenge to his authority, it's better to arrange a meeting where the two of you will be alone. Then confront your boss with something like:

"Bill, is it my imagination, or do you have something against me? Have I done anything wrong? I really want to succeed here; I really want to do a great job, but I have the feeling there's something about me you don't like."

You can't take this approach if you've been ignoring procedure, coming in late, missing appointments, or otherwise obviously not doing your job the way you know your manager wants it done. But if you've been performing well in an atmosphere of resentment, confronting the situation shows a strength of character that often wins respect. It almost forces the manager to explain his or her attitude, or deny any prejudice against you.

However, you may encounter a boss who evades or stonewalls you. Be prepared to quit if you don't get a satisfactory answer.

In any case you're better off to confront reality as soon as possible. See if things get better after you confront the problem. The alternative is to work for thirty to sixty days—or maybe a lot longer—before discovering that there is no chance that things will change, for reasons beyond your control.

NEW SALES MANAGERS HAVE BEEN KNOWN TO CLEAN HOUSE

The reasons why you're getting a new sales manager fall neatly under three headings. The first includes all the obvious reasons: the old manager is retiring, or is getting promoted, transferred, or whatever. The second heading covers politics and power struggles.

The third includes only one cause. But this single reason explains most of the changes made in sales managers (including many changes that officially have a cosmetic explanation).

This single reason is that sales under the old sales manager weren't up to upper management's expectations.

But it doesn't matter what the real reason for the change is. New sales managers always feel heavy pressure to validate management's decision to give them the job. What does this mean to you?

You will encounter cases where the new sales manager is taking over because the old manager was promoted for doing well. The old manager got the sales staff to reach a high sales volume. The new manager, if he's smart, will make few changes.

How this affects you personally will depend on where you stand in terms of sales production. New sales managers tend to divide the sales forces they inherit into three groups: the top third in sales production, the middle third, and the bottom third.

After close scrutiny of the bottom third of their sales force, many new sales managers will start clearing out the deadwood.

The top third they won't mess with.

How they handle the middle third depends on their character, on how secure their own position is, on market conditions, on their perception of the effort, cost, and time involved in recruiting and training new salespeople, and on other management considerations peculiar to their individual situation. In other words, if your production falls in the middle third of the sales force, your job security with a new sales manager is questionable.

Keep in mind that you can't always rely on good sales management from above. But you always can rely on your own good self-management, can't you?

This doesn't mean being a jerk and telling the other salespeople, "I have to do this oaf's job because he's too stupid to know what he should be doing." That kind of thing can get you fired. That would be a very unprofessional thing to do. My goal is to help you become the most professional salesperson you can be by bringing up these situations before they arise and telling you the best ways of handling them.

There must be reasons why your boss is a sales manager—not always good reasons, but whatever they are, you're the salesperson and he's the manager, and his emotional instability at any moment can get you fired. So you need to be smart enough to cover yourself and move ahead. Who knows? Someday you might be in the guy's place.

Most companies are well run by good people. You may never encounter problems of the kind we've discussed in this chapter. Nevertheless it's good to know about such things so that if you do meet with them, you'll know that you're not necessarily at fault.

Many salespeople have held jobs with many different companies in the course of their careers. This increases the likelihood that they'll find themselves working for an exceptionally poor sales manager at some point.

There's really only one solution: Do whatever it takes to push your sales into the top third. If you can't accomplish that, at least work with energy and enthusiasm. Show lots of initiative. Become a self-starter. Don't wait for a whisk from the new broom (your first may be your last). Get out in the field and stir things up.

In the next chapter, we'll talk about the overall effects of having a change in sales management.

CHAPTER SIX

YOUR BOSS OR
YOUR COMPANY

Managerial changes are a fact of life. Few salespeople escape having at least one change of managers thrust upon them before they log many years in the selling game.

Sometimes the change is welcome; sometimes you don't care one way or the other. But sometimes a change rips you with anger and confusion—and even greed. At such times you're very likely to make a serious mistake in your struggle to reach the top or stay there. Let's discuss some of the possibilities and pitfalls.

LOYALTY WHEN YOUR BOSS GETS FIRED

Let's say you have a manager you've worked with for five years, and that manager gets fired. Now is your loyalty to the manager or to the company? This is something you really need to ask yourself every once in a while.

Let's say that you and your boss get along really well. This person understood when you had problems, and did his best to steer you right. Even though he's helped your career growth, you have to maintain an attitude that he's getting paid to do that. It would be different if it were being done for nothing.

This doesn't mean you have to be hard-nosed about it,

but basically you should recognize that your manager is there to do a job. If he's good at it and helps you a lot, naturally you want to give him your loyalty—within whatever limits seem reasonable to your situation.

However, when you first hear that your manager will be replaced, remember that you don't necessarily know the whole story. Perhaps, unbeknownst to you, there are personal problems. Or perhaps there's some other hidden reason why the company feels that person needs to be replaced. Because of the inclination of so many people in the United States to file lawsuits, most companies have made it their policy to give as little information as possible about employment changes in their organizations. So, it's possible you'll never know the real reason for anyone's job change.

But, remember that companies don't replace managers to get practice in firing. Good managers are too hard to find. Unless the company has an idiot in charge, if the manager is delivering the goods he gets to keep his job. That is, he'll keep the job unless a bad move is made in the power struggle that goes on more or less constantly in most organizations.

Would your manager's firing be justified in the eyes of a fully informed but disinterested observer? You'll probably never know. In today's highly regulated personnel climate, with its ever-present threat of costly wrongful-discharge lawsuits, few companies feel they can risk being completely candid in difficult personnel cases.

Nevertheless, if the word is out that your manager is going to be replaced, the people in the office will choose sides—even though they don't have all the facts.

Maybe a third of the office didn't like this person anyway, and had a foot on his back for months, trying to nudge him out the door. You and many others are loyal to this manager.

As a result, there's some pushing and shoving going on in the office. What's that doing to the department's sales production? It has to hurt. Understandably, management is frantically trying to get things back to normal.

In this situation, a top professional would have an attitude that runs about like this: "I like John. I think he's wonderful, and he has helped me. But I work for the company. It's hard for me to imagine they'd fire John for no reason. But I'm not going to stake my family's financial future on what they do in his case."

In other words, if you're happy with the company, don't get dragged into these things. Keep in mind that over a few years you could have several managerial changes. Each time it happens you don't want to take the position that your job depends on a manager's continued employment more than it does on your performance with that company, your earnings there, and the way they treat you.

In most cases, managers move on up the corporate ladder or make a lateral move within the company. You can't expect them to be with you forever.

If you feel you represent the best product or service, if you're doing a good job, if your customers are happy and you're happy—you certainly don't want to lose your job. You might go through three sales positions without finding one that you like as much as the one you have today.

Let's say you have a sales position you're happy with, the company is happy with you, and you're making what you feel is a good income. When everything is going well for you, don't get drawn into office politics and throw it all away. A month from now today's emotionally charged issue will be ancient history—if you've kept on working. But if you're starting over, the effects can be with you for a long, long time.

Another situation can happen when your manager finds out he's losing his job. Sometimes he runs around the office and gets allies to go to the company and say, "If he goes, we go." Then if the manager goes, you may well all go.

If you just use a cool and commonsense approach to most of these problems, you'll know what to do. The key is to step back and look at the larger picture. You don't have to be in sales or sales management to understand that nobody likes to knuckle under to threats, especially upper management people who feel they have position and power to protect.

How is management likely to react when a group threatens to quit? From their standpoint, giving in would involve an unacceptable loss of face and authority. They know that giving in won't solve the old problem and in fact might open up a host of new problems.

But an effective sales force can't be replaced overnight. Their abilities, insights, and connections won't be duplicated merely by signing a purchase order or placing an ad. The strongest salespeople that can be hired have to be given time to develop their product knowledge and customer contacts before they can produce results. And, as any sales manager who has done it knows, building a sales force from scratch involves a great deal of time, effort, and disappointment.

Rarely will upper management opt for letting the whole threatening bunch quit. Wise upper managers will try to talk with the allies individually and help them see the picture a little more clearly—away from the emotions of the moment. They may explain in a little more detail about the reason for this person's dismissal. And, they'll let the individuals make a more clear-headed decision. This will usually dampen the fires of mutiny enough that the remaining allies lose their power.

To avoid making a serious mistake in these areas, you have to be able to mentally raise yourself above the emotional turmoil of the moment. You have to be able to consider these difficulties in the light of what's most important to your basic purposes in working for the company.

Stand back. Look at the situation objectively. Say to yourself, "Am I happy with my job? I like John but am I prepared to let my family see me on the unemployment line to stick up for him? The thing is, I can't be sure that my getting involved will actually help him; but it's clear I can get hurt in this thing."

Maybe some people above John are afraid of him—afraid they'll be fired and he'll get their job. If so, that problem is between the company, John, and the fearful people. In any case it's the company's game. It's not your call as a salesperson. You don't want to get involved even though what happens might seem to be extremely unfair.

CONSPIRACY'S LURE

Another problem arises when a manager decides to quit and wants to take the company's top producers along, either to an established competitor, or to start a new company that will compete with your present employer. This can constitute a conspiracy, so consider carefully before becoming involved.

Let's say that your manager comes to you and says, "We're starting a new company and we want you with us." Hearing a statement like that is exciting; visions of wealth and opportunity suddenly dance before your eyes. You imagine you'll soon be a partner in a rapidly growing enterprise. The future beckons, and it looks brilliant.

Be cautious and take a clear look at propositions of this kind. Sure they're alluring. But are they realistic?

Pretend the new company is started, with or without you. First of all they may have begun by ripping off your present employers, thereby probably giving them cause for an unfair competition lawsuit against the new company.

Start-ups suck up money, usually far more than the organizers planned, even without having to fight a costly lawsuit. There are licenses to obtain and deposits to make, offices to lease and furnish, people to hire and train.

Countless decisions must be made, quickly and sometimes with inadequate information. Inevitably mistakes are made, and some of them are likely to be expensive.

With so many new positions to be filled, round pegs get pushed into square holes. Essential activities get entrusted to people who may lack the necessary energy, insight, or skill to carry them off. Meanwhile, precious time and money go down the drain.

Perhaps new products must be designed, tested, and manufactured, which means that machinery has to be purchased and inventories of parts and raw materials accumulated. And, usually, there are unforeseeable delays of one kind or another all along the line.

The usual, natural way to plan for a new company is with a high degree of optimism and enthusiasm. After all, if the organizers aren't optimistic and enthusiastic, who will be? With this attitude in control, the funds raised for the start-up barely cover the obvious essentials. No provision at all is made for the kinds of unforeseen contingencies and unexpected disasters that so often strike new companies.

For emotional reasons, a new company's financial plans tend to minimize start-up costs, delays, and problems, and to maximize start-up sales, profits, and cash flow. When reality strikes, the bad news often is worse than expected, and the good news doesn't live up to the dreams.

I know of a very successful salesperson who left a sales job with a company he'd worked with for more than eight years to become the vice president of sales and marketing for a friend's new business. Expectations were high because a similar company launched in Australia a few years earlier had grown like wildfire. After a few months of finding and establishing suppliers for the product and developing product literature and displays, they were ready to go. However, they had overlooked one "minor" factor: in the United States, there were already established companies offering a similar product, and in Australia their product line was new and innovative with practically no competition. One year after joining that company, the VP of sales and marketing was working very hard, taking half his salary, and no longer seeing the bright light of glory promised in the beginning. The selling skills that had made him successful with his previous company were not put to their full use in his new position. He didn't know the market before he made the leap. The company nearly folded. He wasn't financially prepared to handle the lesser income for any length of time. Luckily for him, he was able to get back a job with his previous company and get his benefits reinstated.

There are plenty of cases in which making such a change proves successful, but please understand that they are fewer than the unsuccessful cases.

Over everything hangs the relentless pressure of time. Every new company has a limited period in which to control the cash flow involved in a start-up. If that doesn't happen, the new company either gets heavy new infusions of cash, or it fades from the scene.

Often this money comes from new owners or new partners. Will the new people squeeze you out? Will you be happy working for or with them? Your manager's new company may have to change drastically in order to survive.

Will the initial capital investment stretch far enough to keep the new company going according to its original plan? Now there is a payroll to meet—including the compensation you'll probably be depending on to meet your own living expenses if you join this organization.

Unless you become part owner of the new company, what's the percentage in trading a solid job with an established firm for an iffy job with a new firm that may or may not make it?

Okay, so Bill says you'll be a part owner. However, unless you nail the specifics down in writing before you commit yourself, you're probably going to wind up with nothing but Bill's non-spendable promises. You may already know he's capable of deceit and unethical conduct in business just by his efforts to start his new business during hours he should be working for his current employer.

Like a politician running for office, he may make more promises than he can keep in order to float his dream. When the bills fall due, you may be called on to ante up a sizable hunk of cash yourself to help keep the company going.

You're not home free even if you get a written contract specifying your share in the new company. Merely discussing such an arrangement makes you part of the conspiracy; signing a contract about it puts written evidence of that fact in circulation. At some point you not only endanger your present job and reputation, you may also put your personal assets at risk if your old employer wins a judgment for damages.

The moment your manager raises the possibility of starting a new company, you have an uncomfortable ethical problem. First and foremost, if you are approached with such a proposition, tell the manager you don't want to talk about it on company time. Arrange a meeting after work and outside of the company buildings. Nothing says you can't consider new opportunities for yourself. Just make sure everything you are being told is aboveboard. Consider that this manager may be lying to the company about his intentions. If so, how honest will he be with you? Ask how he plans to handle the news of his leaving the company with upper management.

Loyalty to the company you work for requires reporting the conspiracy to them, especially if it's a new business venture that could hurt the company. But that means blowing the whistle on someone who has earned your personal loyalty. It's not an easy position to find yourself occupying.

Yet if you see the manager still there picking up all the information he can, lists of clients and so on, do you feel that he is acting ethically? And if Bill is acting unethically in this matter, what makes you so sure he's going to be ethical with you later?

Let's say the company has been fair with you. Bill is getting ready to leave and take a big portion of the company's business with him. He hasn't told the company what he's doing, of course, and he's still drawing a paycheck from them. If that's not unethical, what is? Would it be wise for you to put your future in the hands of someone like that? Can you be sure he'll be ethical and fair with you later?

You have a perilous decision to make. You can go with Bill; you can believe he's engaged in a rare unethical act; you can convince yourself that he'll be fair with you down the line.

Your best bet, when you know about the upcoming move, is to explain to Bill the position you're in. Whether you go with him or not, you want to handle any involvement in the situation ethically. Try to convince him to "do the right thing" and go to management about his plans for leaving as soon as possible. If he really has some good ideas for how to run a competitive business, maybe they'll make him an offer he can't refuse to stay and implement those plans in this company.

Even if Bill decides to continue operating behind the backs of your employers, let him know you don't want to take a fall should the whole thing blow up in his face. Tell him you won't lie for him or hide facts about your knowledge if asked.

If the situation is causing you to lose sleep, you should consider going to the company that's been fair with you all along and say, "There's a problem you need to be aware of. I don't want to get involved in the politics of it, but Bill is planning on leaving, and I understand he's trying to convince many of your staff to go with him." Then, let them decide how to handle the situation.

It's not good to be considered a "snitch" by your peers, but what if what Bill is doing shuts down the company and you don't want to go with him? After all, the term "snitch" was created by the people wanting to exert pressure over others. If you saw someone robbing a bank and called the police, the robber may call you a snitch, but the police and officers of the bank will call you a good citizen. Now, I ask you, who do you want to impress? You must always remember who signs your paycheck, and that's who you should remain loyal to. You might still be out of a job because of his unethical conduct. He might give your company a wound that it will never recover from. As a result it may fall by the wayside a few years down the road.

You don't know whether Bill's new company will make it, but your present company has a track record. They've survived the desperate first few years that wipe out nine out of ten new businesses. So are you a snitch or are you taking responsible action to protect your own financial future?

If you're happy with your position, you have an obligation to go to management and tell them something's happening. Maybe you can avoid being part of the ensuing witch-hunt. You can say, "Please don't mention my name. I'm not looking for brownie points. I'm happy with what I'm doing and I don't want anything going wrong with the company." Management is certainly going to appreciate that. Whether you get any brownie points doesn't really matter; what counts is that you've taken action to protect your economic well-being.

There's no way you can stay out of it. You work there so you're bound to be affected. In a situation like this you have to take a stand.

Suppose you decide to sit back and watch Bill pull off this caper and leave. You stay. Isn't management likely to come to you later and say, "You must have known what was up. How come you didn't say anything?"

It's no different than if you know someone is stealing from the company and you don't report it. You become an accomplice even if you never touch a cent that isn't indisputably yours.

WHEN YOU KNOW SOMEONE IS STEALING FROM THE COMPANY

It's widely believed that shoplifting, burglary, and armed robbery cause the heaviest losses that business firms suffer from criminal activity. However, companies that employ salespeople usually aren't exposed to those hazards to any large degree; their greatest exposure is to insiders. Employees in this country steal between 15 and 25 billion dollars a year from their employers, according to authoritative estimates.

The overwhelming cause of business bankruptcy is managerial inexperience or incompetence—cited in 92 percent of the cases. What the statistics can't reveal is how great a part undetected insider theft played, but it's clear that many small firms go under because employees steal so much that their profitability is destroyed.

If you know that one of your fellow workers is stealing from your employer and you don't report it, you become an accomplice even if you don't personally profit from the theft. Suppose that Sharon sees Lucinda carrying boxloads of stuff out of their employer's place of business every day. Sharon doesn't want to be involved.

Maybe Sharon hates the company, and says to herself, "It's their problem. Why should I care?"

If Sharon needs her job, she should care. No one ever knows how many losses a company can stand. Thefts by employees, added to sudden problems in the marketplace, have pushed many companies to the wall. If the company fails and Sharon loses a good job, she'll say, "Aw, those dummies. If they were smarter I'd still have a job."

Maybe management was smart enough but they just

didn't believe their own people would steal from them. It happens.

You can take the position that it's none of your affair—but it is, particularly if you're happy with your position in the company.

Even so, you don't want to become the company snitch—every time some little thing is done wrong you run and tell somebody. That's not a good thing to get a reputation for.

On the other hand, it's your responsibility, to your family and yourself, to protect your job. When it gets to a certain point, you have to say, "I can't live with this."

When you reach that point, tell management, "This is what's going on. If you want to do anything about it, it's up to you. I'm not trying to curry favor, but I'm happy and I don't want to see this continue because I'm afraid it might damage my job security."

People have to choose between loyalty to their financial security and company on the one hand, and loyalty to their fellow workers—no matter what they do—on the other. However, if your fellow workers involve themselves in stealing or other conspiracies harmful to your employer, they attack your security. You don't need that, and you don't have to put up with it.

If the idea of being forced to choose between remaining silent and speaking up is intolerable, there's a way of avoiding that painful pinch. Unfortunately the alternative exacts an emotional price too, but you may feel it's well worth it. Here's the alternative:

Limit your exposure to other employees' disloyalty by making it clear that you're a company person. If you make this point strongly enough, thieves and plotters will be careful to do their dirty work out of your sight and hearing. In other words, you won't have to worry whether to tell management what's going on because you won't know what's going on.

How much heat you'll get from your fellow employees will depend on your precise attitude. Whether you come off as a schemer looking for ways to win preferential treatment, or as someone intelligently looking out for his own interests, depends on how you handle it. Taking this route will test your communication and interpersonal skills to the utmost.

Some people, especially those involved in or thinking about hurting the company, will be hostile toward you as a result of your pro-company attitude. However, thieves and plotters are negative-minded. By avoiding them you'll find yourself being drawn effortlessly into closer contact with the company's more positive people. They are making it, moving up, and feeling good about themselves, their jobs, and their futures. Associating with them not only will inspire you, it will bring you many opportunities.

Another way to deal with theft and plots against the company's interest is to put an anonymous note in the company suggestion box. While the anonymous note is a weak way of coping, if you can't deal with the problem any other way, it can be vastly better than doing nothing.

CHAPTER SEVEN

MAKING THE RIGHT STAY-OR-QUIT DECISION

Americans are a restless people. Most of us, particularly early in our careers, make a series of job changes. Even if you're somewhat on the apathetic side, sooner or later you'll probably face the stay-or-quit decision about your job. Should I quit and start over somewhere else, or should I continue to hang on where I am?

APPRAISING YOUR CURRENT SITUATION

Many salespeople are so flattered to get an offer from another company that they'll make a bad decision to leave their old company. It's wonderful to be wanted—but what is often forgotten is that once you're in the new company, you're just like everybody else there.

This means that you have to prove your worth every day, and you're subject to whatever challenges your new company has. If there are incompetent people over you in any of the departments that affect you—sales, shipping, manufacturing, accounting, or whatever—you're stuck with them. If there are takeover problems, a failure to stay on the cutting edge in product innovation, or labor disputes with the hourly employees—you're stuck with them.

All companies have some internal personnel problems

and external competitive problems. Unless you have clear evidence that your present employers have greater challenges than the average company does, chances are good that any change you make won't significantly reduce the strength of company challenges you face. A change will only give you company problems that have different names and voices.

It's easy to jump to false conclusions here. Why? Because you live with your present employer's problems every day. However, from the outside you won't learn much about the problems you'd face at any new company. In this entire area of company complications that make your life more difficult and your work harder, there's only one sure thing: anywhere you work there'll be at least a few problems.

If you find yourself in the enviable position of achieving your highest income earning potential with your company, it's not wise to knock the company or try to change it to fit your financial mode. At that point, you need to analyze if there are other things you could do for the company to earn more income, if that's what you want. If not, don't do what some top producers do by becoming a pain in the backside and letting the whole situation get out of hand.

Some salespeople make moves just because somebody else wants them badly. This happens a lot in the car business. Some of the top auto salespeople in any city are making big circles, going from agency to agency in search of that mythical perfect selling situation. Sometimes they do this because they're too easily offended by management.

At each change hardly 20 percent of their customers follow them; usually about four out of five customers don't bother. These constantly moving salespeople therefore have to make a career of rebuilding their customer bases. Not for them the greater and easier earnings of repeat business—they like doing it the hard way.

You may think, "All right, I'm leaving all my customer problems behind."

Not necessarily. In your new company you'll probably be taking over someone else's territory. What did he or she leave behind for you? Maybe an army of upset customers. There may be all kinds of problems in your new territory, the full extent of which you won't learn until it's too late to do anything except grin and bear it.

Keep in mind that the grass always looks greener on the other side of the fence. Salespeople often give in to a frustration cycle and make a change without fully analyzing the situation. The grass in the pasture you're thinking of leaving will look very lush and green to someone else—because of all your hard work to make it so. Inevitably, a great deal of the personal contacts and product knowledge you've laboriously gained will be lost to whoever replaces you. In the same way, you'll have to reestablish the contacts and learn a new product line before you can function effectively with a different company.

THE TWO SIDES OF JOB CHANGING

Because sales skills are highly transportable, it's comparatively easy to change jobs in the selling field. You take your proven sales ability and a few of your customers to your new position, learn about the new product and, theoretically, that's all there is to it. Away you go.

Yet, as many studies have shown, changing jobs is one of the most stressful things you can do. Why continue subjecting yourself to that kind of stress? Over a period of time it can have a serious impact on your health.

When you change employers you don't change yourself, and you certainly don't change the nature of the selling occupation. In your next position you may be bugged by the same things that bug you now. It may be wise to consider making an attitude adjustment from within before making the external change of getting another job.

I'm not suggesting that you stay with your present position no matter what. But before you change, make sure your reasons are sound, that the change has a high probability of bettering your situation.

You have an obligation to yourself and to your family to put yourself in front of the best product and the best compensation package you can find. It's so important that you study the trade journals and other literature about your industry. You must know what's happening in your field. If a competitor has a feature you don't have and you think that's the reason they sell more than you do, you can't just jump over to that company without serious consideration. If your company doesn't have what they have, ask your company why. There may be a very good reason for it. They may also have the next hot feature to enter the marketplace waiting in the wings and may be in your competitor's position in six short months. The reason I'm going into this decision so deeply is that many salespeople make this decision without adequate analysis. Then everybody loses.

When a company starts you out, helps you build a customer base, and enables you to reach a high income, you have a moral obligation to that company not to leave and take some of its customers. It's something you really have to ask yourself.

Salespeople can find a million ways to justify leaving— and most of them are garbage. They'll make up reasons about how they were passed over, or the company did this or didn't do that. And instead of just going out and making a clean new start in another field, they'll go with a competitor and try to bring their customers along with them.

But in a lot of cases the customers won't make the transfer. This means that the salesperson isn't better off, the original company has been damaged by having a bit of unpleasantness bounced off some of its customers, and the salesperson's new company isn't too happy with him because he didn't bring in the accounts they were counting on. That's often the reason they wanted him in the first place.

When a competitor comes around wanting you, the first question you should ask is, "Do you want me, or my customers?"

It's not really so flattering to be wanted for the customers you can possibly bring. Then where are you if they don't come with you?

Some companies adopt a quick and dirty sales strategy: bring in the competition's top producers and get their customer base at no added cost. To accomplish this they make offers to salespeople they can't sustain over the long pull. By joining such a firm, you become an accomplice in a scheme that's unethical, immoral, and possibly illegal. Can you realistically expect long-term satisfaction and fair dealing from a management dedicated to unethical, immoral, and possibly illegal practices?

Beyond poor ethics and morals, such policies demonstrate that the company trying to hire you away can't meet or beat your present employer in fair competition. If your customers like your present employer's product, they'll continue buying it. The question is, will you be there to sell it to them?

Or will you be coming in trying to switch them from the product you used to tell them was the best? You won't be able to do it every time.

Salespeople almost always think it's them making the sale, not the product's benefits. There's a good reason for this: Selling demands a certain amount of ego because you're hit with rejection every day. It's necessary, to survive in selling, that you build yourself up in your own mind, because some days can be so bad that you need that ego to keep you up. Successful salespeople are especially good at building themselves up in their own minds.

Yet in sales it's easy to get one's ego blown out of proportion, especially when success smiles on your efforts. The fact is, ego-building multiplies the risk of making bad decisions because it can so easily lead us to grossly overestimate our power.

Selling can be a very tough field. Salespeople must face a great deal of rejection to be successful. Therefore, a top salesperson must be an above average person in many ways. However, while it's great to have a large ego and be proud of your accomplishments, it's wise to learn to handle yourself with humility as well.

HOW TO GET THE BEST RESULTS WHEN FACING THE BIG QUESTION

The stay-or-quit question may arise from sudden anger over a minor issue that upsets you, or from the gradually accumulating suspicion that you might be better off else-where. In any case it's an important career decision that should be made deliberately.

Let me tell you about two excellent ways to help you reach the best decision on stay-or-quit or any other important matter. The first is the method given in the Ben Franklin Close that you're familiar with from reading *How to Master the Art of Selling*, or perhaps from attending my seminars.

The Ben Franklin Close is an important sales tool that I won't repeat in whole. However for your convenience here's the part that applies to what we're discussing:

The Ben Franklin Decision-Making Method

Divide a sheet of paper by a line down the center so that you have two columns. At the top of one column write "Yes" and list under it all the reasons for going ahead with the matter under consideration. Head the second column "No" and list under it all the reasons against going ahead. Then simply count them. If there's a preponderance of yes reasons, go ahead; if not, don't.

Benjamin Franklin devised this method, and used it fre-quently. It yields good results as long as there's no reason for or against the decision that's of overriding importance.

For instance, if you're considering buying a second home in the mountains and your wife doesn't like the mountains, you don't need the Ben Franklin method to tell you not to go ahead. But when you're in a genuine quandary as to what decision to make, as all of us often are, old Ben's method can help clarify your thinking.

A SOFT EXIT AVOIDS A HARD FALL

When you leave, make sure your manager doesn't hear it first from someone else. From the first moment you think of leaving, keep a closed mouth on the subject.

And be especially careful about offhand remarks, jokes,

significant looks, and body language. Keep in mind that you can let a lot of information slip by nonverbal or informal means.

During my time as a sales manager, I had one experience in particular which was one of my most difficult to handle. Barry Lang had tremendous potential. We agreed at the beginning of the year on a goal of making him the number-one salesperson in the company. Every time we were together, that was all we talked about—him walking up in front of 300 salespeople, representing a company that at that time was one of the leaders in the industry. It was a red-hot goal we both shared. Every month we saw Barry get closer to the top in the company-wide ratings. In August, he took the number-one position.

Suddenly, I heard rumors that Barry was thinking about leaving the firm, something I couldn't understand. After doing some checking, I found obvious signs that he planned to leave, set up an office as a competitor, and take some of my best people with him.

Although it was very painful for me, I had to confront Barry with this information and fire him. He couldn't believe I'd let my top person go. I couldn't let him continue with us, gaining all the notoriety as top person, and then hurt the company as a whole by going off on his own. We did work out an agreement by which Barry was shortly re-hired. However, he had lost his opportunity to become the top salesperson in the company. He had lost a great deal of the respect of his associates and management, and he probably lost a great deal financially from this setback. I relate this story because it's imperative that you realize the importance of holding to high ethics when you're ready to grow to your next level.

Some of the people around you at work would love to pick up the hint that you're secretly thinking of quitting. Once they've gained that glimmer, they'll start a rumor that management will hear, or they'll tell the boss themselves.

Before you tell your manager you're quitting, carefully plan what you'll say. It's important to avoid sounding arrogant. It's equally important to realize that the new company you're so excited about may turn out to be a dud. Why burn your bridges behind you?

Tell your manager something like, "I've enjoyed working here, but I've got this opportunity that's too good to pass up. I hate to leave because I know I'm going to miss all of you. . . ."

Then hand him your resignation letter, in which you say more nice things.

The point is to avoid burning bridges behind you for no reason. It's possible that things won't work out at your new company. If that happens you may, for your family's sake, need to pocket your pride and try to go back to your old company. Why make it any more difficult than it has to be?

CHAPTER EIGHT

STRATEGIES FOR PUTTING YOURSELF IN A STRONGER POSITION

It's long been said that most people only use 10 percent of their mental power, letting 90 percent of their brains go to waste. Recently some highly respected psychologists came to the conclusion that the correct figure is closer to 4 percent of brain power being used, that most people let 96 percent of their minds wither on the vine.

Imagine how fast your car would go if it used only 4 percent of its horsepower. The engine wouldn't run even with the gear shift in neutral.

Yet that's what some of us try to do: get through life on just 4 percent of our brain power. As a result, we don't move far, or fast. A lot can be done about this. Intelligence and effectiveness are learned skills to an enormously greater degree than most people believe.

GET RID OF SELF-IMPOSED RESTRICTIONS

Most of us are limited by self-imposed restrictions we often don't even realize we've put there. For example, how many people born into a nonacademic family ever think of trying to acquire a college degree? They might be bright enough to do it. But usually they make the career decisions that establish the kind of life they'll lead without ever considering the possibility of becoming a doctor of medicine, law, or philosophy, or an MBA.

Why would anyone want to devote years to gaining a degree? Well, for openers, the average degreed person pulls down half a million dollars more in lifetime earnings than the average high school graduate does, according to U.S. Government figures.

Having a degree is wonderful, but it does not guarantee exceptionally high earnings. For many people, sales is a more direct route to more money than a degree would be.

When you're a teenager, deciding what to do with your life, you're usually working from within the reality of a teenager. Since the basis for most of your life has been school, many people want to become teachers. It's the old "I can do a better job" syndrome. We have an idealistic desire to improve the world and so on when we're young. I'm not saying that's bad, but it can't always be accomplished as easily as young people think. However, once in the working world, many people's shift from wanting to save the world to wanting to earn high incomes. While the degree they planned for since teen years and achieved may have gotten them started in the working world, it may not be enough to transport them to this new level of desired income.

And, over the years, I've encountered a few people for whom academic degrees opened only one door: the door to futility. After failing to cash in big on their educations, they became bitter and imposed more restrictions on themselves than most people do. Being degreed made them feel that most lucrative work was beneath them. As a result they wouldn't do the apprentice-type work that success in almost every field demands. But even brain surgeons at the peak of their careers have to scrub up before performing the operations that bring them their huge fees.

Degreed people share one experience: they all worked long and hard at taking advantage of a proven strategy for putting themselves in a strong position in life. However, few salespeople work diligently at any strategy that could put them in a position of greater strength; most keep their heads down trying to meet their quotas. As a result, even those who work very hard often are unable to move ahead rapidly.

WORK FOR A COMPANY THAT APPRECIATES SALESPEOPLE

Because they operate on an enormously more independent basis than other employees, salespeople have much greater opportunities and tendencies to aggravate management. Nevertheless, nothing happens until someone sells something, which means that good salespeople can be a company's most valuable asset. Destroyed structures can be rebuilt, damaged tooling replaced, inventory replenished, production people hired. All this can be done within a short, predictable time, with little likelihood of failure.

But, since it's rare for an entire sales force to disappear overnight, some managements show a surprising lack of concern about maintaining high morale in the department that keeps them in business. It's possible that you work for such a firm.

The top management of your company should appreciate its salespeople instead of considering them to be primarily a source of problems. If this appreciative attitude isn't stressed in their pronouncements, policies, and actions, you can probably enhance your strategic position and potential for growth by choosing a company that makes it clear, by word and action, that it values its salespeople highly.

However, salespeople can't function by themselves. They must be backed by smoothly operating departments that handle new product development, manufacturing, shipping or delivery, accounting, and other essential activities too numerous to mention. A company that can't provide adequate backup to its salespeople won't be good for them even though it is highly sales-oriented.

Salespeople are the most effective when they eagerly promote their own company by extolling its virtues and accomplishments with infectious enthusiasm. To do that with conviction, they must thoroughly know and sincerely value their company. It rarely happens by accident. They need friendly contact, approval, and sincere emotional support from their organizations in order to offset the heavy rejection that is their daily lot.

Some managements recognize these needs and carry on consistent programs to keep their salespeople's morale high. Many other organizations understand the need but fail to do anything effective about it. The few organizations that, from the top down, deliberately ignore their salespeople's special emotional needs suffer lower sales efficiency, higher sales costs, and higher turnover as a result. Many such shortsighted firms fail—another reason for taking your talents elsewhere.

One of your most important personal responsibilities is to keep yourself up. This vital duty to yourself is far too important to be left to your boss, your company, or anyone else. The next chapter discusses it in depth.

Keeping your morale up can be tough in sales even with a supportive company behind you, and too tough without that support. If you have to fight your own company almost as hard as the competition, give some consideration to putting your career in a stronger position by switching to a firm that appreciates its salespeople more. That's why we gave you the question to ask during your interview about the type and quantity of support and training that's offered to salespeople.

BE PREPARED TO BE A PROFESSIONAL

Auto-action is what we do just as self-talk is what we think. Most of our action is reflexive; we act before, or as, we think.

Consider any competitive sport's action. Winning athletes are thinking athletes. In most sports, it's the quality and quickness of the athlete's thought as much as his or her athletic ability that determines who wins and who loses.

If they're winners, it's mostly because they instantly sense what's happening and then make the right physical move in response: going to the right to tackle the ball carrier, leaping to the left to backhand a hard serve, running in to scoop up the bunt and throw the runner out at first. There's no time for a leisurely weighing of alternatives.

Our daily lives are much the same. When we talk with customers, we can't take a lot of time to decide what we'll say next. We can't spend an hour deciding what product we'll push, what price we'll try for, which close we'll use next. In sales, as in sports, opportunities to score are fleeting.

How can we improve the quality of our auto-action so that we'll make the right moves more quickly and with more success?

There are two elements to consider: (a) Half of the solution must come before the sales interview, and it's called preparation. You can't make the right moves or say the right things if you don't know what they are. Plan ahead, prepare thoroughly, and know your stuff. (b) The equally important other half of the solution comes from training yourself to keep a stream of supportive self-talk going in your head during the moments when you're actively selling face-to-face with a customer. Be sure to use playful, positive, colorful language as you talk to yourself in a happy, childlike way.

Here's a vital point: If you realize you've goofed by doing or saying the wrong thing, be careful about mentally chewing yourself out. Some people won't make the changes necessary to get over a defeat without getting angry. If that works for you, go right ahead, as long as you do it when you're alone. If you're not sure if it works for you, it probably doesn't. Don't waste your time being upset about something that's not going to help you. And don't panic. Instead, think something like:

"That's okay, Albert Einstein made mistakes too."
"I never said I was perfect."
"What did I do right?"

I have taught thousands of students to keep what I call a "Success Journal." In it, I tell them to keep a running description of things that go right for them during every aspect of the sales process. If you are honest with yourself and write down exactly how the right things happened, you'll have a wonderful volume to refer to when things don't go quite as planned. Review a few notes on the area in which you have recently had a challenge. And then return to pumping yourself up as you say something to gloss over the damage. But many times the best way to handle your blooper is to simply ignore it and keep on talking. If you keep talking, nine times out of ten the customer will forget, or won't notice, your mistake.

There's no way I could know what's going on in the average salesperson's head when he or she is trying to make a sale. But from my long experience in many aspects of selling and sales management, I'm convinced of two things: heavy hitters boost themselves up while they're selling; and heavy losers tear themselves down while they're failing to sell.

It all boils down to this thing called "positive thinking." I remember when there was a lot of talk about positive thinking in the '70s, and I know a lot of people who got tired of it. But, I don't know any one successful person who ever stopped doing it once he got started. You see, it's just as easy to put positive pictures in your mind as it is to put negative ones in. And, it doesn't cost a dime to start switching from self-talk that tears you down to self-talk that builds you up, and at this moment I can't think of anything that will put more money in your pocket sooner. But it does take preparation before, and concentration during, the sales interview. Tell yourself, "It's not like me not to be a good salesperson."

Some salespeople have developed a habit of negative self-talk while with customers. What do I mean by that? Well, when you say something to your customer, you have this habit if you hear yourself saying, "Why did I say that?" "That didn't come out right," "I could have said that better." People with this bad habit are constantly evaluating everything that comes out of their mouths. The major problem with this is that you'll find yourself on an emotional roller coaster while in front of your customers and you'll end up emotionally drained just about the time you need your strength to close the sale. You need to make the switch to positive thinking. However, just deciding to switch to positive thinking won't get the job done. In the heat of a sales interview you'll fall back into your old habits. What you must do is work out a very positive self-talk pattern and start using it on yourself all the time. Only then will it become so habitual that you'll naturally carry it into the stress of your selling sessions. Many people get into the habit of saying, "I should have done that or should have done this." That's negative. It makes right now very unpleasant. Instead, try consciously switching from "should have" to "next time." "Next time, I'll try a warmer approach." Next time lets you plan ahead to a positive future situation rather than dwell on the current not-so-positive situation.

If you've been a negative self-talker and switch to playful, colorful, and confident self-talk with enthusiasm and determination, your sales performance can't help but take a big jump up.

PULL AHEAD FASTER USING THE LAW OF EFFECT

The law of effect states that the probability of a certain behavior being repeated is directly related to the consequences that behavior produces. In other words, if you try something new and you like it, you will try it again. If you try a new sales technique and it works, it's likely you'll try it on the next customer. If you try that same sales technique and flub it, not making a sale, will you try it again or not? Most people will practice a little more and give it another go, especially since, as salespeople, we are always looking for better ways to help buyers make those buying decisions.

It's not so easy, however, to know what the rewards are in every situation. In the more simple cases such as eating or sleeping, we pretty well know why we do it, even if we can't explain the reasons in scientific terms. In the more complex behavior patterns it can be difficult or impossible to tell why the behavior occurs. Some salespeople spend a great deal of time trying to figure out what product features cause their customers to buy. More salespeople should start their searches for reasons at the basic points: their customers' appetite for reward and urge to avoid punishment and discomfort. In other words, the benefits the customer will get from having your product or service.

All rewards can be classified as either providing positive consequences or removing negative ones. A powerful benefit for one individual, however, may be the opposite for someone else.

For example, today a young couple may walk into an auto dealership and think all of the state-of-the-art options on a new car are the greatest. They may decide that they have to have them as a status symbol. On this same day, an older couple may see the same options as frivolous and cost-increasing. Tomorrow, it may be the older couple wanting all the special options because they are finally at a time in their lives when they feel they deserve some luxuries. Then, too, the next young couple may want a bare-bones vehicle because that's all they can afford.

Rewards Can Lose Potency

The power of benefits varies constantly. At one time, having AM/FM radio in a car was the greatest thing. Today, we expect it as a minimum. It's no longer a great buying factor because we, the buying public, have become satiated. The benefit then loses its value and the behavior it formerly encouraged often stops.

And we can lose faith in the benefit. For example, a salesperson working for a small firm may be promised part ownership in the business "someday," or "when the timing is right." This promise may inspire that salesperson to greater effort for years. But if the part ownership doesn't materialize, eventually that sometime incentive not only loses its positive effect, it can incite the salesperson to quit in disgust, taking as much of the company's business along as possible.

The "I Can't Afford to Make a Change" Syndrome

Companies change the rules their salespeople operate under from time to time. These changes are usually presented as being non-negotiable, which they generally are if you work

for a large corporation with several layers of managers between you and the decision maker.

In smaller firms the company will make very careful consideration before making such changes because it can't afford
to make mistakes. If you are a top producer and feel you can't
live with these changes, you might be able to negotiate a more
acceptable arrangement for yourself. However, if changes are
made that you feel very strongly about and the company will
not make any concessions, do you have enough money in the
bank to afford to make a change? If not, it's a goal you should
set for yourself. Even if you can't see yourself ever leaving
the company you currently work for, I strongly recommend
that every salesperson keep at least three to six months' income available in savings should an unexpected change occur.

After all, you have certain obligations to meet, and the
odds are that changes will come suddenly, taking you by surprise. Before you can go to your manager asking for favors,
you require a certain level of security in the form of cash in
the bank in case it doesn't work out. Some salespeople can do
it with ten bucks in the vault; others need at least half-a-year's
income safely stashed away.

How much you need depends on your personality, age,
family obligations, how long you believe it will take you to
achieve a similar income elsewhere, and other considerations.

Besides a dispute with the company, you could find yourself looking for a new position for a variety of reasons. Your
present company could be taken over by corporate raiders, or
it could incur huge expenses fighting off a hostile takeover.

Restructuring of the company could be forced by a change
in government regulations, as happened to many large corporations in the airline and trucking industries when they were
deregulated. Your company could lose a monumental product liability lawsuit; it could suffer a regional recession, an
industry-wide decline, or a sudden increase in foreign competition. Security is a life-style and a state of mind, not a job.

Being free of worries about immediate cash for essential
living expenses is an important element of security—one of
our most basic needs. Know yourself and set aside the amount
you need as soon as you can.

PROTECT YOURSELF FROM BECOMING INEFFECTIVE

Personal growth is the process of increasing your knowledge and effectiveness so that you can earn more, enjoy more, and contribute more to the betterment of yourself, your family, and all of humankind. It demands an investment of time, effort, and money. Keep in mind that if you're not moving ahead you're falling behind.

To keep yourself moving ahead, I recommend that you allocate 5 percent of your time to personal improvement. To have the funds to pay for seminars, tapes, books, and the travel expenses involved, also set aside 5 percent of your income for this purpose. Your personal growth won't happen without this kind of commitment.

Can there be any better investment than in your own personal growth? Think about it. I believe you'll agree that anything else you might invest in can lose market value, be stolen, or be seized for taxes. On the other hand, the time and money you invest in yourself will remain with you for life, contributing throughout your career to your self-confidence and to your ability to defeat whatever life sends against you.

But where is the best place to start?

Everyone has strengths and weaknesses: some things are easy for us, some things are hard. Curiously enough, many people take for granted the things they naturally and effortlessly do well, feeling that those things can't be important because they find them easy. People afflicted with this view often spend their lives failing miserably at whatever is most difficult for them instead of succeeding brilliantly at whatever is easy for them.

In the theatrical world it's commonplace for comedians to despise comedy and yearn to do tragedy. Meanwhile many of the great dramatic actors long to do comedy. A few multifaceted people can cross over successfully. Most can't.

While you can grow enormously by doing what you most fear to do, it's vital to remember that you don't necessarily fear most what you have the least ability to do.

For example, studies show that the fear of speaking in public terrorizes more people than anything else they can walk away from. Certainly it was what I feared most when I sold real estate. Then one day somebody phoned and invited me to give a speech to an organization's conference. I agreed to speak because a few days earlier a man I respected enormously had told me, "Do what you fear most and you conquer fear."

Although the idea of speaking before a crowd terrified me, I did it anyway. Not well, though. My first experience at speaking to a large audience was a humiliating disaster.

Somehow I didn't give up, and I continued to speak whenever the opportunity presented itself. Each time it went better, and gradually it came to me that what I had once feared most was in reality one of my strongest abilities.

Explore every route upward. Don't shrink from what you most fear doing, but also study what's both good for you and easy for you. Make sure you aren't blinding yourself to your strong points. Exalt those things in your mind; learn to be proud of your strengths. Concentrate on doing them more often.

Then identify the things you find difficult to do, do poorly, or hate doing. If you give it some open-minded thought, you may be able to find imaginative ways to avoid doing those things at all. If that's impractical, subcontracting or otherwise delegating them will lay several more feet of steel-reinforced concrete over your mental bomb shelter.

SHODDY APPEARANCE CAN KILL YOU IN SELLING

Many salespeople lose a lot of sales by not being sensitive to appropriate dress and careful grooming. An acquaintance of mine shared with me how dramatically his business improved when he switched from casual wear to stylish suits. His upscale clients immediately began treating him with more warmth, listening to him more intently than before, taking his advice more often. And he found himself suggesting—and selling—the better and more lucrative alternatives more frequently.

He dresses as he wishes in his free time after work, on weekends, and on vacations. Due to the increased business he's generating, he's now enjoying more and better vacations.

DRESSING YOURSELF RIGHT OUT OF SALES

While it's always a good idea when you're working to be dressed professionally, seeming overdressed can make your prospects feel inferior and defensive—and antagonistic to the thought of buying from you.

If you're cold-calling, or meeting someone for the first time for an appointment you made by phone, you won't know much until you get there about what sort of person you'll be meeting. However, as soon as you see the building you'll be going into, you can make last-minute adjustments before you leave your car that will probably put you more in tune with the situation.

If your appointment is in a prestigious new high-rise, it's a safe bet that your suit will give you the best shot. But if your prospects are headquartered in a run-down old industrial building, they probably dress casually—and will feel more comfortable if you do too.

Leave your suit jacket in the car for this one. Perhaps change into more casual shoes too. For women, I suggest a lower heeled shoe. Men, keep a pair of loafers handy.

Salespeople generally work with a variety of customers and prospects every day. This makes it difficult to select one set of clothes that will make the best impression on everybody they see all day long. But some days you'll have one appointment that's of overriding importance. This solves the problem: Choose what's best for the one important situation and make do with minor adjustments (such as taking your jacket off) for the other customers.

Some clothes lend themselves to a variety of modes; others do not. The pants of many suits look fine by themselves, depending on your shirt choice. The right outfit will allow you to dress correctly for a formal appointment, and later easily modify it so that you will feel right in a more casual atmosphere. By taking off the formal attire of tie and coat and slipping into a sweater or sport jacket (for women, dress slacks), in a couple of minutes you can be well but casually dressed and well tuned in to your most down-home customer.

Wardrobe Selection

One of the most important aspects of dressing well is color coordination. Try a new look you've admired on someone else. Have fun with changes in fashion. Every year sees a wide range of interesting new looks that will give you a savvy but professional look.

If you don't feel comfortable with wardrobe selection, get help. Some of the better department stores have wardrobe coordinators on their staffs to assist customers. You might also ask an acquaintance whose taste you admire to help you, take an evening course in wardrobe selection, or hire a professional dress consultant.

Shoes

Organize a shoe-shining and cleaning kit at home that you can set up and put away quickly. Be aware of the condition of your shoes; keep them in good repair and polished. Shoe repair shops can handle both tasks for you, and if you have problems with bunions or tight shoes, they can also stretch them for you. It's easier to be relaxed, alert, and in your best selling mode if your feet don't hurt.

Grooming

Before you call on a customer, check in a mirror to make sure your hair is in place and there's nothing on your face you didn't put there intentionally. Women should inspect their eye makeup to make sure the color is even.

Keep a refresher kit in your car with moistened towelettes, travel-size toothpaste and brush, breath mints, deodorant, comb, safety pins, needle and thread, a supply of buttons, spot remover, a nail file, hand lotion, and tissues or a roll of paper towels. Both men and women should know that a warm handshake is marred by rough hands.

I'm not going to preach here, but if you smoke, please be aware that the odor of cigarette smoke is offensive to many people. Never smoke in front of a client! And, if you smoke in your car between appointments, try to keep the car window open so the odor won't cling so heavily to your clothing. End of speech.

Posture

As you wait, avoid slouching in the chair with papers scattered around you. When you're directed to the conference room or office, walk confidently with your shoulders back.

Accessories

An attractive attaché case or briefcase is a must to keep your order forms, calculator, and catalogs handy and in good shape. Your business case doesn't have to be expensive, but it shouldn't be suffering from overwork. If it looks like you've used it to dig out of the snow, some of your customers will wonder if you're good enough to handle their account—after all, it seems like you aren't making much money. Also invest in a classy business card holder so you won't have to hand out dog-eared cards. Use an elegant pen. If you're asking a client to authorize paperwork for your product, making the final close, don't ruin the picture of excellent service you've given them by handing them a dime-a-dozen disposable pen. Or, worse yet, don't give them a pen from the local hotel you may be staying at. Keep the image professional and positive by investing in a few very nice pens of your choice. These small things set you apart from the average salesperson. Business is often won or lost for small reasons.

Let Your Appearance Build Your Confidence

When you look your best, your self-confidence is high and your presentation will be given with more flair and enthusiasm. Looking your best takes time and money, but the effort will pay off in higher sales production. As I mentioned, appearance counts with your personal hygiene, clothing, and business accessories. However, don't forget your car. Be sure to keep your car clean. It could be pretty embarrassing to have the need to give your client a ride in your car and have it filled with fast-food lunch bags, baby toys, and dirty dry cleaning. Going to the expense of having your car cleaned professionally each week should eliminate that worry. And, believe me, the peace of mind that little extra expense brings you is well worth the investment.

CHAPTER NINE

TRANSITIONS AND CHANGES

Why am I devoting a full chapter to coping with transitions and change?

Because more promising sales careers are wrecked by out-of-control personal problems than by poor sales performance.

Everybody has personal problems; some are unique to you, some you share with everybody on the planet. Therefore it's unrealistic to think in terms of solving all your personal problems. What is realistic? Seeking to control your personal problems so that you can enjoy life to the fullest and still achieve your goals.

How well you handle life's daily transitions has a lot to do with whether or not you're able to keep your personal problems under control. And, since some kind of change usually comes before, accompanies, or follows close behind every personal crisis, the art of coping with change is a basic survival skill.

Moreover, some sales jobs often involve difficult hours— evenings and weekends—and call for heavy travel. The impact of these two pressures on the family can be disastrous. It can be, but doesn't have to be. In this chapter we'll look at ways to avoid this disaster, and the others we've hinted at.

THE LIFE-THREATENING DIFFERENCE BETWEEN WORKAHOLICS AND THE WORK-DRIVEN

Some people think staying on top means you have to be totally absorbed in your work. All the interest and pleasures that well-rounded individuals enjoy must be crowded into the fewest possible hours.

For most people, however, forcing themselves into total absorption in their work leads directly to physical or emotional burnout. In some cultures today, it's not uncommon for the working spouse to devote 60 to 70 hours per week to their jobs, including having business dinners or meetings nearly every night of the week. That leaves little time for their personal lives and their families. However, working those hours is the only way for them to get ahead. The nonworking spouse accepts it as a way of life and handles every other aspect of their mutual lives. By current American standards, that doesn't allow for much in the way of relationships and wouldn't be widely accepted. Many Americans would view this style of working as undesirable.

On the surface, being work-absorbed appears to be classic "Type A" behavior, and "Type A" behavior is often associated with high income. "Sounds good," you might say. "I'll take the money now and worry about burnout when and if it hits me."

Think again. "Type A" behavior has been identified as one of the most deadly risk factors in heart and circulatory disease, the number-one cause of death in the United States. The work-driven don't seem to grasp how little point there is in being the local graveyard's richest resident.

However, there's a vital difference between being a workaholic and being the work-driven sort who exhibits "Type A" behavior.

Workaholics love to work. Nothing else gives them the enduring excitement, the lasting fun, and the emotional satisfaction that working does. Everything else quickly pales and, no matter what, the workaholic is soon back at work. Workaholics aren't driven, they're pulled.

People who display "Type A" behavior—that is, who force themselves to keep working when their minds and emotions cry out for rest and relief—are not workaholics. They are work-driven.

Workaholics thrive on work; they glory in it. Instead of being exhausted, they usually leave long work sessions refreshed, smiling, and ready for fun. By contrast, the "Type A" work-driven person often emerges from a long work session emotionally and physically exhausted, ill-tempered, tense, and in no mood for company.

I'm a workaholic. I know intimately the joys of being pulled by the challenge and satisfaction of work. At times in years past I've also been work-driven, so I know how little satisfaction that condition gives while it breaks you down and multiplies your problems.

If you're work-driven to an unhealthy degree, how do you change yourself into a happy, healthy workaholic?

That's a huge question because every work-driven person is different. All I can hope to do here is to give you a star or two to steer by. Your work-drive probably springs from deep within you. If so, reaching an understanding of it may require professional counseling. But if you feel sure you have time to cope with your work-drive, here are those stars to steer by:

- Make sure you're being pulled by achievable written goals that excite you, goals that you have chosen, not goals someone else—your parents, spouse, friends, whoever—imposed on you.
- Make sure that when you achieve a personal goal, you always take the reward you promised yourself.
- Communicate with yourself until you understand what makes you feel driven. Then decide whether that drive is healthy. If you decide it's not, reorganize your thinking to adjust that drive to something that *is* healthy.
- Restore balance to your life. Unfortunately, too many people think of goals only in financial terms. They set their money goals first, work hardest at them, and worry about everything else later. That's not a healthy way to approach

goal setting. Setting goals for balance in your life should be your highest priority. Exercise more, eat less; laugh more, grind your teeth less; give more, take less; find interesting people to spend more time with, be with negative people less; attend your spiritual needs more, think about your material needs less.

Here are some sample goals for achieving balance in your life:

Physical: I walk two miles each day for health and relaxation.

Emotional: I spend time each day talking with each of the special people in my immediate family.

Financial: I make ten new contacts each day in order to reach my monthly income goal of $3,500.

Spiritual: I schedule time each day for reflection on the good in my life and thinking of ways I can contribute to the lives of others.

MINIMIZING THE IMPACT OF BAD HOURS AND HEAVY TRAVEL

Working weekends and evenings makes it rough in any family. If it's a two-income family and the other spouse works regular hours, it's worse than rough.

Throw in some travel during the week and what's left? Possibly not enough to sustain the relationship—unless you take extraordinary measures. Here are some of the things you can do:

- Invest part of your extra earnings. Your evening and weekend work might bring in extra money. If so, invest some of it in keeping your family happy—that is, in fun things they especially enjoy.
- Make family appointments. Set aside time each week that you hold sacred for the members of your family. Put your family appointments on your weekly schedule and tell ev-

eryone else you're not available then. No matter what, don't let business interfere with spending quality time with your family at those appointed times. Without this time your family can count on, plans can't be carried out. Their frustrations will grow, and the resulting family problems may have a bad effect on your sales performance.

- Stay involved. If you must be away during special events for your spouse or children, be sure to call beforehand, if possible, to give support, and afterward to hear how things went. Even if there are not special events going on while you're away, be certain to spend a little one-on-one time with each family member upon returning home. This helps them to know how much you care and it helps you get back into the "home" feeling as soon as possible. No one likes feeling as though they're an outsider in their own home.
- Make the important phone calls. In today's jet age, mail may not beat you home. Keep in close touch by phone, fax, or overnight mail.
- Acknowledge your spouse. Don't ever forget to let your spouse and other loved ones know how much you appreciate their job of holding down the fort while you're gone.
- Give thoughtful gifts. Thoughtfulness and personalization count for more than cost. Most people prefer small things given more often to bigger things given at long intervals. Try these ideas:

> Go for unusual gifts.
> Make your gifts fun.
> Send a gift to your spouse's office. The ooh's and ah's from the people he or she works with will pack a lot of emotional impact into your gift.
> Send a rose a day. If you'll be away during a special occasion, before you leave, go by the florist and make this arrangement. Write a brief note to go with each flower. What you write yourself is a hundred times more emotional than the same words in someone else's handwriting.
> Balloon bouquets. Your spouse may associate flowers with funerals and see balloon bouquets as being more fun.

Mylar balloons last for weeks, latex balloons only for hours or days. A good balloon store will deliver a bouquet bulging with heart-shaped Mylar balloons for the price of a floral bouquet. But, long after flowers would have wilted, Mylar balloons will still be bouncing around on the ceiling saying "I love you."

- Set family goals. Get your family involved in your goals and the rewards that achieving them will bring. This way they'll feel that their sacrifices to your schedule are worthwhile. Make the reward for winning a sales contest a family treat and they'll give you constant support during the contest. If the reward is good enough, they won't want you home at all. They'll give you all the support you need to reach this goal.
- Get your children involved in your work. Those of us who are of non-Asian extraction can learn a lot about a wonderful way of intensifying family bonds from the Asians we're happy to have in our population. Go into any business operated by an Asian and you'll probably see the owners' small children playing in a corner or helping out with simple tasks.
- Invite your spouse on extended business trips. When you're away for more than a week, arrange for your spouse to fly out and join you on the weekend if at all possible. Chances are you two can enjoy a mini-honeymoon away from your usual preoccupations.

TRANSITIONS

How do you make swift, effective transitions from work to the other roles you play? How do you put aside the massive concentration on your job that pushed you to the top so you can become the spouse, parent, companion, or friend you want, and need, to be?

Success here is essential. Without it you can't maintain your mental and physical well-being, take care of your loved ones, and draw strength and purpose from them. In fact, without reasonably good transitions, losing your family to divorce becomes a real possibility.

A recent study of the presidents of large, profitable companies revealed that as a group they have longer marriages and more stable family relationships than middle managers do. Compared to lower-level executives, successful company presidents also live longer and enjoy better health, and their children have lower rates of emotional disturbance.

A popular misconception is that success and family problems go hand in hand. This erroneous idea persists because the mass market enjoys believing it; stories of family problems among the rich and famous sell newspapers. Yet success in business and success in family life clearly stem from the same sources.

Most company presidents don't get ulcers, they give them. But few were born presidents; most of them worked their way up. Studies indicate that throughout their careers the company presidents somehow found time and energy for family, friends, and a variety of outside activities.

How did they do that? They gave high priority to their non-business life. They understood at the beginning of their careers that doing so would enhance their performance over the long pull, not diminish it.

And, as the years passed, these steady, family-loving men and women with wide-ranging interests moved swiftly up the ladder. On the way they climbed easily past more narrow-minded people who had little interest in anything but business.

This happened for many reasons. The men and women who would become presidents impressed those they met with the broadness of their understanding. They seemed capable of more growth because they were already dealing effectively with all aspects of their lives. Since they devoted time and energy to a variety of causes and concerns, they were more experienced than people who knew nothing but their work. And they radiated the solid emotional strength that having a family gives.

If you currently live only for your work and avoid outside

interests, shortchanging your family and yourself in the amount and quality of time you spend with them, I hope you'll consider the implications of this study carefully. I'm convinced that nothing can do more for your career than lavishing care and attention on your family, your religion, your health, and your other non-business interests. Ideally you would do those things for themselves, but better you do them for ambition's sake than not at all.

THE ART OF MAKING QUICK SWITCHES

The transition I'm talking about is simply the act of switching quickly and completely from hard-nosed business and money-making activities to soft-hearted family and recreational activities. How do you make swift, effective transitions from one area of your life to another? Here's how:

Take control. Unless you control each transition, other people and avoidable complications will delay or confuse the transition. As a result, you'll get even more frustrated and tired.

Plan how you'll do it. The smoothness of your transitions depend on how you mesh with your spouse and children or the other people in your life. Put yourself in their shoes and lead off with something you know they'll like.

Use every aid you can. Effective opening moves for a good transition from the work day to the family can begin as soon as you reach home. Help cut up veggies for dinner, or serve cookies and milk for kids. Set aside time to sit and talk over refreshing soft drinks, cheese, and crackers for mom and dad. Think about your loved ones individually and use what works with each of them.

Begin your assembly of effective transitions by identifying your most common and troublesome transition point. For most of us that's what I call Typhoon Time.

TYPHOON TIME

If you're a working parent, Typhoon Time hits hard and fast after work, doesn't it? That's when you switch from the pressures of work to the pleasures of parenting after hitting the ball all day.

Most of us would like to make the change in a leisurely fashion. We've worked hard; now we'd like to relax, maybe take a shower and change clothes, check the mail and the answering machine, phone a friend or get dinner started.

But in today's world the luxury of leisure is hard to come by. If you try to ignore your kids, you'll turn this transition into a nerve-wracking disaster. Why? Because a natural part of being a kid is to be self-centered.

Your children may have been alone for several hours after school when you first see them. Or maybe you dashed in and picked them up at a child care center. Either way, they want your attention badly, and they want it now.

Fortunately, there's a good side to this: they usually want the same things every day. So organize yourself to give those things to them (assuming you feel good about what it is they want).

They may need a hug or a few minutes of your undivided attention while they tell you about their latest exploit. Maybe they need a glass of milk, a cookie, and the TV turned on to their favorite program. Sure, TV is a crutch. It's also an aid, and every working parent needs all the wholesome aids he or she can get.

But you don't have to let advertisers determine what your kids will watch. Use your VCR. A lot of interesting and educational videotapes that your children should see are available from libraries, church groups, public organizations, and private companies.

In many families, the worst thing about Typhoon Time is that everybody seems to fall apart then. Day after day, children pick Typhoon Time to throw their worst tantrums. The parents, just home from work and feeling frazzled, sometimes have difficulty maintaining a high degree of self-control.

"Every day my four-year-old was like an angry little bear when I picked her up after work," Marie Stevens, a top-selling rep, says. "I couldn't figure it out. I thought she hated me for leaving her at the child care center, but she was always sweet in the morning. Then, when I came for her after work, whammo—tears, screeching, the whole bit. Try sticking that on top of a tough day."

Desperate for help, Marie talked with a counselor. She was told that her daughter's regular afternoon tantrums had their healthy side.

"Children learn very early to choke down their negative emotions in public," the counselor said. "So they keep their bad feelings canned until they're in a safe situation—at home or in the family car. Being on their own all day at a young age is tough on youngsters, and they need a safe outlet for their bottled up angers and frustrations. So they let good old mom have it with both barrels as soon as they see the whites of her eyes."

Once Marie understood why it was happening, she got less upset, and her daughter's tantrums soon dropped to a tolerable level. Within a few days, Marie learned more about how to ease through the stressful moments. Hugging her daughter helped. Sympathetic questions, and listening carefully to the little girl's answers, helped. And Marie's new attitude, warm and empathetic instead of cold and impatient, helped even more.

Why Typhoons Hit Us Too

One of the reasons Typhoon Time hits adults is that we, even more than little kids, have to bottle up our anger and frustration most of the time when we're in public. When we come home, we feel like we have the right to be our "real" selves: no more pretense, no more holding in, dump it all out on anyone handy.

Unfortunately, that means dumping on the only people available, our loved ones. It's not a good formula for insuring long-term stability in the relationships.

So in the typical two-income family, two bottled-up adults get home just when a couple of bottled-up kids come storming in. In this situation bad moments often follow. Yet it doesn't have to be that way.

Most of us won't ask for help when we need it. We don't analyze why things are getting out of hand; we just react. But Typhoon Time is a particularly bad hour to let frayed emotions control our actions.

Remember your own childhood. Mom was always there with cinnamon rolls, or a delicious slice of hot homemade bread, when you got home. The house was warm and quiet and she always had time to listen to your terrible troubles. And she wanted to listen.

But now, with your own kids, you just want them to shut up and stop asking for things. You want to relax and get organized to make some use of your precious few free hours. And that selfish feeling frustrates you even more, because you want to be a good parent.

"Why can't I be like Mom?" You know the answer. Your mom didn't work outside the home, and she lived in a less hectic era.

Typhoon Time is a rotten hour to leap into a frenzy of activity—catching up on the mail, leafing through the newspaper, firing up your dish and clothes washing machines, letting the TV blare with the latest bad news nobody needs, making phone calls that could wait, and giving your spouse a list of errands that need to be done before the stores close.

Of course the scenario varies if there is a spouse at home. It's unfortunate, but the stay-at-home spouse, even if he or she works out of the home, will often greet the other spouse with a list of everything that went wrong during the day. The stay-at-home spouse may be anxiously awaiting another adult to talk with, especially if there are small children at home. It's natural to turn to the person you know you can most depend on when you've had a bad day, but don't unload the moment your spouse walks in the door. Test the waters first to determine if he or she is in better or worse shape than you are. If you feel you need to unload or explode, tell your spouse so. Don't just jump right into your problems. Doing so at an inopportune time will only add fuel to the fire that's often created during Typhoon Time.

How to Tame Typhoon Time

Few things can equal typhoon-taming for improving family relations and easing parental stress at low cost.

Accentuate the Positive

Give everybody a snack as soon as they come in. Next, make a game of who can change quickest and pile into the car first. Then:

Go to the neighborhood park. Run around, throw frisbees, push the kids on the swings, or play catch for a few minutes. Do something together that allows the whole family to yell, jump around, and generally blow off pent-up emotions.

Go swimming if you have access to a pool. Many neighborhoods have pools, and some cities have public pools with special family rates, and there are a lot of fun things to do in the pool.

Take the whole family on a brisk walk around the block. Assuming that your neighborhood is safe and the weather is good, this can be the quickest and easiest way to tame Typhoon Time.

OR

Get everyone out into the backyard and play tag or toss a ball around. Play croquet or badminton if your family enjoys those types of activities. Get active and get everyone together.

De-emphasize the Negative

It takes planning and determination to see these ideas through, but you'll find they're well worth the effort.

Let the mail and the answering machine wait until after dinner. You'll save time by giving them your undivided attention at an hour when you can wrap up each item as you go.

Don't run errands after work. The stores are crowded then with tired, frustrated people, so you'll spend too much time standing in line. Instead, organize your errand-running so that you can take care of it all one evening a week.

Better yet, take care of errands during your working hours. One of the perks of being an outside salesperson is that you can pop into stores when they're not busy and get your personal business done quickly. Your schedule and unfortunate canceled appointments may give you a few moments of down time so that you can take an early or late lunch break and get a few things done. Don't cheat yourself out of this valuable time saver, but more importantly, don't abuse the privilege either.

Plan meals on a weekly basis. Perhaps on errand night you should all eat out. Maybe you can combine your meal stop with your errands, and allow the children to help with them.

And in General

Don't let tradition and rigid thinking decide every detail of how your family operates.

Design dinner to meet your family's present needs. Some parents try to impose the tradition of a sit-down family-style dinner every night long after their children's outside activities have destroyed all the kids' interest in, or need for, that particular form of togetherness. If the sit-down dinner isn't working because everybody wants to eat at different times or on the run, you can reduce the strain by preparing dip-out and scoop-up foods—chili, all sorts of stews, tacos with beans and rice.

Being a good parent requires constant adjustment to rapid change in your children. In just ten short years a heavily dependent four-year-old becomes an eagerly outreaching fourteen. What worked beautifully on that vanished four-year-old is certain to drive your teenager up the wall.

Suit your typhoon-tamer to your children's ages. Little kids love going to a park or the gym with their parents; teenagers are likely to hate it.

BETTER WORK-TO-FREE-TIME TRANSITIONS FOR EVERYONE

The important thing is to have a definite plan for making the transition from work to free time. Showering and changing into casual clothes is one of the most effective ways of unwinding from work. It's nonfattening, quick, and almost universally available.

If you don't exercise first thing in the morning, right after work is usually the next best time. Since your work as a sales representative is mentally and emotionally stressful, your transition plan should include physical activity—biking, rapid walking, running, swimming, or any other aerobic exercise that will drain tension away while giving your heart and health a boost.

This type of activity will often help clear your mind of the problems that were upsetting you during the workday. This will allow you to discuss them rationally with your spouse if you still feel the need to do so.

CHANGE

Change is one of the most stressful events people undergo—even when they go into one with a positive attitude and the change is beneficial and pleasant. I'm sure you are well aware that change is inevitable in your personal life. However, it's just as likely to occur, perhaps even in higher ratios, in your sales life.

The key is acceptance. When a chapter of your life closes, sit down and concentrate for however long it takes to grasp the full meaning of the change. Don't dwell on it. Dwelling on the various aspects of change only makes things seem bigger than life and tougher to accept. Learn to accept the blow that's involved and let the whole thing go for all time in one big swoop.

Such sessions can be painful. They can be wonderfully cleansing too, especially if you let your emotions run. It's not only okay to cry if you've suffered a painful loss, in many cases it has to happen before you can let go. By giving yourself time to get over things in private, you can face the future calmly, determined to succeed in other ways.

Accepting and letting go must come sooner or later after every irretrievable loss and unavoidable change. In extreme cases denial comes first, then anger, and finally acceptance.

With some people the letting-go never happens. As a result their loss clouds their minds as long as they live.

Handling Changes That Are Too Tough to Face All at Once

Life often drops changes on us that we simply can't face all at once. Grief over the loss of a loved one falls into this category. If you're emotionally disabled by any loss, get professional help in coping with it.

There's no special honor in bulling through these trials on your own. And, in cold financial terms, you'll save money paying for help as opposed to burdening your sales production with your personal sufferings for a lengthy period.

Can the Emotional Impact of Favorable Changes Be Ignored?

We're likely to assume that any change we can't handle in a single face-the-music session must be bad news. Curiously, this is not always the case.

In other words, just because you're reaching your goals doesn't mean you won't feel the pain of change. You still need to develop your skills at coping, or your continuing success will run into ever larger emotional barriers to further progress.

As this happens, the usual incentives lose their power to move you. As a result you settle into a comfortable niche somewhere. You'll do this not because you lack the ability to rise higher, but because the pain of change has become too great. The key to continuing on a path of positive change in your life is to set goals.

The Pace of Change

The world has been changing faster and faster for 800 years. Today armies of scientists and engineers are busily researching and inventing all over the world; a hundred years ago no more than a handful of people were similarly occupied. Given these facts, the pace of change will continue to speed up.

This constant acceleration means that even the experience of change is changing. We can't avoid becoming more skilled at handling change because we are constantly exposed to it in the products we buy and use, and in how and where we travel.

However, these general changes in the world have only a slight impact on us compared to the personal changes that take place in our lives. Personal changes usually involve three distinct stages: Something ends. The ending is followed by a period of confusion and distress that leads to a new beginning.

Even when we choose the change, and labor long and hard to bring it about, its arrival is still likely to be accompanied by change's favorite traveling companions: confusion and distress.

People generally concentrate on the new beginning and try to ignore their feelings of confusion and distress. But if they don't take time to mourn the passing of the old way, usually it's not truly over. It lingers in the mind, ready to stab our emotions at unexpected moments, each time giving us a stiff push toward making a bad decision.

It doesn't come easily to mourn the passing of the old when we're excited about the new. We have a built-in barrier to facing the fact that a favorable change can be painful: we don't want to question the wisdom of the new course we're pursuing.

Keep in mind that it's not necessary to put down the old way in order to change to the new. All that's really required is to recognize that, all things considered, the new is better than the old. You can and should still honor your old convictions and loyalties, take pride in your former accomplishments and possessions; and, by all means, treasure your memories and friendships.

CHAPTER TEN

WHAT STRESS CAN DO TO YOU

Being in sales exposes us to all sorts of stresses—stresses that the "mass of men" would shudder to think of encountering on a daily basis. Yet, we salespeople diligently plod on through the torrential rains of stress inducers, somewhat oblivious to the damage they wreak on our bodies and our minds.

STRESSED OUT? WHO, ME?

I want to list here some of the things that cause stress in a salesperson's life. Once you realize how many there are and how often you encounter them, we'll help you learn how to relieve those stresses.

If You're New to Selling

In considering a career in selling, you put yourself under the stress of making a decision to change. You must weigh all the factors involved. Are you ready to handle a change at this time of your life? Are you willing to go for it all the way? Will you put forth the effort required to learn all about your product and develop proven selling skills? Will you be satisfied with learning to be an average salesperson or will you put pressure on yourself to become a top achiever? Can you live with a relatively unstable income until you make your mark in selling? How will you handle the criticism from your family and friends who think sales is not right for you? How will you find a product you really enjoy selling and can earn a good income from? What kind of company will hire you with little or no selling experience? What if you're not dressed right? What if your car breaks down? Oh, no, you can't find the building. The appointment was yesterday? You brought the wrong information.

If You're a Veteran

(Note to new salespeople: Add these stressing questions to your list once you have a selling job.) Where will your next lead come from? How will you get an appointment to meet with this person? How will you handle the rejection if you don't make this sale? What will you do to make up for this lost lead? You've got to keep moving, contacting a certain number of people each day to meet your sales quota. What if you don't do it today? What if you're late for this appointment? How do you handle this angry client? Why was this order filled improperly? Are your sales meeting quota? Will you win the contest? Will you keep your job?

When I first entered selling, I made a mistake, as do many people who go into our business. I decided to try sales. Now, what's the mistake I made? Try. Do you know how many people are *trying* selling? Do you know how many people get into selling as if it's something you can just kind of try and maybe you make it, maybe you don't?

You will agree with me that there's no such thing as a brain surgeon trying his vocation. He doesn't wake up one morning and say, "I think I'll try a little brain surgery, get a feel for it, see if I like it. I'm starting part-time, though." Even bricklayers and secretaries need to get some training before they're competent enough to make a living in their chosen field.

You show me anyone who earns a higher than average income in any field and I can tell you they have totally committed to their profession. They have burned bridges to their past professions. They're committed to being professional in that vocation. That's why they earn so much. That's why so many salespeople have incomes that are among the highest in the country—because they've made a commitment to this wonderful profession.

I hope you're ready to do that today—to commit to becoming a professional salesperson. Not just by title, but by example, by your skill level, by your ability to achieve, earn a higher than average income and cope with success if you are blessed with it. Because many people can't handle success any more than they can handle failure.

The worldwide tragedy that's causing salespeople to fail is their inability to understand and cope with stress. The word stress, in my opinion, has been somewhat overused. You may have read a book or two on stress and feel you have an understanding of it. I thought I knew a lot about it too, until I started doing research and found out that the stress that most of us have been taught about in the current books is not the stress that we in sales go through. You see, most of the books or tapes developed to cover the topic of stress were not made by, or for, salespeople. Most of them say, for example, that traumatic experiences create overwhelming amounts of stress, which lead to a certain state in which you will flee or fight. I don't disagree with that point. However, it doesn't cover the major stress areas that ruin our lives in selling.

If you are mentally and physically sound, you begin each day filled with energy and emotions to do your job. If I were to take a .357 Magnum and shoot it at a target at close range I would totally destroy it. Well, that's like what happens in major stress situations. A divorce. Death of a loved one. Financial reversals. Those are traumatic, but that's not what happens on a daily basis.

What I want to talk about is cumulative stress. Cumulative stress involves all the little things that happen in a selling career—things that bother you, but aren't traumatic enough to knock you down. These little stressors could be likened to darts. For this explanation, visualize little darts with streamers on them. We'll call them stress darts. And if you are in selling, from the moment you wake up in the morning they are coming at you. Many of us have learned to duck out of the way of some of our stress darts. However, many of them stick.

Their little streamers represent a flow of energy and emotion that leaves your body each time you get hit with a stress dart. I'm sure you will agree that being hit with a dart is painful, but not life-threatening. The pain may slow you down, but not for long. But, what happens when six or seven of these darts stick in you each day? Think of how much energy and emotion they drain from you.

If you have ever had a job that involved physical labor, you know how tired you can feel at the end of the day. Believe it or not, the selling business is a draining business. Many new salespeople are surprised to find they are more tired at the end of their selling days than they were during their physical labor days. Selling will take away all your energy and emotion if you don't know what's happening to you.

Realize that in sales you are a professional problem solver. You have to be aware that there are things that happen all day to cause you stress. I have learned over the years that you must play a game with yourself in order to keep the most common little darts from striking home and draining all your energy and emotion. If you stay in selling and don't learn to cope with these things, you are going to have all kinds of negative things happen to you physically. Too many people suffer and die young because they did not learn to cope with this thing called stress.

Sales Stressor #1

The first stressor is guilt. Guilt is a wasted emotion. Many of you know what you should do, don't do it, and then feel guilty. Or you know what you shouldn't do, you do it anyway, and again, you feel guilty. Now, I'm going to ask you: If you're feeling guilty over something you've already done, forget it and move on. If you know you're going to feel guilty *before* you do it, then don't do it. This is called maturity.

If you know you should do things and you aren't going to do them, you're probably lacking a very important trait. It's called discipline. Discipline is the "fountain of greatness." If you don't already have discipline, don't set a goal to get it in a short amount of time. It's not that easy. Begin by setting one small goal such as getting up every morning when the alarm goes off—not 10, 15, or 20 minutes later. Once you've successfully gotten yourself out of bed with the alarm for 21 days in a row, you will have developed a new discipline. Seeing it written on this page may sound simple, but if you are like most people, when the time comes and that alarm goes off, it will be tough to set your feet on that floor.

Once you've accomplished that one new discipline, then you will be ready to try another. Do yourself, and the loved ones who live with you, a favor and don't try to change a lot of things at once. The shock may be too much for them and they may fight you. It's tough enough to discipline yourself without having others give you feedback that might reinforce the habit you're trying to break. Also, don't try to increase the discipline in others without their consent. If you decide it's time the whole family got up at 5:00 A.M. every day and they don't agree, you're creating a whole new stressor for yourself and them.

Let's go back to guilt. What happens when we feel guilty? First of all, we dwell on it. We know we're not doing what we should do. You see, the problem with selling is that you can act like you're working and not really be working. You can play busy with lots of movement. "I'm a salesperson. I got up and got dressed. That's just like work. I got in a car and drove somewhere. That's just like work. I sat at some desk, just like work."

Work, in selling, is only the time you spend in front of someone who is qualified to say "Yes" to your product or service. Everything else is preparatory to work and most salespeople do not spend anywhere near 40 hours a week working. They float through their day hoping someone will ask them if they have any more product.

If you're serious about your career, you're going to start looking in the mirror at the one person who's decided who you are at this point. It's not your family, not your friends. It's you, based on the decisions you have made, or not made, because life is nothing but a matter of choices and if we want different results, we must get real serious about different choices.

Sales Stressor #2

The second stressor is something that is the staple of selling. It's called rejection. Gang, rejection is part of your business. That's why you can make so much money. You see, the average American is so afraid of rejection that he finds jobs where the rejection is very low.

You go into sales and whatever you call yourself—consultant, network marketing specialist, whatever clever name you've gotten to hide what you really do—your life's blood is your ability to cope with rejection. To handle more of it. To expect it. To know that it's not bad. It's good. You see, you've also got to realize that no one's ever rejected *you*. They've rejected your proposal or offering at that point in time. It's nothing to be taken personally.

Please realize, also, that most of you do not face daily anyone who has ever rejected you in the past. So, we've just got to lighten up with it. Make a note to yourself on your daily planner each day: "I won't take it personally." You've got to do that with rejection. It's a big game.

Sales Stressor #3

Our third stressor is disappointments. You work so hard for people. They promise you the business. If you're like most salespeople, you've worked very hard and given good service. You call to follow up, only to hear the prospect say he's bought from your competitor. And what do you say? "Congratulations. I hope you'll be happy with it"?

What do you really want to say? Nothing like that, I'm sure. Many of you are holding this in. I want you to learn how to release it creatively. By that I mean you must learn the game. Learn to say these words, "Oh, you felt after research that buying my competitor's product was best? Well, fine. I'm curious, however, were you at least happy with the time and effort I spent trying to give you good service?"

Most of them will agree you were great. They'll be the guilty ones now.

"Since you were happy, may I send you three of my business cards that you can place in the hands of three other people who are qualified to hear about my offering?"

Most will agree, intending to throw your cards in the trash. But, we forestall that by writing a letter, "Dear Jim, Thank you for your gracious offer of giving me three pre-qualified referred leads. I will keep in touch on a weekly basis and wait to give excellent service to these fine people." Then, you file their names in a file labeled the "OWE ME" file.

The funny thing about salespeople is that we want to be thought of as professionals. We want to dress and act professional, but we don't always live the lives of professionals.

For example, lawyers and medical professionals know how much money their day is worth. They know how much they can bill per hour. That's the first key to success in selling. Set an hourly rate that reflects your worth and demand it from society for quality service given.

By the way, if you go to a psychiatrist and after therapy you still go nuts, guess what, he still sends you a bill. He's earned the income. It's the same with you. I believe that if you give quality service to people you have a right to get referrals. And if they weren't interested, someone else will be if you just learn how to ask and to use emotional obligation. Have fun with it.

Call those people back. Those cards will become like stones in their pockets. They'll get you those leads. You might laugh about this, but in my career, someone would occasionally come in with a beat-up old card of mine and I would find out that they had been referred by someone because of my follow-up.

A word all salespeople must learn to use is the word *lose*. You might as well get more creative and go after business you've earned, because what have you got to lose? You've got nothing to lose. I want you to learn to stretch and do a little bit more than you've ever done. Overcome the fear of being rejected instead of sitting back and saying, "Well, I'll talk with someone else." Let's follow up, follow up, follow up, follow up until they buy or die.

Sales Stressor #4

The fourth stressor is a major enemy not only in our selling careers, but in our personal lives. One word: FEAR. "Oh, I'm afraid." You see, fear is what keeps people from going after what they really want in life. Their fear of failure. Their fear of rejection. And many times if you are pleasant and nice, it doesn't happen. Live by these words, "Do what you fear most and you control fear." That's what successful people do. They overcome fear and become strong and successful.

Sales Stressor #5

The fifth stressor is schedules—a commitment to time. Many salespeople lack the discipline to write down what they're going to do every day and then do it. Or, they don't like paperwork and schedules that regulate their time. In a "regular" office job, schedules are less of a reflection of what your income will be. You are expected to be there 40 hours per week and do your job.

Successful people realize that scheduling and paperwork in this society are a major part of selling. You don't have to like it, but you must learn to do what you hate and most want to avoid, as early as possible in your day. If you get up in the morning and have paperwork that needs to be done, get to it right away. The rest of the day you'll be free because you won't be dwelling on it.

Sales Stressor #6

Number six, I feel, is a disease. It's unfortunate, but this disease is rampant in society. It's called procrastination. You've no idea the number of people who don't get what they want because they're always putting off what they need to do in order to get it.

Let me give you the definition of procrastination quickly. It's living yesterday, avoiding today, thus ruining tomorrow.

Many people are literally living their lives this way instead of taking control. I've had people tell me it's one of their biggest problems.

I want to share a little secret I've learned over the years about some of the most successful millionaires. They procrastinate too. But they do it when they've planned to do it. It's called pre-planned procrastination. They choose a date or time when they're going to do absolutely nothing and they do it very well, whereas average people are always looking for ways to put off doing what they know they should do. The discipline it takes to overcome procrastination can be developed by living by three small words: DO IT NOW. If you take twenty-one days, as I've mentioned previously, and commit to changing as you want to change, just watch what will happen.

Sales Stressor #7

Number seven is something that a lot of people in selling have problems with. It's quotas. Many companies have established quotas that, unfortunately, devastate their salespeople. Others create quotas so low that they don't motivate their people.

While some salespeople look forward to getting their quotas, to others it's the equivalent of having their teeth pulled without the benefit of painkillers. Other people are highly motivated by quotas. You must analyze yourself to determine how quotas affect you.

I found myself motivated by quotas. It was like being dared to do something, and most companies know that giving quotas is a good way to handle a highly competitive salesperson. However, if the quotas we are given are so far above what we consider to be our current level of abilities, we tend to get intimidated. And, intimidation often brings its negative cousins, procrastination and guilt, which we've already discussed.

If you truly believe a quota given to you is unrealistic, ask to sit down and review it with your sales manager as soon as possible. If for some reason the issue is not flexible this time, just let the manager know you'll do your best and then get out there and do it. Don't dwell on it. Dwelling on problems or challenges in selling wastes more time than anything else.

Sales Stressor #8

The eighth stressor is deliveries. This is the date or time your customer is supposed to get his product or service. One of the challenges we have in selling is that sometimes we will say anything to make that sale. If they want it at a certain time, we'll say we can do it even though we know the company could never make that delivery date. Don't do this. As a professional, you must learn how to anticipate an objection, such as a delayed delivery date, and handle it during your presentation. As I teach in my selling course, brag about the objection.

"Mr. Johnson, as we get ready to discuss the opportunity to serve you with our fine product, I must tell you that we are in a very advantageous position. Let me explain. With most of my competitors, if you said you wanted their product, and they told you they could deliver it right away, I guess that probably means not very many people want their products. With our product, because of the demand, if you want it, you'll have to be patient because everybody wants our product or service."

If a situation arises in which your company cannot make the delivery date agreed upon when you made the sale, do not, I repeat, do not hesitate to call your customer about it. The sooner he knows, the fewer problems you'll have about it. Don't worry about giving him a lot of details as to the reasons. Just give him the plain facts and wait for his response. If the delay causes him some tremendous challenges, try your best to work with him. Arrange for a partial delivery if you can. See if your company will pick up the shipping charges and ship it a faster way. Be flexible.

Sales Stressor #9

Number nine is customer stalls. "It's not in the budget." "We're waiting for things to get better." "Get back with us in a few months." In my selling courses, I teach the best methods I currently know for handling situations in which these stalls come up. However, there will be times when we just can't do anything to move the buying process along. When that happens, we need to step back and stay in touch until the customer's buying desire heats up.

Sales Stressor #10

Number ten is peer attacks. A peer attack is what happens to the people in your company when something you do, usually something that outshines them, threatens them. How do they react? We've already covered this but not as a stressor. Always remember this: You'll probably never have problems with the people who are working in positions above or below you. It's those on your level that you have to watch out for.

Sales Stressor #11

Canceled appointments are just part of the business, and they drive us crazy. When you are a salesperson you get to be the first one canceled if anyone is going to get canceled because your prospect gets too busy. It's something you have to live with. That's why I suggest you do what doctors and dentists do. Have someone confirm every appointment during the day. Or, do it yourself. Don't just call and say, "I'm calling to see if we're still on." That gives them an out. Call with an assumptive attitude and say, "I know we're getting together today at 2:00 and I have spent so much time in preparation and am so pleased with all my research and findings that I'm sure you'll consider it time well spent. I wanted to remind you, I'll be there promptly at 2." That way, if they were considering canceling your appointment, they'll be more likely to go ahead anyway. Or, if they truly must cancel, they'll be more likely to reschedule a time with you at the next available date.

Sales Stressor #12

Finding leads. If you work for a company that does not provide you with leads, do yourself a favor and don't give yourself the whole world to look at. It's the opposite of the old adage, "Can't see the forest for the trees." You want to see those individual trees. Isolate faces for yourself. See the people you know in your mind's eye and think about whether or not they qualify for your product. When you run out of people you know, you'll have to begin testing a system of prospecting which will lead you to the right group of people for you to work with.

Sales Stressor #13

Finding locations of appointments. If you are going to a new area or have been assigned a new territory, don't think twice about asking your client for directions to his location the first time you go there. Nothing makes a worst first impression than being late because you were lost. It shows a lack of preparedness.

Sales Stressor #14

Equipment breakdowns. If you must rely on your car or a company car to get you to and from appointments, schedule regular maintenance checkups and don't miss one. The time you spend with the car in the shop for preventive maintenance will be more than repaid by having a reliable car that gets you to important sales appointments. The same goes for any audiovisual equipment or communication equipment you use. Keep it in good repair.

Sales Stressor #15

Traffic jams. This one is practically inevitable in sales. We have to look at it as a game we play. If you know there's always a traffic jam along a certain route, do your best to find an alternate route, leave extra early for an appointment for which you must go through this area, and keep motivational or training tapes handy so you can make the most of this otherwise "down" time.

Sales Stressor #16

Misplaced items. Whether it's your car keys, a piece of product literature, a news item, or an order (which, by the way, should never get lost), misplacing anything is a waste of your valuable time. You'll probably spend more time looking for it than it was worth in the first place. So, do your best to stay organized. If it's really a weakness for you, it may be worth your while to hire someone to help you get organized. There are some very good companies conducting highly profitable businesses helping people get and stay on top of things in their lives.

Sales Stressor #17

Getting or giving poor phone messages. Misunderstandings that arise from poor communication cost businesses billions of dollars annually in the United States alone. When taking information over the telephone or making notes in a presentation, don't use any abbreviations or take any shortcuts that you won't understand two weeks from now. It's better to take a little longer to be accurate the first time than to make a costly error down the road.

When giving information verbally, whether it's in person or over the telephone, have the person read it back to you so you can be certain they're understanding what you said. One of today's advantages in telephone communications is the widespread use of answering devices by which you can leave very specific messages for people, not relying on a third party to communicate the proper information for you.

HOW STRESS HITS

David Harold Fink, M.D., author of *Release from Nervous Tension,* writes, "Nervous tensions do not exist within a vacuum. They do not exist exclusively within the nervous system. They exist within all the organs of the body. When there is an emotional tug-of-war within the individual, there is a pull of one organ against the other. Nervous tension is physical. This is the reason that so many sicknesses are caused by emotional conflicts."

Many authorities agree that stress invites illness into the body. Months or years may pass before the malady takes on a physical reality. When that happens, the ailment often requires medical care, perhaps even hospital treatment and major surgery, as in the case of the stress-caused oxygen shortages and blood-flow problems that lead to heart attacks.

However, stresses resulting from frustrations, large or small, often strike in the form of annoying tics and twitches years before they develop into serious forms of disease. You can easily rid yourself of these minor irritations.

A PILL FOR EVERY PROBLEM

Fighting stress with any type of drug is a screaming danger signal. Many people use alcohol or prescription and illegal drugs to counteract something else they're doing that isn't good for them.

For example, many people ignore or even scoff at what healthier people know: Vigorous exercise is nature's way of relieving emotional and physical symptoms of stress. Instead of taking health-building exercise, these people take health-punishing sleeping pills. The next morning they skip breakfast because they're too groggy to be hungry. Usually they gulp coffee to start their engines.

Caffeine on an empty stomach jangles their nerves so much that by mid-morning they have a headache and take an aspirin or something stronger. By lunchtime they're starving, so they eat a heavy meal and often reward themselves for getting through the morning by having a drink or two.

Back at work at last, they dismally contemplate an afternoon that seems to stretch out endlessly before them—too long to be endured, too short to accomplish all they must get done. Soon they're fading fast, so they start hitting the coffee or soft drinks harder and harder until at last they feel the caffeine-fueled rush of energy. When their workday finally ends, they're so delighted that they feel like celebrating with a drink or two.

More alcohol, poured in on top of a day already too heavy

in attacks on their central nervous systems, leaves them in no mood to do anything smart. That night when their scheduled slumber time arrives, they're too jazzed up to sleep, so they go for the sleeping pills—and the whole cycle starts over again.

How do you break out of a whirlpool like this that's taking you down? Instead of a tranquilizer, take a brisk 15-minute walk. Instead of coffee, drink fruit juice. You break out of negative cycles by doing something positive at every step.

CONSTRUCTIVE AND DESTRUCTIVE STRESS

Stress is an essential part of activity. You can't stand up without tensing muscles. Life is a trade-off of stresses. For example, eating puts stress on your digestive system; going without food when you're hungry inflicts even more stress. Tension of this kind is "constructive stress." It's positive.

Constructive stress doesn't cause heart attacks, muscle spasms in the back and legs, or stomach ulcers. Marathon runners undergo vast amounts of constructive stress, but no one (except for a few individuals born with abnormal hearts) has ever died of a heart attack within seven years of running a modern marathon.

Another kind of tension, "destructive stress," inflicts the damage. Or, to be more exact, our internal emotional reaction to the external destructive stress that life hurls upon us inflicts the damage.

When the term "stress" is used from now on, it will refer to the destructive variety, not the constructive natural kind.

You can't reach the top without subjecting yourself to a great deal of stress for long periods of time. Many exceptionally successful people are convinced that without high stress there's no high performance.

Yet stress can kill you, although people often discount this possibility. However, the devastating part that stress plays in heart disease has been proven beyond all possibility of doubt.

Unquestionably, stress contributes to the development

of hardening of the arteries in some people. In fact, among nonsmokers over 30 years old who aren't significantly over-weight or underexercised, stress is clearly the most dangerous controllable risk factor for heart disease that they face.

Although not as well documented yet, stress is believed to count heavily in the development of a wide variety of other illnesses. It's long been a cliché that stress pushes some people into alcoholism: The phrase "drove me to drink" is at least a century old. In our time, many alcoholics speed up the process of self-destruction by abusing illegal drugs in addition to abusing the legal drug alcohol. In the coming decades, medical research will reveal many other life-threatening effects of stress.

WHY IS STRESS SO DANGEROUS TO SALESPEOPLE TODAY?

What makes stress so dangerous to salespeople today? Unlike those in most other occupations, salespeople in today's fiercely competitive marketplace go directly from one stressful situation to another with little or no relaxation in between. Their days become one long stressful experience instead of a series of short stresses offset by short periods of relaxation. It's no wonder many salespeople end up in doctors' offices with symptoms which are the result of stress overload. They complain of headaches, rapid heartbeat, fatigue, anxiety attacks, ulcers, and so on. The sad truth is that most people can learn how to control stress and avoid these maladies altogether.

Think of yourself as a rubber band. If you stretch to the breaking point once in a while and then return to your normal relaxed state, you can go on stretching and relaxing indefinitely.

But if you keep your rubber-band self stretched tight for long periods, your rubber band will snap. You'll go off the deep end one way or another. You may even have a heart attack.

Yet we can't avoid stress in today's competitive world—not even if we're only trying to get by. And certainly those who aim higher must function effectively under heavy stress of long duration.

CAUSES OF STRESS YOU CAN ELIMINATE

Since stress is such a sneaky and constant killer, it makes sense to give priority to eliminating every cause of stress you realistically can. Here are a few removable causes of deadly stress:

Lack of Personal Goals

If you don't have goals that excite you and give your daily activities purpose, you're running the race of life at a distinct disadvantage. Goal-oriented people make quicker and better decisions that get them there faster. People without goals have a tough and frustrating time trying to compete.

Family Not Involved

If you fail to get your family or other loved ones involved in your goals, you're asking for stress-producing family squabbles. But if the family understands and is enthusiastic about what you're doing, they'll help you in every way they can. The difference can be enormous.

Give high priority to involving your family in your goals. This probably means that you should give them a large voice in setting those goals. What you're looking for is enthusiastic, heartfelt support, not only for your own exclusively personal goals, but for your team, family-type goals.

Life-Style Pitfalls

Not getting adequate exercise. Eating too much of the wrong things too often and too fast. Relying on drugs and chemicals to give us courage or consolation, wake us up, put us to sleep, move our bowels, and cure the colds we wouldn't get if we took better care of our health.

THE WRONG WAY TO COPE

Many people drink, smoke, or pop pills to cope with stress. Whether the drug is alcohol, nicotine, speed, or cocaine, its first use is usually driven by the stress of peer pressure—the urge to belong or a weakness to give in to temptation. Once one is addicted, the stress of physical craving comes into play. Generally this stress is reinforced by another: the stress of denying the obvious: that enormous harm is being self-inflicted.

Yet few addicts to booze, tobacco, or illegal drugs realize they are reacting to stress when they ingest their drug. Most of them just don't think about what they're doing at all.

It's widely believed to be enormously difficult to break these habits. The term believe is the key here. It's only as difficult as you believe it is. For example, researchers announced this year that the nicotine in tobacco is more addictive to many people than are many illegal drugs, yet millions of people have quit smoking on their own because they believed they could.

CHAPTER ELEVEN

POSITIVE SYSTEMS FOR BEATING STRESS

In the previous chapter we talked about how dangerous and widespread stress is in America today. Now let's talk about how salespeople can defend themselves in positive ways against the hazards of stress. The best defense against the negative effects of stress for any salesperson is education. If you have a problem, pick up a book. Listen to an audio program or attend a seminar on the subject. Heaven knows there are seminars and classes available today on nearly any subject you can think of. Find one that you think will help you.

Once we are aware of the problem, we are capable of finding a solution for it. After all, problem-solving is a way of life for salespeople. All we need to do is turn our persuasive, problem-solving powers on ourselves to find the appropriate solution.

Instead of tearing you down the way coping with stress in negative ways does, the methods suggested in this chapter will make you mentally, emotionally, and physically stronger. At the same time they'll help you control the dangerous consequences of the stresses, anxieties, tensions, and frustrations that are an inescapable part of business competition.

By admitting, even if it's just to ourselves, that we are in need of help or need to make some changes in order to be happier or even to survive the stressors we are currently facing, we have taken the first step toward cure. We need to then investigate different stress reducers to get to a position where we can think clearly about our stressors, then relieve them. In many cases, there is nothing physical we can do about the stressors in our lives.

So a prospect cancels an appointment. Focus on what can be done rather than on what cannot be done. First of all, reschedule the appointment. Then, look around you: Are there any other businesses in sight that may have a need for your product or service? If so, why not cold-call on them rather than spending the time until your next appointment brooding on one lost opportunity?

If you have a real challenge with planning and scheduling your time, there are hundreds of good books written on the subject. Several companies that market time planning devices include seminars on how to use them. Take advantage of all the information you can gain and put to use what works for you.

If customer stalls are a problem, you need sales training. In my first book, *How to Master the Art of Selling*, I teach seventeen powerful ways of getting customers to say yes. If reading isn't your thing, the material is available in live seminars, on audio, or on video tape. There's always a source for the information you need to know. It's just a matter of applying yourself to finding it.

If you don't want to take the time to investigate the resources available to you, call your local library. Most information desks will be happy to research a list for you and it's usually at no charge. What more could you ask for?

In the balance of this chapter, we'll be talking about the stress reducers we must take advantage of in order to clear our heads, calm ourselves, and come up with the real, specific solutions to relieve the stressors that are bothering us.

THE POWER OF PRAYER

It may seem a little odd to discuss prayer in a chapter on stress—as though religion is just another bottle of pills in the medicine cabinet. Yet the curative powers of prayer have been praised by history's greatest leaders for 2,000 years.

As a Christian, I believe that my religion is far more to me than simply a cure for troubles. I try to live it every day, and through my religion I gain not only relief from pain and uncertainty, but also purpose and an abiding knowledge of where I fit into the universe and time's swift flow.

On the other hand, many people lead productive, worthy lives without prayer, without religion.

To the rest of us who believe, religion can be a tremendous force in our lives that propels us ever higher. But sometimes we may allow our beliefs to fade into the background, from which they only emerge on special occasions. In the daily press of making a living and meeting all the other demands on your time, it's difficult sometimes to avoid drifting away from your religion.

I hope you won't let that happen, that you'll realign your priorities so you find a prominent place for your religion in the forefront of your thoughts and activities. If you have a faith, a religion, stay true to your beliefs and use it for strength and perseverance. If you don't, start a search to find out how God can be a true source of peace and happiness in your life.

Because, in the long run, your religious beliefs encompass everything that really matters. Millions of people around the world daily use prayer as a restorative force.

WHEN MOST OF YOUR STRESS COMES FROM ONE PERSON

What do you do about someone who causes you stress? If you're married to that person, obviously you can discuss the situation and try to resolve it or, if the problem is beyond solving, get a divorce. I don't recommend divorce as an escape or as an easy out. However, after all other avenues have been tried, it may be necessary.

If a client puts a lot of stress on you, it must be handled quite differently. You will have to evaluate the importance of his business and determine whether or not it's worth putting up with the stress to have that business.

If your business stress comes from people in your office, such as your superiors or peers, you may have to consider whether or not you want to live with this situation.

However, it often happens that getting a business divorce—that is, quitting your job—simply isn't in the cards. Career or financial considerations may rule it out. After all, there's always the hope that the problem will be solved by the stress-giver's departure for one reason or another. Or maybe you'll get promoted or reassigned out of that person's reach. In many cases, a problem of this sort can be resolved once it's out in the open.

Hope is no substitute for action, however. What can you do now to relieve the stress that person is dumping on you?

Begin by trying to figure out exactly why that person is stressing you. Some people are just passing along stress they've received. It's very difficult to receive stress and turn around and calm down. For example, a sales manager receives a call from his division manager saying that sales aren't quite up to snuff. He then passes along the stress received to the next salesperson he encounters. Is he or she doing it deliberately? If so, for what purpose?

Some bosses have nothing in their managerial toolboxes except a variety of stress-giving systems that supposedly push salespeople into higher performance. Some customers routinely try to stress salespeople to cut a better "deal."

If those seem to be their reasons for causing you stress you can't complain much about their purposes, but you don't have to go along with their methods. If it's one of your peers who is bugging you, the problem is more complex. Let's discuss each of these situations.

WHEN YOUR BOSS GIVES YOU TOO MUCH STRESS

Trying to build a career at a company you don't believe needs you as much as you need the job is a basic mistake. All sorts of problems are certain to flow from that mistake. If you're constantly afraid of losing your job, you can't throw your total power into the work. Unconsciously you'll hold back the extra bit of effort that success demands. How come?

Because floating somewhere in the back of your head is the thought, "Why bother? I probably won't be around to reap the benefits."

And fear of losing your job can damage your judgment, leading you into mistakes you wouldn't make if you were more confident of your future.

The way to get a stress-giving boss off your back is to make yourself valuable to the company. Then ask for a private meeting with the boss and say, "I'm under more stress now than is good for my production or health. Here are the specific problems, and I need you to tell me what can be done to correct them." Then calmly inform your boss exactly what's troubling you. Also be aware that your challenge with your boss may not disappear overnight just because you've brought it out into the open. It may take some serious rethinking on your part and the part of your boss before the situation can be cleared up. If this approach doesn't get the boss off your back, you may have a stay-or-quit decision to make.

WHEN ONE OF YOUR CUSTOMERS OVERLOADS YOU WITH STRESS

Recognize that everybody rubs some people wrong. If one customer gives you a great deal of trouble, it may be for reasons you can't change. If that's the case, there's no reason why you should allow the circumstances to bother you. Instead, consider this to be one of the stressful situations that you're going to resolve promptly.

Maybe you can trade your problem customer for someone else's problem customer; new faces may eliminate personality clashes on both ends. Possibly you can simply stop calling on that customer if it's not worth the hassle. Check with your manager first when the account is important enough to be missed. In organizations that provide quality products or services, fewer than three percent of the customers will cause more than fifty percent of the problems. And nobody makes money selling to the troublemaking three percent. Your company may be better off giving them to the competition.

FOLLOW THE BOY SCOUT MOTTO AND *BE PREPARED!*

New salespeople are prone to additional stress simply because they're unprepared. They're unprepared for nearly every aspect of selling at first. They lack the self-confidence that comes with experience and sales success. This stress can be easily lessened by taking the time to be very well prepared for each aspect of your day. It will be slow going at first, but once you develop the preparation habits, you'll feel a lessening of stress and a greater desire to continue being prepared. That's when it gets easier.

Sometimes heavy stress hits salespeople because they don't think they're in the same league with the customer. They sit there too tense to think straight, afraid they'll do something wrong and blow the deal. So usually they do blow it.

Why are they suffering all this trauma? Because they've decided the person they're trying to sell to is so much better than they are that they can't possibly identify with them.

This can happen when salespeople deal directly with entrepreneurs (company owners), or with celebrities and high-level executives. Some of these people do their best to intensify a salesperson's feelings of inferiority in hopes of driving a tougher bargain. And, usually, there are other reasons. Behind the posturing, the self-styled big shots are often a lot less confident and secure than they want you to believe.

Here are some tip-offs that your customer is insecure:

- His office is arranged so that he sits with a window behind him, making you squint into the light.
- You're placed in an uncomfortable chair, or otherwise put in an awkward or uncomfortable position.

- He attacks your product's quality, or your company's reputation, owners, and policies.
- No matter how good a price you offer him, he tells you, "You'll have to do better than that."

Some people experience a great deal of stress just being with a salesperson. They're wary of you. They don't want to be sold anything. They don't want to let down their guard and start to like you, lest they won't be able to say no. Take into consideration your client's position. If he's a purchasing agent for a fairly large company, he does little other than meet with salespeople. Granted it's his chosen field, but we all have days when we can't stand doing our job for one more minute. Top salespeople take a few moments to allow the decision-maker to clear his mind from the previous meeting. They take time for small talk. They try to relieve tension and discuss something soothing to the decision-maker. Then, they will help the decision-maker focus on the reason for the meeting and get on to business with a clear head.

REACTING TO INTENTIONAL STRESSORS

How do you deal with these or other intentional stress-giving methods?

First of all, be aware that by using such tactics, customers tell you they need what you're selling more than they want you to think they do. Rather than fall over yourself offering new concessions, start backing away. Exactly what you say will depend on what's true and seems reasonable given the general situation at the time.

Some companies suggest you talk up a competitor's product. Obviously you'll praise the one you figure is the least desirable to the customer. He knows about that product and he doesn't want it—or he wouldn't be spending time trying to stress you into giving him unreasonable concessions.

Mention that you're worried about delivery. Labor disputes or temporary shortages of parts and materials can hit almost any industry at any time. Tell him that your company may have to put limits on how much you can supply your customers. This can be very effective; poor delivery may be one of the stress-giving customer's greatest fears.

Talk about price increases. Obviously this is no good in a soft market, but if there's anything on the horizon that indicates the possibility of higher prices in the near future, use it to push the customer into a more businesslike attitude.

Question the customer's authority. When you've lost all hope of obtaining an order on profitable terms, you don't have anything more to lose, do you? So rock the customer back on his heels by asking whether he has the authority to make the decision. He might be so surprised that he'll fall off his high horse and buy from you to prove he can.

Question the customer's credit. This can really test your confidence. But again, what more do you have to lose? Ask him for references to other suppliers he has paid promptly. This can only be considered on a first meeting with a prospect. You will most likely only have one opportunity to use it because it'll work or you'll never see this person again. So, please use this only as a last resort. Also, it must be handled in such a manner as not to ruin your reputation or that of your company.

STRESS DUMPERS

When customers try to pass some of their stress over to you, you're mistaken if you see this as a display of power. In reality, it's a revelation of weakness—a cry for help. Use that to your advantage. Help them—on your own terms.

Successfully coping with customers who dump stress on you calls for risk taking. Weigh what you have to lose through passive submission against what you could gain by taking a strong position.

In many such situations, it's quickly clear that the prospect either doesn't want what you're selling, or prefers to buy it elsewhere. This means you have nothing to lose by asserting yourself.

If you always try to find a strong response in these cases, sometimes you'll succeed. However, taking the course of least resistance—passively accepting the customer's stress-inflicting tactics—puts you out on the street empty-handed every time. Speaking up strongly offers at least a slim chance that you may make a sale and gain a long-lasting customer.

Many buyers feel that timid salespeople are that way because they know their product or service isn't of the highest value. They take the personal confidence of other salespeople to indicate their conviction that they offer the best price and quality available.

In other words, to many buyers your confidence level is an important element in determining what they think of your product's quality and price competitiveness. Govern yourself accordingly.

In truth, you have a lot to gain by challenging the stress giver. By doing so, even if you don't get his business you'll probably gain confidence instead of losing it.

WHEN THE ONE DUMPING STRESS ON YOU IS A COWORKER

Make sure of your ground. Be certain that you aren't overreacting to the other person's reasonable exercise of his or her privileges, and that the problem isn't something you can and should ignore. But if you know you're in the right, act. A stressful situation of this kind can damage your work performance and income, and possibly even attack your health if you allow it to go on and on.

Confront the person. Do this when the two of you are alone. Tell him exactly how he's affecting you and ask him politely to stop. As you do so, be ready to help him save face in every way you can without retreating from the position you've taken.

Remember that what he says when you confront him isn't as important as what he does afterward. Many people will bluster aggressively when confronted, and then quietly stop doing what's been bugging you. It's a matter of saving face. Let him.

And keep in mind that you're calling on him to change his view of you. Maybe he didn't think you could hit the floor with your hat before; now he is beginning to realize that you can't be trifled with. Give him a little time and space to adjust. Above all, don't threaten him.

What if nothing changes after the confrontation? Your next step—before you seriously consider quitting or seeing an attorney—is to ask your boss to take corrective action.

HOW TO EASE A STRESSFUL MEETING'S IMPACT

Your meeting may be with the boss or an important customer. In your mind, turn the stressful meeting into a funny situation. One way is to imagine that the stress-inflicting person is sitting there wearing a clown's mask. Your lively imagination will suggest other ridiculous scenarios that may work better for you. I don't mean by this that the situation should be taken lightly; however, don't take things too seriously either.

Some people enjoy stressing anyone they can; others have so much stress themselves that they can't help but pass some of it along.

BASIC WAYS TO BEAT STRESS

Here are several key methods for controlling stress in positive ways that also advance your general well-being.

1. Exercise
The vital element is frequency: get in at least three workouts a week. However, if you're over 35, be sure to see your doctor before increasing your physical activity.

Begin your exercise program without straining, and increase your workouts in easy stages. Maybe you'll start with some fanatics who are yelling, "No pain, no gain," words that have led more people to injury than any other peacetime slogan. Your fanatical friends will probably ridicule your slow starting pace. Grin and bear it because before long you'll be making steady progress and they'll be limping around nursing hurts.

Nothing washes emotional stress away better than vigorous exercise that's well within your physical capacity. The two essential requirements in any successful exercise program are that it fit your needs and physical condition and that it be something you'll keep on doing.

A brisk walk, a jogging session, or a stretch routine—there is a vast array of exercises that can provide quick tension-breakers. It doesn't matter what exercise you select, as long as: it's vigorous enough to give you a good workout, it's not competitive, and it's not frustratingly difficult to do acceptably well. Walking, in my opinion, may be one of the lost arts in our civilization of drive-in everything.

2. Weight control

Overeating is one of the most popular bad ways to cope with stress. However, few overweight people are willing to consider this possibility.

The idea that they have been getting fatter and fatter because it's their way of handling stress is too simple and direct to be acceptable. So they continue to search for the magic diet that will enable them to shed pounds without having to change how they deal with stress.

It can't be done. Every year millions of Americans prove that point by starting and quickly dropping the latest fad diet—usually without keeping off a pound.

Permanent weight loss is more likely to happen after people adopt the principles of low-stress living (discussed earlier in this chapter) and learn how to cope with stress without eating more than their bodies need.

3. Use a journal

Write down each day, or at least each week, what's bothering you. When you have a few weeks of this kind of stress record, your self-analysis can be very illuminating.

It's amazing that it takes so long. If we had started keeping a record in our teens of what foods bother us, we'd reach a better diet many years sooner. I find that eating ice cream makes me feel terrible. There are a lot of foods I don't eat anymore and I feel much better. For example, I've been off cheese for a long time. Recently I ate some; it felt like I'd swallowed a bowling ball. This may not be true for you, but for me, cheese is out.

Learning what to avoid is a big part of rising to the level of a thinking person instead of remaining a purely reacting person. Pay attention to what works for you. Spend some time finding out what makes you feel good and happy, and then avoid the other things.

THE COMPELLING NEED FOR RELAXATION SKILLS

Some of these techniques may sound like the latest guru nonsense out of India by way of Hollywood. If you react that way, these exercises may make you feel uncomfortable. They shouldn't.

You may be wondering why I'm spending so much time on stress reduction. Stress is a major factor in any selling career. It especially affects those who achieve success in their careers because successful people do what failures won't do. That alone causes stress and its effects can't be ignored for any long period of time.

Many businesspeople, and especially those in sales, live under almost constant stress. As a result their bodies rarely get out of the fight-or-flight mode.

These people never relax. Instead they travel from one stressful situation to another. Always their bloodstreams are supercharged with adrenaline, their jaws set with determination, their muscles tensed to no purpose. When they take time off, they find ways to turn it into a competition.

Even the popular music they like throbs with unremitting tension, pumped-up emotion, and high energy. These people are stretched tight at all times. Instead of alternating between periods of stress and periods of relaxation, their tension level varies only from stretched to stretched to the point of breaking.

A few years of this constant stretch has serious physical consequences: Hypertension, strokes, heart attacks, ulcers, mental problems, or burnout follow as night does day.

You don't get to take your pick, the maladies pick you. All you can be sure of is that you'll be visited by one or more of them if you keep yourself always stretched tight.

There's no two ways about it: Unless you learn how to take the stretch out of your rubber band from time to time, stress will snap it—and you'll never be the same again.

QUICK FIXES

You may already have discovered the best way you deal with stress. If not, rummage through these items and see if there's anything that will help:

- If you're having trouble falling asleep, put an electric fan on low. Then just listen to the hum. Every time a different idea floats through your consciousness, tell yourself you'll think about it tomorrow and go back to concentrating on the hum.

  You may be bothered by suddenly remembering something you're afraid you'll forget. If so, get up, make a note of it, and go back to concentrating on the hum.
- Music. The best thing is relaxing music. Get a tape you enjoy and keep it in your car so you can play it when your stress threatens to get out of hand. There are plenty of prerecorded relaxation tapes available on the market today.
- White noise. Listen to tapes of falling water, surf breaking, and birds singing. This is wonderfully relaxing. Make your own, or buy these environmental tapes from a store that sells wilderness books, camping gear, and back-to-nature stuff.

- Calming down. Simply taking a swim, hot shower, or bath is enough. In chilly weather, try a hot tub or sauna.

LOWER YOUR OVERALL STRESS LEVEL: MANIPULATE STRESS

Stress poses a great threat to almost everyone's ability to stay on top. You never want to forget that stress not only can burn you out and chop your income, it can break up your family and injure your health. And it can easily kill you.

While stress reduction can ease specific difficulties with excessive tension, it's not the complete answer. In fact, if you can make stress manipulation work, it shows that stress is already getting to you. The next physical blow may be far more severe.

What's the solution? In dealing with stress, you have three choices. You can:

(A) Mask your stress problems with tranquilizers, alcohol, and other drugs, whether legal or illegal, and take the consequences of your actions when they hit you.

(B) Ignore your tensions and anxieties and try to bull through them with flip remarks such as, "If stress is going to kill me, so be it." However, this attitude is rare among first-heart-attack survivors.

(C) Develop relaxation skills using some of the techniques covered in this chapter and move toward the kind of low-stress life-style that will allow you to enjoy living more and still have a satisfying and rewarding career.

Lowering your stress level will probably call for changes in the way you think, live, and act. We all tend to resist change, but in this case the required changes will probably be in the direction of learning to enjoy a variety of life's opportunities more, not less. Isn't that what we should all be striving for?

Here are some guidelines for enjoying life more so that you can get rid of excessive stress before it gets rid of you.

33 WAYS TO LIVE A LOW-STRESS LIFE

You may want to add items to this list of compressed ideas, rephrase some of the rules, or drop others that don't apply to you. After you settle on a list of rules for living a low-stress life, review it frequently. Make your individualized list part of your basic rules for conducting your life with style, imagination, and success.

1. Don't let stressful situations drift. Heal a troubled marriage or get help, professional help. Solve your problems at work or quit. Softly drift away from the people in your life who bring you trouble disguised as friendship. If you have legal worries or financial difficulties, make the hard choices that are required and settle those matters. Do the same with any health worries you may have. You can live with the facts of reality more easily than with the nightmares of ignorance.

2. Many times the best thing to do is nothing at all. Problems that would go away by themselves if ignored often become even more stressful if they're attacked aggressively. Try ignoring the problem for a few weeks before you attack it. If the problem still worries you after that time, make the hard choices it takes to resolve the matter.

3. Exercise to blow off frustrations. Vigorous exercise (that's within one's capacity) is humankind's most positive way of coping with pressure. Establish an aerobic exercise habit. Swim, bike, run, walk briskly, or choose other aerobic workouts that you'll perform regularly. Exercise to reach a high level of conditioning that will build your health.

4. Don't drink alone. If you use liquor at all, drink on social occasions only. If you use it to drown your sorrows and wash away your frustrations, liquor will use you—roughly.

5. Value time. Train yourself to look on time as a precious resource, not as a merciless taskmaster.

6. Distance yourself from negative people. If you now associate with people who belittle your opinions and attack your feelings of self-worth, drift quietly away from them in the least stressful manner possible.

7. Find positive friends. Seek out and make friends with gentle people who accept and affirm your independence and worth as a person.

8. Take up deep relaxation. Acquire the skill of deep relaxation and practice it daily.

9. Live a balanced life. Avoid putting too much energy into any one area—and that includes your career. Go after rewards in all facets of living.

10. Enjoy your work. You spend too much time working not to enjoy it. If you don't enjoy your work, figure out why. Then develop and execute plans that will make the emotional satisfactions you derive from your work as important to you as the money you make.

11. Seek a variety of challenges. A low-stress life presents a variety of challenges and rewards. If all your challenges come from your work, your career dominates your life too much. Find other outlets for your energy and intelligence.

12. Lean yourself out. Get going on a sensible program to gradually get your weight down to a level you'll be comfortable with. Then keep it there.

13. Learn to like food that's good for you. Teach yourself to prefer the foods that are good for you. Use sweets only as an occasional reward, cut down on junk food, and ease up on the empty calories that beer, wine, and hard liquor put into your body as fat.

Millions of people have acquired the taste for grains, fruits, vegetables, and fish. They've learned how to prepare tasty meals that exclude red meat, fatty sauces, and high-cholesterol dairy products. The results are already in: Wise eaters live longer, more active lives than careless eaters do.

14. If you smoke, stop. In addition to the physical stress that smoking imposes on your body, today's widespread opposition to breathing someone else's smoke dumps a lot of mental stress on a smoker's emotions. Chapter Fifteen of my book, *The Official Guide to Success* gives a simple, surefire mind game that will allow you to quit cold-turkey with a minimum of emotional stress.

15. Eliminate "recreational" drugs from your life before they eliminate you from the living.

16. Throw off the chains of chemical dependency. Don't use tranquilizers, sleeping pills, headache pills, and other central nervous system depressants. Instead, reorganize your activities. Drop nonessentials and reduce the excessive demands you've been putting on your system. Relax, get into balance, and start enjoying life while you keep your career booming along.

17. Allow your body to work the way nature intended. If you've been using laxatives, throw them away and use nature's remedy. Eat fresh fruit—nature's cleansing agent—then switch to a balanced diet that will normalize your digestive tract. If you've been using antacids, throw them away too. Use deep relaxation techniques and low stress living to cool the fires in your stomach.

18. Don't poison your body with phony remedies. Several consumer organizations, a number of medical researchers, and the Federal Drug Administration—all people who have no ax to grind in this regard—say that over-the-counter cold remedies don't work, and often make things worse. Free yourself from feeling dependent on patent medicines.

19. Get a physical checkup every year. It will give you peace of mind.

20. Don't give up your personal rights. If you've allowed pieces of your personal rights to slip out of your grasp, do whatever has to be done to get them back. Insist on the right to select your own companions, the right to choose your life's goals, the right to love the person you choose if that feeling is mutual, the right to worship, think, and believe as you wish; the right to organize and spend your time in ways that you feel return the greatest satisfactions and benefits to you.

21. Have a brief renewal session every day. Reserve a little time each day to renew your dedication to your goals, your uniqueness, your purposes, your faith. These sessions can be as short as two minutes.

Make these brief interludes times of complete privacy. Free yourself during these moments from your career's demands and be alone with your thoughts.

After you've experienced the power of these renewal sessions, consider whether more than one a day will lower your stress levels and speed your progress.

22. Insulate yourself from the killing pace of change. You don't have to be trendy in every aspect of your life in order to keep up. On the contrary, you'll find it easier to run at the front of the pack if you keep in touch with your roots, honor who you are and where you've come from, and keep a clear vision of where you're going.

Some people maintain stability zones in their lives by gathering information about their ancestors. Others rely on simple personal rituals and comfortable old ways of doing things. A few satisfy this urge by acquiring antiques. Keep your emotional stability by using whatever works for you.

23. Celebrate holidays, family events, and personal anniversaries with gusto. There are no better shields against the stresses of future shock than enthusiastic participation in your traditions, and in emotionally marking each event and anniversary that's important in your life.

24. Put some of your time into pure relaxation. Occasionally engage in pastimes that return nothing tangible. If you insist on having something to show for everything you do, you put the fullest kinds of relaxation beyond your reach.

25. Actively seek new ideas and experiences. Open your mind. Try doing things you've never done before, sample foods you've never eaten, go places you've never seen.

26. Cultivate your mind every day. Read interesting books and magazines that present unfamiliar viewpoints. Search out new fields to study. Your mind needs exercise just as much as your body does. Read books and articles that give you new ideas and challenge you to rethink old positions.

27. Learn from listening. Learn from other people by trying to see the world through their eyes as you listen to their opinions. If you make the effort to open your mind to other points of view, you'll often be rewarded by gaining valuable insights you might otherwise miss.

28. Find and cherish fine friends. We all need friends. Work at developing one or two high-quality friendships with individuals you can trust and be yourself with.

29. Give your obligations an annual checkup. Review your obligations at least once a year. Make sure they're still bringing you satisfactions and rewards that justify the time, energy, and money you're putting into them. Dump the ones you decide no longer further your goals, or in some other way aren't good for you anymore.

30. Get rid of negative cues. Posters, slogans, and cartoons that excuse or affirm negative ideas don't belong where a positive-minded person like you spends time. Let the world—and more importantly, yourself—know that you're fully committed to life's positive side.

31. Surround yourself with positive cues. Slogans and cartoons displayed where you work, on your vehicles, and where you live are a powerful form of propaganda. Use them to help you visualize your goals. Include some that remind you to relax and unwind occasionally.

32. Find the point where you're most effective. That point lies somewhere between blind obstinacy and wimpish indecision. Accept the fact that you'll never have the perfect answer to every question, and make a habit of searching for challenging new concepts and opinions contrary to your own. But never lose sight of the fact that without decisions based on careful analysis or an emotional conviction, nothing gets done.

33. Set goals so that you will have a positive sense of direction no matter how much chaos is going on around you.

CHAPTER TWELVE

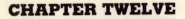

BURNOUT

There is no precise medical definition of burnout. Perhaps we won't see a widely accepted definition for some time. Defining burnout precisely would be difficult in any case, but the task is complicated by the fact that burnout comes in several varieties.

Nevertheless, burnout does have some widely accepted symptoms. These include irritability, fatigue, alcohol or drug abuse, poor performance, low morale, and absenteeism. Other symptoms are a heightened level of anxiety and a lowered level of genuine involvement in one's work. However, not all these symptoms will be present in every case.

Each occupational category has its own typical form of burnout. Burnout among managers may be signaled by uncharacteristic instances of forgetfulness and inability to communicate effectively. Salespeople may be unable to concentrate or seem overwhelmed by details.

People in the final stages of burnout are likely to experience intestinal distress, frequent illness, rapid pulse, lack of concentration, and an unusual craving for sweets. Smoking and alcohol use also tend to increase.

Many people who are burning out don't think it can happen to them. Sure, they know about burnout, but it's something that only "hits other people, not me."

So we both know you're not burning out. But, just to

humor me, please take ten minutes to rate yourself on the twenty questions that follow.

IS IT HAPPENING TO YOU RIGHT NOW?

Sit down at a table or desk with pencil, paper, and your watch. Use the watch to pace yourself: Consider each question for about half a minute before deciding on the number you'll give as your answer.

Use 0 for no, never, or none and 10 for yes, always, or a lot. In most cases, a number between 0 and 10 will be closer to reality for your situation today; if so, put down than number as your answer. Here are the questions:

1. Are you spending less time with your family and close friends than you did a year ago?
2. Are you having trouble finding time for routine business activities such as returning phone calls and reading reports and memos?
3. Do you feel that you're having more colds, aches, and pains this year compared to last?
4. When your day's work ends, are you unsure of what to do with your free time that evening?
5. Do you sometimes feel like chucking your career or current relationship and starting over somewhere else?
6. Do people seem anxious and ill at ease around you?
7. Do people ask you if you're all right?
8. Do you think you're working harder and getting less done?
9. Do you feel tired early in the day?
10. Has your emotional involvement in your work decreased?
11. Do you feel more cynical today than you did a year ago?
12. Do you feel sad for no reason you can put your finger on?
13. Do you forget appointments, promises, or deadlines?

14. Are you more irritable than you were a year ago?
15. Do you feel that sex isn't worth the trouble?
16. Are you more disappointed by your friends and associates than you were a year ago?
17. Do people tell you that you don't look so good lately?
18. Does it anger you to be the target of good-natured joking?
19. When you're with a friendly person who has no connection with your work, is it hard for you to carry on a conversation without talking shop?
20. How often do you feel that life is boring?

THE BURNOUT METER

Add up the points you've marked down for the twenty questions and use the total to place yourself on the Burnout Meter given below.

If you score high, keep in mind that a questionnaire of this kind can only provide a rough guide. So don't be alarmed, but don't ignore that result either. In any case, the mere fact that you're reading these words proves that you have time to take corrective action.

0–10   You are burnout-proof unless drastic changes hit your life and attitude.

11–20   You're doing well.

21–30   You're doing fairly well, but you should give serious thought to how you can ease stress and pump more reward and relaxation into your life.

31–40   Unless you change direction, you have burnout in your future.

41–50   You're slowly incinerating yourself. I recommend that you immediately start working hard at cooling your burnout fires.

51–60   You're melting down. Mount a massive effort to beat burnout, or find professional help without delay.

61–100 You may be burned out. Recovery must now become your top priority, but you're far past the point where you can deal with this problem on your own. Consider getting professional help at once.

DOES BURNOUT AFFECT WOMEN AND MEN DIFFERENTLY?

Dr. Joyce Brothers says that one of the greatest stressors on working women is guilt. "No woman can work and raise children and not feel guilty," she claims. Many working women feel that it's a no-win situation whatever they do. If they stay at home they feel guilty about not bringing in money; if they work outside the home they feel guilty about neglecting their children and marriages; if they work part time they often feel guilty in both places.

Some women who have never worked outside their homes suffer burnout. The stresses of raising a family can be deadly for many women because it's a 365-days-a-year, 24-hours-a-day job.

And for working women and single parents, a weekend off from work often turns into a mad dash to do a week's chores in two days. It takes careful planning to meet these problems successfully.

THE GATEWAY EFFECT: THE GOOD SIDE OF DEALING WITH BURNOUT

Burnout is a painful and destructive experience. It can even be disabling. At the very least burnout will be highly distressing, not only to the people who suffer it directly but also to their families. Often their friends, clients, and associates will also be blistered by a burnout's flame.

Yet burnout can be overcome. Beyond that, if properly handled, burnout can also be the gateway to a richer, fuller life for its victims.

The reason lies in the nature of burnout itself. This condition can only develop when someone concentrates too closely on his work or on a single problem area in his life, weakening or entirely losing the ability or desire to participate in and enjoy life's other opportunities and satisfactions.

When this basic cause of burnout is understood, the cure becomes obvious: Get back in balance! Pursue goals and satisfactions that have nothing to do with your career, or with any other troublesome problem area that may be pushing you into burnout.

The goals and satisfactions that will allow you to escape burnout may lie in family life, in personal artistic expression, in spiritual activities, in exercise and sport, in a hobby, or in any other activity that produces nothing except enjoyment and relaxation while consuming time and energy.

Most of us will agree that it's better to learn how to enjoy life without going through the pain and turmoil of burnout. But if overcoming burnout is the only way this vital lesson can be learned, better the hard way than not at all.

STRUCTURING YOUR LIFE TO MINIMIZE BURNOUT RISK

Taking the trouble to restructure your life to cut down the risk that you'll burn out is well worth doing, but not only because burnout is such a devastating experience. Great mental stress always accompanies burnout, and that stress can physically attack you in dangerous ways. It can plug your coronary arteries and cause a heart attack. It can give you strokes or ulcers. And it can speed up or cause a wide range of other illnesses.

Let's look at some of the basic elements in your life that can be restructured—that is, changed—to help minimize your risk of burnout.

Marital Status

Studies have shown that you're less likely to burn out if you're married, most likely to burn out if you're single. If you're divorced, you fall in between the other two groups as to risk.

If you're married and your marriage fails, it's vital to realize that the losses extend beyond the physical. Your spouse was, or should have been, your friend too, and perhaps you relied on that emotional support more than you realize. If you lose your closest friend in a divorce, move quickly to find someone else who can at least replace the friendship aspect of your relationship. Be careful, though, to look for that friendship in the appropriate places. As Dan M. found, work might not be the right place to look.

> After I split up with my wife, I got more sensitive at work. After that if my sales manager didn't jump up and down when I brought in a big order, I'd sulk for days instead of going right back out after another one. Naturally that kicked my sales performance in the teeth.
>
> I was trying to make my manager do what my wife did whenever I got a big order—praise me to the skies. Of course my manager never cared as much because the thirty other salespeople around here also want all the attention they can get.
>
> I should have seen right off that the kind of emotional support I'd lost in my divorce wouldn't come to me from a business relationship. But, with all the turmoil and pain of the split-up, driving that simple point through my head took a long time.

Even though married people as a group are less likely to burn out, it's important to note that counselors often work with spouses whose burnout is caused or accelerated by a stressful marriage. From the standpoint of burnout risk, you're better off single than in a bad marriage.

Having Children

Having children instantly exposes you to a new, higher level of personal stress. Most people adapt to it willingly because of their desire for and love of their children. Once they achieve comfort with the new stress level, many of them also find themselves better able to cope with the non-child-related stress in their lives. That's why most parents are more resistant to burnout than childless people. If you think of children as needful little creatures whose incessant demands can never be adequately met, you may doubt this assertion. In fact, if you're even slightly hostile to the idea of having children, becoming a parent may increase rather than decrease your susceptibility to burnout.

It's common knowledge that parents vary widely in their willingness and ability to cope with and provide for children, and in their devotion to them. These qualities are difficult to measure. Probably for this reason, no researcher has yet published an evaluation of their effect on the burnout risk of parents.

We must therefore take it on faith that good parents gain strength from their families because they regard children as precious enrichments to their own lives, and that bad parents don't because they regard children as burdens.

If you want to be a good parent, you can be. However, it can be a tragic mistake to think that parenthood won't drastically change your life. But you only have to take it one day at a time.

Other Activities

Burnout strikes most often at ambitious single people who avoid activities that don't further their careers. Those least likely to burn out are married, have children, and pursue many interests outside their careers.

Social Support System

People who are burnout-proof understand where and how to get effective social and emotional support, and they don't hesitate to go looking for it when needed.

The burnout-prone, on the other hand, get little or no emotional support from spouses, other family members, friends, business associates, or from membership in clubs and congregations.

The burnout-prone's failure to obtain emotional support may come from not knowing how to get it, not knowing where, or from the dangerous and false idea that only the weak need it. Later in this chapter I'll discuss how you can build an emotional support base.

UNHEALTHY DEFENSES AGAINST BURNOUT

We're all familiar with people who turn to one or several forms of self-destruction to find temporary relief from their problems. Drug addicts, alcoholics, and heavy smokers know very well that what they're doing will shorten their lives— the image of living dangerously is one of the things that attracts many of them to their addictions.

But we're not going to discuss those kinds of desperate problems here because what I have to say about them appears in other chapters. Here we'll talk about how burnout affects the way its victims work with the rest of the world.

Burnout is a state of emotional exhaustion that results in reduced personal effectiveness. Since almost everybody must get along with other people to do their job, the first sign of approaching burnout often is reduced effectiveness in dealing with other people.

There are some specific signals of approaching burnout that can show up in the daily activities of salespeople and sales managers.

Typecasting

The most effective way to deal with people is to treat each one as a unique individual who has special abilities, sensitivities, and needs. Doing so requires caring and involvement, which is to say it's time-consuming and emotionally demanding.

When those emotional demands approach the breaking point, the potential burnout draws back from individuals, puts the people he or she must work with into categories, and from then on responds to the category instead of to the individual. It happens almost as an instinctive reaction.

A famous Hollywood director once said, "All actors are cattle and should be treated as such." Shortly after he said that, burnout sent his career into a rapid decline. His last pictures were ongoing battles between him and the actors, none of whom liked being treated as cattle. When the word went out that he was big trouble on the set, investors stopped backing his films. His career was over.

Sales managers skating on the edge of burnout often find refuge in typecasting. "All salespeople are crybabies," they might say, or "I've got a bunch of slow ponies around here. It'll take dynamite to make them gallop."

When the dynamite explodes under the entire sales force, the best half of it immediately quits. To the dynamiter's cost and consternation, only the least productive salespeople stick around.

When they're close to burnout, salespeople sometimes tell themselves something like, "All my customers are deadbeats, chiselers, and double-crossers. I'm not going to worry about those bums anymore." With that attitude, can a hefty drop in sales be far away?

Personality Change

One of the signs of burnout is that the affected individual's personality seems to change—that is, he or she is to some extent depersonalized. The burned-out individual feels a sense of unreality, and may occasionally express surprise at his or her own behavior.

Although this symptom is often difficult to detect in someone else, surprise at your own behavior, and strong feelings of unreality, are danger signals to watch out for in yourself.

Becoming a Bureaucrat

When the emotional pressure of dealing with customers as individuals becomes too great, some salespeople fall back on doing it by the book. They suddenly become experts on why it can't be done; "it" being whatever the customer wants, whether that's quicker delivery, modified specifications, or

special pricing. Generally bureaucratic salespeople also reduce their personal customer contact to the minimum.

For every lost sale they have a perfect excuse backed by
some petty rule they've applied. In detail their performance
is justified; in general it's miserable. When the sales figures
are examined, many of the burned-out bureaucratic salespeople get fired.

DOES BURNOUT COME FROM WITHIN OR WITHOUT?

Is burnout internally caused, or is it the result of external
conditions? An extreme case will illustrate my view. A soldier
emerges from a foxhole after being under prolonged artillery
bombardment. Although physically unhurt, he's in shock and
can't be made to obey orders. His company commander sends
him to the rear, where he's treated for battle fatigue by a
psychiatrist.

It's clear that had the artillery bombardment not oc-
curred, the soldier would be happily horsing around with his
buddies instead of suffering acute mental distress in a rear-
area hospital.

On the face of it the artillery barrage caused his break-
down. But did it? He was physically unhurt: his only "injuries"
were therefore self-inflicted by his well-founded fear during
the barrage that he would be killed or seriously wounded at
any moment.

Although conditions are rarely so dramatic, in civilian
life we also undergo prolonged bombardments of events that
threaten our mental health and ability to perform. But it's
never those external events that burn us out, because they
can reach our brains only through our own perceptions and
senses. Therefore, it's our internal mental reaction to the
outside events that does the damage.

The distinction is vital. To the extent that you blame
outside events that are beyond your control for your mental
exhaustion, you hide from the true cause of your problem:

your own internal reaction to those outside events, something that is under your control.

In civilian life the outside events that exploded on our careers like incoming shells are many: job pressures; the relentless demands to produce more and do it more quickly; the frustrations and disappointments involved in our work; rumors of takeovers, plant closings, and downsizing; the insensitivity of superiors and the incompetence of subordinates; office politics; and the sheer volume of details that must be handled with sensitivity, accuracy, and speed.

Again I say, burnout can be eased or pushed back by comparatively minor changes in your attitudes toward your work and your life. Let's look at some of these ways now.

COPING WITH BURNOUT IN POSITIVE WAYS

No one wants to go through the pain and punishment of a burnout. Yet many people who are clearly on the brink of one steadfastly refuse to change the behaviors that are threatening their performance, their careers, and their mental health.

Because burnout is an internally caused condition, it can be eased internally. Often this can be done by achieving one or two minor changes in attitude.

Some of these changes may at first glance seem likely to reduce your income dramatically. Actually in the long run, and often in the immediate future as well, they'll protect and even increase your productivity and income. How much will you make if you burn out and quit, or burn out and get fired?

Deciding to change careers and start over in some other area can be great. I've done it several times without ever regretting a change. But you want to pick your time and leave with all your flags snapping in the breeze. That's a lot more fun than scrambling to cope with a dismissal, or struggling to pull your life back together after a painful burnout. So give careful consideration to these ways to reduce your risk of burnout.

Try Different Strokes to Swim the Same Pond

You don't have to change jobs or leave town to get away from tedium. In any selling position, whether in-house or out in the field, the possibilities for doing things differently are almost limitless.

Unfortunately, many salespeople repeat their routines over and over year after year, some of them getting no better in the process. In many cases, they gradually get worse as boredom chips away the last bits of warm spontaneity in their presentations.

Certainly stick with the tried and true if it's working for you and you enjoy repeating it. However, it's not a bad idea to start working subtle variations into your presentations long before you start to get bored with them.

Continually polish your material to make it work better. You can find a great deal of challenge in rephrasing your points in better ways, in adding newer, tighter language, and in perfecting your timing.

But if you're already fighting hard against tedium, take drastic action before the problem turns into a full-blown case of burnout that forces you into an unplanned and unwanted job change. You have your own way of selling that's unique to you. It grew out of your basic personality and background and the accidental events that shaped your early experiences as a salesperson. Every other salesperson in your company gets the job done in his individual ways. What does this mean? That other salespeople use selling methods that are different from yours. Some of these differences will be slight, others will be major. Some of their ways won't be as good as yours, others will be better. Find out what those differences are and try them out yourself. This can be profitable fun that will help you beat tedium and drive burnout back.

Set Realistic Goals

Setting unrealistic goals is a common mistake. Consider the old saying: "Meeting any challenge that doesn't kill me makes me stronger."

This dangerous oversimplification can be true. It can also be false, as in the case of mountain climbers who lose toes to frostbite but not their lives.

The saying ignores most of the unrealistically high challenges the vast majority of us set for ourselves. Failing to meet those challenges normally isn't fatal or even the least bit dangerous, but any failure can push one toward taking fewer risks and accomplishing less.

Chapter Six entitled "Learn to Love 'No,' " in my book *How to Master the Art of Selling* is largely devoted to methods of rising above failure. I urge you to become familiar with those techniques.

There are two main reasons for setting goals: to organize your priorities and focus your efforts on the most important ones and to raise the level of your performance. Goals that are unrealistically high discourage effort instead of guiding and intensifying it. With that in mind, set your goals at a level that will encourage you to reach higher but won't make you fall on your face.

Work Less and Easier

When feeling overwhelmed by demands, a common reaction is to dig in and work harder. Meals are rushed or skipped entirely. Time off goes by the boards. Family life becomes a dim memory. Only work counts. But problems and demands continue to intensify and multiply. Can burnout be long delayed?

Instead of grinding your teeth and working longer and harder, step back and force yourself to take time to examine your priorities. Everything doesn't have to be done right now. Start working smarter, not harder.

There can only be one MIP (most important project) that you must complete first. Find that one MIP, make everything else wait while you complete it, and when you're finished go on to the next MIP. When quitting time comes, stop working and leave. Go do something that has no relation to your job.

Later that evening when you're feeling relaxed, give a few minutes thought to tomorrow's MIP, jot it down on a piece of paper along with any ideas about handling it that come to mind. Then forget about the whole thing until tomorrow.

You know what? The world won't end. You won't get fired either.

Instead, you'll start having effective days because you're working effectively on one project at a time and accomplishing a great deal. When you've run that string of effective days into an effective month, you'll not only be money ahead, you'll be happier and healthier too. And so will your family.

Take Short Breaks

If you feel so pressed that you never take a five-minute break away from your desk, or stop at a park and smell the roses, you're not running your job, your job is running you— straight to burnout city. It's a good habit to get into in the selling profession. Schedule fifteen minutes other than travel time at least twice a day to stop. Find a park between your two destinations and relax for a few minutes. Go into a book-store and browse. Check out an antique store or ethnic shop. Go to a batting cage or driving range and hit some balls. You must be careful not to get too carried away and spend more than your fifteen allotted minutes. You'll be amazed at what you can learn in such a short time and how it helps you clear your mind before psyching yourself up for your next appointment. You'll go into your next meeting with a fresh outlook and maybe even something new you've discovered that your client would have an interest in.

One of the many advantages of taking a few quick breaks each day is that it gives you a chance to put your immediate concerns into perspective by briefly stepping back from them. Many people racing toward burnout work furiously at tasks they can't complete, or that would make little difference even if they did accomplish them.

By making it a habit to step back from their work several times a day and reflect on what they're doing, potential burn-outs would be able to see many demands that could be dele-gated, delayed, shortened, or even eliminated.

If you can't schedule in those breaks, at least listen to

some positive tapes or relaxing music in the car between meetings. It's essential that you get rid of a failure or subdue a success so you enter the next room on an even keel.

Dwell on the Fun Side

Every job has positive and negative elements—the fun side and the boring side. It's true, though, that in some positions it takes quite a bit of inventiveness and determination to find the fun part.

Perhaps you can't find any real pleasure in your work. Even so, you can still choose to spend more time thinking about the parts you like best rather than dwelling exclusively on your job's least pleasant aspects.

Give High Priority to Other Activities

The habit of concentrating on one's work too much is one of burnout's primary risk factors. It's also one of the most easily controlled. When you give all your attention to work to the extent of begrudging anything, be it family, friends, or exercise, that takes time away from your career, you're dangerously out of balance.

Get back in balance by rediscovering your old outside interests, or develop new ones. To make this stick, the outside interests must satisfy some urge or interest that you have. The activities with the best chance to satisfy you are the ones you used to pursue, or wanted to pursue, before you became addicted to your career.

However, for this to work, one requirement must be met: You have to make time for your outside activity or activities. This means that some things you've done yourself, or supervised personally, will have to be dropped or delegated. You can't just jam your new activity into an already too hectic schedule and expect miracles. You have to rearrange your life to comfortably accommodate the nonbusiness activity, or it won't happen.

Let's say that you decide to renew your interest in the arts and start going to the opera, a concert, or a play every Friday night instead of working late. Meeting this goal involves doing two things well ahead of time: organizing your work so you can leave on schedule, and making all the decisions and arrangements for your night out. If you look on it as a fun kind of want-to instead of as a laborious have-to, you stand an enormously better chance of staving off burnout and at the same time enjoying life more. But without advance planning done on a priority basis, your attempt to turn your Friday nights into enjoyable burnout-beaters will become nothing more than one more failure on your pile of frustrations.

As you consider the importance and practicality of developing outside activities to balance a heavy concentration on your career, keep in mind that increasing your ability to escape from work will increase your capabilities at work.

Larger Changes That Prevent or Cure Burnout

Recognizing that this emotional problem can rob them of their brightest people, more than two out of three of the Fortune 500 corporations now provide anti-burnout training for some of their employees.

Yet in many other companies you'll still hear things like, "I don't want any burned-out people on my team. Anybody who can't stand the heat around here had better get out of our kitchen." In these companies, burnout is a dangerous thing to be suspected of.

If you feel that you're at some stage of burnout and are unsure of your company's attitude toward such problems, step carefully. If possible, deal with it yourself, quietly, without attracting any more attention at work than you already have to the pressure you're feeling.

What can you do if you suddenly realize that you have a serious problem with burnout? Here are some ideas:

1. Accept the Challenge and Take Action
Beating burnout may well be the greatest challenge you'll face this year. Make no mistake about it, if you're in a high-pressure job (who isn't?) and you work long hours, you're running some risk of burnout.

If you suspect that you have a touch of it, you probably really have a performance-cutting case of burnout already. Burnout doesn't cure itself. But it does yield to treatment, sometimes very quickly.

The first step is to recognize that you have to make some changes. Then decide on a course of action and carry it out. It's important. Your career, and your family's future welfare, may depend on how well you cope with your risk of burnout in the coming months.

2. Take a Long Break

Like aspirin for a headache, the most obvious treatment for burnout is to schedule the soonest and longest vacation you can manage. What if part of your problem is money, so that an expensive vacation is out of the question?

A vacation for someone whose career is endangered by burnout is the best investment that person can make. If necessary, borrow to finance it. And your vacation doesn't have to be expensive.

Anyway, if you've been in the city's high pressure cooker too long, an active and inexpensive vacation will probably be your best choice.

3. Make Your Short Breaks Count

When Peter Ueberroth was given the responsibility for organizing the 1984 Summer Games of the Olympics in Los Angeles, he took on an almost impossible task. His instructions: Stage the best Olympics ever and make a profit doing it. No way would Los Angeles stand still for going half a billion dollars in debt for the Olympic Games as Montreal, Canada did in 1976.

Ueberroth not only had to build a central staff of highly competent people—all of whom knew their job was only temporary—he also had to recruit thousands of volunteers to work for little or nothing. He prevailed upon the top talents in Hollywood to donate their time and talent to stage the spectacular ceremonies that did so much to make the 1984 Los Angeles games the memorable event it was.

Along the way Ueberroth had to reconcile the often conflicting demands of many different groups. The International Olympic Committee, the tv networks, the L.A City Council, his volunteer workers, dozens of international organizations that oversee each sport, and representatives of the many participating nations all had claims to make and agendas to push.

There was no budging his deadlines. And on top of it all, he had to find the money to keep the whole vast project on track.

We're talking industrial-strength pressure here—an enormous opportunity to succeed splendidly or fail miserably before the entire world. You'd expect that Ueberroth would feel that he had to work straight through all his weekends, all his lunches, to forget he had a family and outside interests.

Did he? No. Ueberroth took every weekend off while he piloted the spectacular Los Angeles games to a hundred-million-dollar profit. His family life didn't suffer a bit, and it's doubtful that he experienced any distress from increased tension.

Certainly he didn't burn out. When the games closed, he went right into another high-pressure position: commissioner of baseball.

What did Ueberroth say about working weekends? "I never do it, because it's counterproductive. When you work through the weekend, your mental attitude is flat on Monday. You need the time off to recharge your batteries."

Compare your job to organizing the Olympic Games the next time you think the world will screech to a halt if you don't work on the weekend. Then when Friday afternoon rolls around, close up shop and buzz off. Do something completely different from your work that you and your family or friends enjoy.

Leave your attaché case—the one that's jammed with work you think you should do at home over the weekend—sitting right on top of your desk where you'll see it first thing when you come in brimming with relaxed energy on Monday morning.

You have to decide to do this on the Monday or Tuesday before the weekend so that you can organize your week to end Friday afternoon at 5:00—or sooner. If you decide to take the weekend off late in the week, you'll probably waiver on your decision when it comes right down to it.

If you put in a solid Monday–Friday work week, take the weekends off. There's no other way. You've got to recharge your batteries or one day your motor just won't run. It'll be totally burned out.

What if weekends are your best time to make money? I know about this. In my days as a real estate agent I had no choice—I worked every weekend because that's when most of the best business was done.

After a few years of not taking any time off at all (in your twenties you can stand a lot) I locked onto having Wednesdays off. To make it work, I printed it on my business cards and told all my clients, "You can't reach me on Wednesdays, but I'm available every other day. This card has my office and home phone numbers. Call me any time except on Wednesdays because I won't be available." It worked beautifully.

BUILD AN EFFECTIVE EMOTIONAL BASE

Think of your emotional base as a table with a solid top and four legs. The top is the emotional support you must have to function at your highest level, given to you by the people you love—parents, children, spouse, friends. These are the people you know will take your side when you need them.

This is not to say that they will never grumble when you make a mistake, or will always fight your battles for you. But when you really need a kind word or a helping hand, they will always extend it.

Your table top is composed of all the emotional support you received as you grew up, plus the emotional support you've been receiving over the past few days and, most importantly, the emotional support you feel certain you can obtain in the immediate future should you need it. Thus your emotional support has a past, a present, and a future. All three elements play an important part in determining who you are and who you're capable of becoming.

Think about the four legs that support your emotional base so you can build up any that are weak. They are:

1. Technical Appreciation

When you nail down an important order under difficult circumstances, you want to be praised in addition to drawing the commission involved. If your good work goes unappreciated, you're probably going to lose some of your motivation.

There's an important requirement for technical appreciation: it must come from someone knowledgeable in your field so that it has the ring of truth. Otherwise it's like having your music praised by a deaf man.

The logical person to give you the technical appreciation you need is your manager. If you're not getting the technical appreciation you deserve from your boss and it bothers you, consider what other affiliations and options are available to you.

2. Technical Challenge

Pushing the same old stuff in the same old territory burns out a lot of salespeople. So does using the same old presentation on new folks year after year. You're not challenged, you can do it in your sleep, and pretty soon you're not doing it as well—or making as much money—as you did at first. Boredom sets in and the time comes when you'll make almost any sacrifice rather than continue selling the way you liked at first but now hate doing.

The solution is to find new challenges without losing your boring but rent-paying basic business. It's easier if you start branching out before you settle into a dull routine, but it's never too late to experiment with new routines, new ways to sell, new types of prospects, new uses for your product or service.

3. Listening

We all need to be listened to at times. Not the glazed-eye variety of suffering-in-silence listening, but active listening that is intelligent and sympathetic.

It isn't easy to find someone who will do you this great service. Generally speaking, you can't get good listening support from a friend or your spouse unless you give it when the other person needs it.

When you need a good listener, you need someone who will let you "get it off your chest." Unfortunately, if you look for a good listener in the most convenient group—among your fellow salespeople—you're probably going to run into a topper, a snitcher, or an advice-giver.

The Topper

Before you've finished your tale of woe the topper interrupts you with, "Hey, that's nothing. What happened to me this morning was a thousand times worse. This guy comes in and says . . ."

The Snitcher

You're just blowing off steam, but somebody sees it as an opportunity to snitch. So the snitcher gives what you're saying a couple of twists to make it sound worse before planting the result where he thinks it will do him the most good. That's exactly where it will do you the most harm.

The Advice-Giver

Many otherwise capable listeners can't resist the temptation to offer an instant cure for your difficulties. Oddly enough, they can't solve their own problems but they always have the perfect solution for everybody else's. Make yourself this promise: "I'll never take advice from anyone who's more messed up than I am." You'll be amazed at how this promise affects who you talk to and about what.

Finding good listeners is like buying fire insurance—if you wait until the barn is on fire, it's probably too late. Work at developing good listeners before you need one desperately.

You may need to give your listeners some practice from time to time, and some gentle instructions to the effect that you don't want advice, and you don't want to be topped.

Good listeners are made, not born. Look for them among

your friends and family. If you don't know anyone who can fill this function for you, perhaps you should consider enlarging your circle of friends.

4. Emotional Challenge
The kind of burnout that often hits pro tennis stars after about seven years can also hit top-producing salespeople in about the same span of time.

Bjorn Borg swept the world's courts and then suddenly his competitive fires went out. He wasn't hungry for fame and fortune anymore because he already had it all.

"I don't want to keep on practicing four hours a day," Borg told his coach one day. The coach knew instantly: Bjorn Borg's tennis career was history. And so it proved to be.

Other tennis stars burst onto world tennis, only to fade after a few years. Thousands of star salespeople similarly shine for a brief period before losing their drive to one form or another of burnout.

Unless you keep on finding new ways to stretch yourself, new challenges and new and higher goals, decline is likely to set in. The most difficult feat of all is to fly high and level through a long career.

CHAPTER THIRTEEN

POOR HEALTH= POOR SALES

GOOD HEALTH FUELS SUCCESS

Selling is a high-energy business. That's why it's so important that you keep yourself healthy. You can't maintain a positive, high energy level with your customers if you're not well. Also, since the first impression is so important in selling, every salesperson needs to look his overall best. Think about it. Would you buy anything from someone who looked as if his next stop would be a hospital? Most people who are smart enough to be in selling are smart enough to know about keeping themselves fit. They don't want their customers noticing their flaws or anything that would take their concentration away from the presentation or close of the sale.

For example, it's become obvious to most salespeople that smoking is a no-no in front of a customer. Years ago, our society wasn't as health conscious as it is today and it was common for a salesperson and client to "share a smoke." Today it would be foolish to risk such a thing.

I can see you pulling back and thinking, "If I want health information I'll see my doctor. Anyhow, what does staying healthy have to do with making money?"—Oops. I think a light just went on. Next you're thinking, "Maybe Hopkins has a point. If I'm sick, how can I keep on making money? And all those fast-track guys with their names chiseled on stone in the cemetery aren't getting much out of their success."

So we're agreed that staying healthy is a vital part of staying on top, aren't we?

The challenge of improving your health (or maintaining the health you have now) is divided into two parts:

- doing positive things such as exercising intelligently, eating right, and learning to cope with stress, and
- eliminating negative things such as being too heavy, smoking, eating foods that are high in cholesterol, and drinking too much.

Meeting either half of the challenge may require some minor changes in your life-style. Although these changes are minor, they won't happen unless you change the instructions you give yourself every day about who you are and what you do.

To smokers only: As a reformed smoker, I understand and sympathize with your antagonism toward putting up with any more preaching on the subject. So I'm not going to preach; I'm just going to point you toward a way to make quitting easier. You don't have to listen, my friend, but it's your life we're talking about.

THE EASY WAY TO QUIT SMOKING

Years ago I was a heavy smoker, a habit picked up long before the evidence was in that it's so very harmful. I liked to smoke; I felt it helped me keep my weight down and cope with the heavy pressure of the strenuous work schedule I maintained. I didn't realize then how offensive it was to some of my customers who didn't smoke.

Once I realized the health and career detriments of smoking, I cut down, but quitting was out of the question. I was a smoker, and I had a thousand reasons why I couldn't (read "wouldn't") quit. For a time I told myself that if I didn't smoke very much, extra exercise would compensate and I'd be as well off as someone who neither smoked nor exercised. Instead, I found myself missing out on the extra exercise but not on the cigarettes.

Finally it dawned on me that I was continuing to smoke only because I was still telling myself that I was a smoker. By this time, of course, I really wanted to quit. So I started changing my view of myself with a self-instruction that soon made it impossible for me to continue smoking. As it turned out, quitting smoking was surprisingly easy after that. I had suddenly become a nonsmoker!

The exact self-instruction I used is given, word for word, in *The Official Guide to Success*. If you have really decided to quit smoking, I guarantee you one thing: within 30 days you'll either quit smoking or you'll quit using the self-instruction that worked for me. It's that powerful—if you really want to quit.

EXERCISE WORKS OFF STRESS

Many people think of exercise as running, playing racquetball, or lifting weights. All those things are fine if you're already fairly fit and well under forty years old. If you're out of shape and on the high side of thirty-five, think walking.

Walking

Walking is almost a lost art in this country, yet it's one of the best exercises known. If you're not in great shape aerobically, get your doctor's okay and start walking every day. Walk a little farther and faster each day, working up to at least a brisk 30-minute walk. The key element is regularity. You can easily get in the habit of rolling out of bed, throwing on some clothes, and getting your walk over with before the rest of the household wakes up.

When you walk with a vigorous stride, you're not only working your heart and legs, you're also working your arms. Everything is in balance, and you're not jarring your skeleton the way you do while running.

For many people, especially those who have avoided exercise for years and may be somewhat overweight, walking is the ideal, low-impact way to start moving toward greater fitness.

In places where heart attacks are almost unknown—always in third-world countries—people routinely walk twenty-five or more miles a day just getting where they need to go. Of course they're breathing clean air and their bodies are lithe and lean; it's hard to be pudgy when you're walking or running twenty-five miles a day.

Other Regular Exercise

It's been proven repeatedly that exercise eases stress and strengthens the heart. What counts is regularity. To get regular exercise you have to select a program that won't lay you up frequently with injuries.

Recent studies have established that people who exercise regularly have quicker memories than nonexercising people of similar age, intelligence, and background. The exercisers don't remember more, they just remember more quickly—an important consideration to everyone in sales.

No matter how demanding it is, exercising only on the weekend is not enough. Studies have revealed that after just sixty hours of inactivity during the following week you start losing endurance. If you are a weekend athlete, you need at least another hour of vigorous exercise on both Tuesday and Thursday to maintain the fitness level you've already achieved.

Without those midweek refreshers, your stamina decreases, no matter how hard you exercise on the weekend. The greatest danger comes when your weekend activities get more strenuous while your endurance is dropping due to week-long inactivity. If you allow this to happen you're setting yourself up for a heart attack.

The Best Exercise Programs: How to Save Your Heart 10 Million Beats a Year

The best exercise programs don't limit themselves to just one aspect of fitness such as strength building. Recently a heavily muscled weightlifter failed the physical examination to be a policeman.

Despite the fact that he had a body like a Mr. America contestant, the treadmill test revealed that he couldn't run a block without putting a dangerous amount of strain on his heart. The man found it difficult to believe that heavy weight-lifting hadn't given him adequate endurance, but the short bursts of effort his workouts required had accomplished nothing for heart conditioning.

Aerobics Is First

The foundation of any good exercise regime must be aerobics training aimed at building or maintaining a high level of endurance. The dance exercises that are so popular with women are excellent; fortunately it's now socially acceptable for men to participate in them too.

Other fine aerobic exercises are walking, running, rowing, swimming, biking, and cross-country skiing. Regularity and frequency are the most important elements, so choose an exercise or variety of exercises that you'll enjoy doing—and will have the opportunity to do—for an hour at least four times a week.

The importance of aerobic training to your general health can hardly be exaggerated. One vital aspect that's often overlooked is how dramatically aerobic exercise can reduce the demands on your heart. Here's how it works:

Quite a few people who get little or no regular exercise and maybe smoke and drink a bit have a resting heartbeat of 80 or more per minute, which works out to about 42 million beats a year.

When they quit smoking, eliminate alcohol abuse, and get into an aerobics program many people with a resting heartbeat of 80 can cut their resting heartbeat to around 60 per minute, or about 31.5 million a year. In just ten years that drops your heart's workload by 105 million beats—a gigantic reduction in wear and tear.

Stretching Comes Second

Once you have conquered the challenge of maintaining a consistent aerobics training schedule, you're in a position to consider additional activity aimed at improving your health and stamina. The second type of regular exercise that you take on should be a stretch routine aimed at expanding the range of motion of your body and limbs. Stretching exercises increase your agility and performance in the fun sports and reduce the likelihood that you'll pull a muscle or injure a tendon while enjoying them.

Stretching exercises must be done gently. Forcing your body into a position that's painful invites an injury that will set your exercise program back by several weeks, possibly by several months.

Give your unused muscles time to adapt to the new demands you're making on them. Keep in mind that it can take years of slowly increasing stretching to reach your maximum flexibility.

My partner, Tom Murphy, has this to say about a stretching exercise program:

"I never really leave business. I'm always thinking about what's going on at the office—it's just the way I am. At home at night sitting around, I tend to eat. One of the things that has really helped me lose weight is the stretch class I'm in.

"It takes about an hour and while I'm doing that, I'm not thinking about business. The exercise calms you down so much, and you feel so good when you get through with that class. As a result, I just feel great all the time now.

"Another wonderful thing about stretching is what it does for your breathing. My 30 minutes a day on the bike are a whole lot easier since I've been doing my stretches because you've got to do a lot of deep breathing to get the muscles to stretch a bit more.

"Get into stretching—nothing else is on your mind when you're doing it."

Strength Building Should Come Third

Once you're firmly on the road to greater endurance and flexibility, consider strength building, generally done with weights or resistance machines in the traditional "workout at the gym."

But get one thing straight: The motto "no gain without pain," is for full-time athletes only. Unless your reasonable and attainable goals in life include world-class athletic performance, you don't have the slightest need to put your body under a painful amount of strain to increase your fitness, agility, strength, and general health. On the contrary, pain and strain will slow the process down by sidelining you with minor injuries and aches.

And, before you tear into an overly ambitious training program, give a moment's thought to how long you've allowed your physical condition to slide downhill. Give yourself at least a month of sensible—that is, gradually increasing—physical training to recover from each year you went without an effective exercise program.

DUMPING TONNAGE

People who pack extra pounds into their skins tend to avoid exertion as their bodies expand. Every additional ounce of fat makes it a little bit tougher for them to get up off the couch and start moving around. With heart-saving exercise out the window and too many globules of fat circulating through their arteries, they're hurt two ways. Carrying too much weight also gives them a poor self-image, and that means they're hurting three ways.

You certainly don't have to go hungry to lose weight, but you do have to cut back on foods that are more than 15 percent fat. Read the labels before you buy.

You can eat so much of the good foods that you won't have room for the bad stuff. It's another case of allowing the good to drive out the bad, the best possible response after years of eating so much of the fatty foods that there's no room for the leaner, healthier fare. Hundreds of books have been written in the last ten years about eating healthier. Educate yourself and try some of the excellent good-for-you recipes that abound today. Their flavor and ability to fill you up may surprise you.

In the last twenty years, deaths from heart disease have decreased by twenty percent. Cardiologists credit this happy result to a variety of causes: the boom in aerobic exercise, the jogging craze, a huge decline in the numbers of smokers, and a massive shift in our diets.

Lou Hall's Hike in His Backyard

Lou Hall felt he was solidly on top of the heap. Money was pouring in, he and his gorgeous wife enjoyed a wonderful relationship, and they luxuriated in the things they wanted most: a prestigious hillside home in West Los Angeles, a Jaguar, a Mercedes, and frequent vacations to exotic places.

Lou loved his work. By delegating the tasks he didn't like doing, he was able to concentrate on what he did best: close sales and make money.

All this success gave Lou a deep sense of power and an overriding confidence. He didn't let anybody tell him what he could or couldn't do. He had stopped getting annual check-ups ten years earlier because his doctor always told him the same thing: stop smoking, lose weight, get more exercise.

Lou knew he wouldn't go on a diet, and the suggestion that he stop smoking just made him mad. He liked to smoke! Exercise? Forget it; it's boring. Who has time for that stuff anyway?

Lou believed he was one of the lucky ones, and he felt that nothing could touch him. Bad things happened to other people. Life was too good, time too precious to waste thinking about negatives that were mere possibilities.

One Sunday afternoon Lou climbed down the slope behind his home. Coming back up, he stopped to catch his breath. That's all he remembers.

Lou's luck held. A neighbor saw him fall and called the paramedics, and they were able to get there within minutes. But by that time Lou's ghastly blue face told the story—death was only moments away. The paramedics worked feverishly.

Several hours later Lou woke up in a hospital, where it took him a long time to accept the fact that he'd survived a heart attack. Lou had believed he possessed an iron constitution and was in perfect health. His doctor, the man he'd ignored for ten years, came in and told him, "Maybe this is a good thing. It might knock some sense into your head."

Suddenly Lou saw the wisdom of quitting smoking, losing weight, and getting regular exercise. He enrolled in the hospital's cardiac rehabilitation program and made the necessary changes in his diet. It was no big deal.

The combination of an intelligent diet and regular exercise took thirty pounds off in a few weeks. Today, two years after his heart attack and two years since he's smoked, Lou feels great. He's learned to enjoy exercise, he's made a few other adjustments in his daily routine, and he's still on top. It sure beats the alternative.

Your first priority for staying on top has to be the simple but necessary act of staying alive. An obvious statement? It wasn't obvious to Lou Hall, who certainly is no dummy. After all, he had the smarts to reach the top.

The Special Life Threats of Success

Success often breeds a feeling of invulnerability. It also provides more opportunities to gratify ourselves with unhealthy things. As a result, successful Americans tend to be at least slightly overweight, and usually they're more than slightly underexercised as well. Some of them still smoke.

Success tends to drive physical activity out of our daily routine. If we delegate life's physical drudgery to others, we must substitute regular exercise for ourselves. Physical inactivity and a rich diet are a deadly combination. Add the multiple insults to the body that nicotine and alcohol deliver and you have a recipe for a short life, not a long healthy one.

Our highly computerized and industrialized life-styles diverge in important ways from the primitive patterns our bodies are adapted to. Staying alive today demands that we make use of the medical knowledge that's been accumulated in recent years to cope with that divergence. The consequences of our choices can't be escaped. If we continue to blindly follow the self-indulgent life-style that's so easy to fall into, we'll blindly stumble into early graves.

CHAPTER FOURTEEN

WHAT YOU DON'T KNOW **CAN** HURT YOU

WHAT A SALESPERSON SHOULD LEARN

You can never learn too much about your product or your customers. Beyond that, you will profit greatly by learning:

1. How to give better service.
2. How to close the sale better.
3. How to keep aware of your company's goals.
4. How to help your company accomplish those goals.
5. Exactly how you can help your company most this month, this week, this day.

You just took a quick but significant test on how secure your future is with your present employer.

How's that again?

It's my contention that unless salespeople have good feelings about their company, they won't be able to reach their full potential with that firm. So, when you read the last three items on the list of things a salesperson should learn (3, 4, and 5 above), what was your reaction?

If you were insulted by the suggestion that you should study how to help the company reach its goals, either you have an attitude problem or you aren't working for the right company.

The same holds true if you were amused at the idea.

What would indicate that you have a future with your present employer? That you were immediately in agreement with the idea of helping the company reach its goals. The stronger that feeling, the more likely it is that you'll be with them for a long time.

SET UP YOUR OWN LEARNING CENTER

Ideally, you would set aside a corner or a room in your home as your learning center. It would be furnished with a well-lighted desk or table, a comfortable chair, and storage space for files, tapes, and books. Don't worry if you can't do this right away, but start with something. I remember back when I graduated from my first real sales training program. The last thing we were asked to do as an assignment, something we were asked to do, in fact, for the rest of our lives, was to develop our own personal reference library.

When you think about that, think about the people who live in multimillion-dollar homes. They usually have rooms in their homes average Americans don't have. These are rooms they take great pride in. Their libraries hold their books, their references, all the training systems and educational materials they've built their careers on—careers that have generated the income to allow them to be able to afford those million-dollar homes.

Don't wait; start today. I started that day the assignment was given with a board held up by two bricks. This makeshift shelf held the class materials I received during that seminar. When that shelf was filled, I got two more bricks and another board. I kept investing in educational materials and pretty soon, I was able to afford not only a beautiful bookcase, but a beautiful new home to put it in.

Master the Art of Making and Breaking Habits

What determines whether you'll do smart things and avoid doing dumb things as you go about your daily activities?

Your habits? Yes, but that begs the question. What causes habits? If you think something like, "I cause my own habits; I'm responsible for them," go to the head of the class, and please accept my heartfelt congratulations.

However, if you didn't think that, it doesn't mean you're a loser. After all, I didn't warn you that I'd ask questions. But if you blame anything or anyone except yourself for your habits, you're dead wrong.

All your habits, good or bad, are yours solely because you maintain them with self-talk. Now we're getting close to the truth about the cause of doing smart and avoiding dumb. Self-talk.

Few salespeople realize the full extent of the damage that negative self-talk does to their careers. It's enormous and I don't know of a better explanation of why so many salespeople aren't more successful.

Negative ideas bombard us from the world outside our skins, and they furnish some, but by no means all, of the raw materials for our negative self-talk. By far the most destructive self-talk is generated within our own minds—primarily from junk that's been rotting there for years.

Few of us are as conscious as we should be that while we're awake, a constant stream of thought, symbolized by either words or images, flows through our gray matter. If we wanted to stop that flow for even a short time, and without falling asleep or taking drugs (alcohol is a drug) make our minds register a complete blank, we wouldn't be able to do it without meditation. Anyone who knows how to reach a state of meditation or deep relaxation can shut off the flow easily.

But for everyone else, a stream of emotional thoughts is running through our heads all the time, even though we usually aren't conscious of it.

Become conscious of what you're telling yourself. Make a real effort here because this is the key to controlling your future. You may be amazed to discover that you're almost continuously beating yourself up, putting yourself down, and telling yourself that you can't do it. Whatever it is that you're tempted to try, you tell yourself it will turn out badly, people will laugh at your clumsy mistakes, and even if nobody can see what you're doing, you'll be sorry you tried.

Why do we do this? Why do we fight change even when it means improving ourselves? It all boils down to fear. We are afraid to leave our comfort zones. We are afraid to make mistakes. We are afraid of looking foolish. What we must first do is realize that we only progress through the acceptance of change. We can't just decide we must do something better and have it happen instantaneously. We must grow through learning experiences. Once we face that fear and learn to push it aside, we can accomplish anything.

When people put themselves down on a continuous basis during almost all their waking hours, the cumulative effect over a period of months or years is catastrophic. This often works in subtle ways. For example, a California psychologist gave IQ tests to a public school class. Then he ignored the results and divided the class into two groups at random with no reference to their IQ level.

The first group, he told the teacher, was considerably brighter than the second group. However, in fact there was actually no difference. The children were never given his conclusions and the teacher was told to treat all the pupils the same. At the end of the school year the grades of the two groups were compared. The first group had grades nearly a third better than the second group and their IQ's measured higher.

The teacher insisted that no reference had ever been made to the different intelligence levels that she supposed the two groups had. Nevertheless she had quite unconsciously communicated to the first group that she had a higher expectation of them and to the second group that they were not expected to do as well. And both groups performed as their teacher expected.

Millions of people demonstrate the power of the mind in humdrum ways. By constantly putting themselves down, they perpetuate their own poor performance. The result is low income and a growing dissatisfaction with themselves that continues to feed upon itself.

Is the solution to constantly tell yourself that you're a superperson and that you can do anything, that there are no limits to what you can accomplish? No, it's very dangerous to go from one extreme to the other. Your mind has enormous power over your body and your destiny. You can monitor what you're telling yourself and begin to swing yourself into a sensible can-do attitude instead of a defeated can't-do attitude.

Habits are part of our controllable personalities. They are maintained by the instructions we give ourselves; therefore new ones can be built or old ones broken by new self-instructions.

I've noticed that many people resist this idea. They like to think that "It's the way I am and I can't do anything about it," or "It's how I do things," as though a flimsy notion of that kind could excuse any habit, no matter how stupidly harmful to them it might be.

It's my belief that people who claim that self-instructions don't work are simply afraid to try them wholeheartedly—because they might work! They just don't want to change.

Will self-instructions help people who want to lose weight, lick addiction to alcohol, drugs, or gambling, or cure laziness and apathy?

Let me put it to you this way: No one who defeats any of those things ever does it without first changing the self-instructions that got them into trouble in the first place. Notice that I stop well short of claiming that revised self-instructions, by themselves, can cure all bad habits in all people.

The first requirement always is that they want to change; this desire must come from within and not be imposed by someone else. There can be no hidden determination to resist the change. Given that, a great deal can be accomplished in every case.

Educating Yourself

Babies are born with completely blank memories, but within a few years they speak their native tongue fluently. Yet an adult trying to learn a new language will study for years without gaining the easy command of a language that children acquire in less time with less effort.

We tend to shrug this off as being the natural state of

affairs; children's minds are like sponges, we think. They simply soak up enormous amounts of information effortlessly.

Yet when adults intrude into natural childhood development and force-feed preschool children with mathematics, reading, and other subjects, the results are not impressive. In fact, it quickly becomes clear that the children don't have such sponge-like minds after all.

Have their minds changed or is it because we try to make them learn? Obviously, young children learn their native tongue in their own way. They don't try to memorize lists of words; they don't take tests on grammar. Instead, they pick up words a few at a time and figure out the structure by themselves.

Within the last few years a small movement has been growing that recognizes a simple truth. The fastest way to learn is the way young children teach themselves.

It's not possible for adults to recreate the infantile learning situation for themselves. Nevertheless, the closer we approach that ideal, the faster we'll learn. And, fortunately, new adult skills allow us to approach the speed of childhood learning.

Let's look at some of the reasons why small children learn language so quickly.

1. They have a tremendous desire to learn and are highly involved in learning their parents' language. Big people talk and they want to be like big people.

2. Few children below the age of five are much concerned about making a learning mistake. They'll try and try again without being inhibited by the fear of failure.

3. Children naturally use rhymes, games, and jokes to speed their learning.

By contrast, consider a group of salespeople who are obliged to familiarize themselves with a new product line or a new price list. Will they be emotionally involved in learning that price list? Will they be seriously inhibited by the fear of making mistakes in front of their peers? Will they use rhymes, puns, or any memory-aiding techniques at all to speed their learning?

We can accelerate how we learn significantly and get it done with less effort than we're now putting into learning poorly. This can be done through any of the hundreds of methods taught in books available in your local public library or college library. The result is that we can learn more, and retain it longer and better, by spending no more than 25 percent of the time an untrained learner takes.

GETTING STARTED ON LEARNING MORE, FASTER

Make a commitment to yourself that you will learn more, and learn it faster and better.

Why bother to learn more? Because knowledge is power, and power can readily be converted into extra cash in your bank account. There is a saying that goes, "What you don't know, won't hurt you." Believe me, that saying doesn't apply to sales. In sales, what you don't know can completely wipe out your chances for a successful career.

You can't know too much about the world in general, and you certainly can't know too much about your product or service, your industry, and your customers.

Let's dispose of an effort-killing idea that some people have. This is the misconception that their brains will only hold so much material—and they've already packed them full. Personal computers sometimes run out of storage space, but human brains never do. There are no cases on record of people being unable to learn more because their brains were too full. Unwilling, yes, by the millions; unable, never.

Every human memory can store billions of bits of information and nobody's is chock-full. Everybody's memory is ready for more input—and your brains are no exception.

As a matter of fact, the more we learn the easier it is to learn more. Few people are competent in more than three or four languages, but there is a record of one man who learned how to speak and write more than 60 different languages fluently. And the speed with which he could learn a new language continued to pick up throughout his life.

PLUG INTO YOUR CLEAREST CHANNEL

Channelling is a powerful tool you can use on your own brains to learn more quickly, more easily, and better.

The concept: There are three powerful channels through which we acquire most of our new information. In every person, one or another of these channels is dominant. Each of us learns quickest and best through sight, sound, or action.

What about the other senses—touch, smell, and taste? With rare exceptions, these senses are never dominant in people living in industrialized societies.

One of your first tasks in training yourself to learn faster is to determine which of the three powerful channels you're most responsive to.

Sight-Dominant

You're reading this book, so there's a very good chance that sight is your dominant channel because most people, even those who never read books, learn best by visual means.

Being sight-dominant doesn't mean that you'll learn everything best through your eyes. Touch typing is learned on a keyboard. Nobody ever learned how to drive a car, ski, swim, or play tennis by simply reading about those activities.

However, even with activities that are action pure and simple, learning speed can be increased by using channels other than action. Many people learn more, and learn it better and faster, by supplementing action (practice) with instruction that comes to them through their ears and eyes from an instructor, or from books and visual aids.

Sound-Dominant

Even if your best learning channel is the auditory one, you're probably often forced to rely on books. An immensely greater variety of material is available in print than on recordings; you can also buy the printed word for much less than the same material in recorded form would cost.

When their source is a book, the best study method for sound-dominant people is to read the material into a tape recorder, and then play it back as many times as they wish.

Action-Dominant

If your dominant channel is action, seek out seminars and classes that emphasize student participation. However, you won't have this option often because much of the knowledge you'll need in business will have to come from the printed word.

Here's the solution: Tear the books apart. Put the chapters that don't interest you right now aside. Then reorganize the remaining pages in the order of their importance to you.

Perform all the exercises that are given in the books. Discuss what you're learning in detail with your friend or spouse. Teach the subject to someone else. Create your own exercises, tests, and review materials. Put what you're learning into use whenever you can. In other words, miss no opportunity to make learning the most vigorous activity you can.

A GENERALIZED LEARNING PATTERN

This section applies best to the sight-dominant majority. If you're sound-dominant or action-dominant, adapt the steps to your situation as suggested above.

Let's say that your company recently acquired a new product line—or you have a new job. You soon realize that the key to making money is a knowledge of chemistry, a subject you know little about at this time.

Your sales manager mentions a certain book and tells you, "It will give you everything you need to know."

When you look at the book your stomach turns over: it's 900 pages of technical matter. But you're highly motivated. This is an opportunity to better yourself considerably if you can acquire a thorough grounding in chemistry quickly. How do you go about it?

Jargon

It's enormously easier to learn about something if you understand its special vocabulary. In fact, you can't get a solid grip on any subject until you do understand its jargon—the words and phrases that are peculiar to it. One of the definitions for jargon given by Webster is "the technical terminology or characteristic idiom of a special activity or group."

The downside of jargon is that it's often used to awe outsiders; the up side is that it's essential to the practice of many arts. Without an understanding of the jargon of medicine, doctors couldn't communicate with each other quickly or accurately. Without the jargon of flight, pilots would crash before controllers could make them aware of their danger. An important skill to develop is to learn early in your presentation how well your particular client understands industry jargon. A doctor would obviously be "up" on medical terms. However, a purchasing agent, assigned the task of buying computers for the accounting staff, may not have the technical knowledge to understand computer terminology or even accounting terms.

Conquering Jargon the Easy Way

There are two kinds of jargon: odd words you've never seen before and common words used in special ways. Usually the easiest to deal with are the odd words because they announce themselves as jargon. You just look them up in the dictionary and make a flash card.

When learning a new subject, if you hit a new term, write it down on a 3 × 5 card. After you've collected several cards, sit down with a good dictionary and look all the terms up at one time. You may need a special dictionary that defines the terms used in a particular field. Write the definition and pronunciation on the back of each card.

Tip #1:

Always form some kind of association between a word and its meaning so that you'll remember it easily. As an example, for the word exothermic, associate exo with "exit" and therm with thermos bottle for "heat" and you get the word's meaning: the chemical change that accompanies the liberation of heat. Jot the association on the back of the card too.

Tip #2:
Look up jargon terms in an unabridged (large) dictionary. Smaller dictionaries have to omit many technical words or give definitions that are too short to be of much help.

Tip #3:
Learn the jargon words first. Then every time you come across one of these new terms in your studies you'll be encouraged instead of discouraged.

Your jargon cards are a flash deck that you can review as often as necessary. Look at the word on the front of the card and recall the definition, pronounce it correctly (checking both items against what's on the back of the card), and perhaps make up a sentence using the word. Review your deck of jargon cards twice a week, setting aside those that you have learned so that you can concentrate on the ones whose meanings and correct pronunciation don't instantly spring to mind. Review your jargon flash deck of learned words after one week and again after a month. If you've made good associations for each jargon word, you'll be delighted at how quickly they become part of your working vocabulary.

Proceed as follows:

1. Set up a study schedule. Can you give it one hour in the morning and one hour in the evening? If you're working a full-time job that requires some paperwork or planning in the evening, two study hours a day is probably the most you should attempt.

Before every study session, do two things:

Clear distractions. Take a moment to consider what might interrupt your study session. If necessary, jot down notes of phone calls you should make and other duties you're putting off until after your study session. The idea is to clear your mind of distractions so that you can give your full attention to your study material.

Psyche up for learning. Take one minute to psyche yourself up for the study period. Review in your mind what you're trying to achieve by learning the material. In other words, what goals are you trying to achieve? Picture yourself receiving the benefits of having this knowledge. Use this minute to fully involve yourself in an emotional way in learning intensely.

2. Use time controls. Use a timer so that after thirty minutes of study a buzzer will remind you to take a five-minute break. On your break, get entirely away from study. Take a walk, watch TV, glance through a book on a different subject, do something that will take your mind off the material you've been studying. Also set the buzzer so that your break won't last more than about five minutes. Return for another half-hour study session, then call it quits for that study session.

3. Skim before you dive in. Read quickly over the table of contents and chapter sub-headings to quickly get an idea of what you're going to be learning, what chapters you should study first, and which you can skip entirely.

Is the book organized so that you have to study the chapters in numerical order to be able to understand the later ones? Or can you jump around, taking first the parts that interest you most?

Alternate between learning the jargon you find by skimming a chapter, and learning the material in that chapter. Avoid getting ahead of your knowledge of jargon; if you try to wing it with technical terms, you may make costly mistakes.

4. Create a test flash deck as you study. As you read the material, write down important points on cards, one to each card. (Use cards larger than the usual 3×5 for this purpose; you need at least a 4×6 card; a 5×8 would be better.)

On the other side of each card, write a question that will test whether you know that important point. Then take a moment to make an association between the question and the answer. The more bizarre and ridiculous these associations are, the better you'll remember them.

These cards become your test flash deck.

5. Review your test flash deck. Review your test flash deck (Step 4 above) every fifteen minutes during your study session. This helps fix the material in your mind and also points out any areas you haven't yet committed to memory. Reread the book to fill any gaps in your information that are revealed by this review.

6. Begin each study session with a review. At the start of each study session after the first, begin by reviewing all you've studied up to this point, using your diagrams and test flash deck to speed and intensify your review.

Too many reviews? Wrong. Reviews are the fast way to achieve the spaced repetition study that knocks most of the inefficiency out of learning. Experiments have proven that material requiring sixty-eight repetitions in one day could be mastered with only thirty-eight repetitions if they were spread over three days. That's a reduction of nearly half; the test questions with ridiculous associations further reduce learning time.

Sharpen Your Memory

It seems that we have at least two memories: short-term and long-term. The short-term memory handles most of the daily work.

For example, if you do some mental calculations or plan your best route to several locations, you'll use your short-term memory to get the number answer or the route answer. In both cases your short-term memory will draw on your long-term memory for information. The same thing happens when you see some people you know and try to remember their names, or when you talk about a program or movie you saw.

As you read this sentence, your short-term memory retains the beginning words long enough for you to grasp the meaning of the entire sentence. Then the meaning of the sentence—not the individual words—is transferred into your long-term memory.

In one of the examples just given, selecting a route to several locations, the short-term memory works out the route by calling on the long-term memory to furnish images and other information about the locations. This is to say that the short-term memory analyzes and the long-term memory synthesizes, both working together to blend old facts with new situations at incredible speeds.

Anyone familiar with desktop computers will see the similarity between human and computer memories. A computer has a Random Access Memory (RAM) which does the processing and calculating, and a storage memory, called the Read Only Memory (ROM). When you turn a computer off, the RAM contents vanish just as short-term memory disappears from the human mind overnight.

All day long you looked at and talked to people, and did various commonplace things. Your memory of this routine activity will whisk out of your mind unless it's registered on your memory by emotional impact, or by deliberate mental effort on your part. In somewhat the same way, information that is only in the RAM memory of the computer must be saved on disk in order to be stored permanently.

What deliberate mental effort will fix the details of routine happenings permanently in your mind? Psychologists call it "registering," educators call it "learning," and for the most part you and I would call it unnecessary.

We don't want to register or learn the minute variations of our daily activities, we want to recall only very small bits of the total. We want to remember names, faces, commitments, and what actions we need to take. Fortunately, there are systems that will enable you to remember anything you really want to remember and, more importantly, recall it whenever you choose.

Are those systems easy to learn? I'll answer that question with two of my own. How easy is it to scramble around trying to cover up for simple details you've been forgetting? And how easy do you really want it to be? If learning memory systems were extremely easy, everybody, including all your competitors, would already have learned them.

To give you a straight answer, learning how to remember better is just difficult enough to discourage those of faint heart, but not difficult enough to really matter.

MEMORY IS A THREE-WAY ACTIVITY

Most of us think of memory as being one thing but actually it breaks down into three distinct phases as we memorize something. These can be called registration, retention, and recall.

Instant Registration

Most of us will remember an insult or some injury done to us for a long time without making any effort to remember it. This is because emotion registers that memory on our minds with a hard edge.

Compare the hot feeling we get if someone insults us to the situation when we set out to learn something we think is not very exciting. Unfortunately, "not very exciting" describes some of the business information all of us feel compelled to learn from time to time.

It doesn't matter that other people find the same material fascinating and highly charged with emotion; it doesn't excite us. Since our memories only react to our own feelings, our boredom with the material means there won't be any emotional imprinting of it on our minds.

I'll repeat how important it is to visualize the benefits you'll gain from learning the new material, whether it be interesting or not. Having goals for learning and for the increased power of the knowledge gained will help keep even the driest material from becoming boring.

Retention

Unless information is registered, we won't retain it. Take for example the common habit of not paying attention to the name of the person we're introduced to. We don't even try, and a few minutes later we feel a little stupid when that person calls us by name and we can't reciprocate. We can't remember the other person's name because we didn't pay any attention to it when it was given to us. No registration, no retention. So the first rule of remembering anything is to pay attention to it.

Recall

Registration and retention aren't of much use unless we can recall the information when we want it. Dependable recall occurs when something we want to remember is registered and retained with associations that we can trigger in a systematic way. Without the system, we'll often flounder; sometimes we'll draw a total blank, at other times we'll know the information we want is floating around in our head just out of reach.

Systematically retained information doesn't behave that way. We pull the association trigger and our long-term memory shoots the information into our short-term memory where we can say it, think about it, or do something with it. It's instant, utterly reliable, and cost-free. Where else but in your own brains can you get a deal like that?

But, unless we know how to make it easy, if we're determined to learn something, we're thrown entirely onto grinding mental effort to fix the material in our minds. Making this type of learning—the hard kind—easy is what we'll be discussing next.

LEARNING THE HARD STUFF

What does "the hard stuff" include? Whatever you want to remember but can't when you need to.

Motivation helps. If you can clearly see how recalling something will put money in your pocket, it should do the trick all by itself, shouldn't it?

Not necessarily. Certainly it's a lot easier to remember names, prices, model features and so on if there's a lot of money hanging on what you can dredge up out of your memory.

Yet when the information to be remembered is more than a few items, and they came at you fast, it turns out that motivation isn't enough. It doesn't help to chew yourself out for being dumb when in fact you're not. At worst you're just ignorant in the area of using good memory technique.

On unexciting material, the retention process of the human mind doesn't approach the mechanical perfection of the computer. Nothing bores a computer, and computers will store vast amounts of crushingly boring data in seconds, after being directed to do so with a few keystrokes.

But computers cannot yet match our ability to understand the complex patterns of speech, a process that demands lightning-fast retrieval of previously stored information about what the sounds we hear mean in the present situation.

Indexing Your Brains

Your memory is much like a library. If your library had thousands of books stacked without any system, you would find it difficult to locate a particular book. But if the books were arranged systematically, by subject and author, for example, then you could quickly locate whatever you wanted. In the same way, you can speed your recall of wanted information by associating it systematically with things you already know.

Registering information is like dropping a bit of information into a file folder. Associating that bit of information to something you already know is similar to typing out a library index card.

If you register each new piece of information strongly at the beginning by associating it systematically with something you already know, you will be able to recall it when you want to. Psychologists agree that the better you register new information, the more quickly you'll be able to recall it. Registering better means creating vivid associations with the new material.

Since learning consists largely of acquiring facts, figures, and relationships, it can be said that learning is largely a matter of memory. Of course, many subjects we want to master involve doing things with remembered information and learned skills.

The Distribution-of-Practice Effect

The time taken to learn something is substantially less if learning is spaced rather than done all in one shot. For example, learning a task that would require an hour if learned all in one day would typically take 44 minutes if spaced over two days.

This only saves 16 minutes. That's not very impressive until you realize that it reflects reducing learning time by more than one-fourth, just by making this simple change in your learning routine.

Taking Short Breaks Speeds Learning

Some psychological studies indicate that the most efficient study period is about thirty minutes, followed by a five-minute break. It appears that taking more than five minutes off provides no learning benefit.

The Magic of Seven

All over the world local telephone numbers contain no more than seven digits. The people who run telephone companies tend to be practical; they know the average person finds it difficult to remember numbers of more than seven digits.

Sure, telephone numbers have 10 digits, including the area code. However, the telephone companies have very cleverly added the 3-digit area codes without violating our limitation of seven. This is because area codes are always associated with geographic locations. And most calls are local calls that don't involve an area code.

However, later in this chapter I'll tell you where you can find a system that will allow you to easily remember numbers of any length.

You may work for a company that has a stock number system consisting of eight or more digits. If so, you can be sure that its employees know fewer of those numbers than in a company where the product numbers don't exceed seven digits.

Not surprisingly, the federal government ignores this principle. Social security numbers have nine digits and practically no one has them memorized. Army serial numbers are eight digits and it takes a considerable amount of coercive force to make soldiers memorize their individual numbers.

The magic of seven extends to many other fields. General managers can only effectively supervise seven departments; group vice presidents can only effectively supervise seven subsidiaries. Which leads us to the subject of "chunking," one of the most effective techniques for speeding your learning.

Chunking

While it's hard to remember more than seven items, each of the items can be quite large and detailed. In other words, you can chunk a great deal of information into any one of seven divisions and use the magic of seven to recall all of them.

For example, you could associate something you wanted to learn with the days of the week. By thinking of Tuesday, you would then have brought into your mind all the information that you had associated with that day of the week. You could use other memory keys to chunk material under, number one through seven, colors red, green, blue, yellow, black, white, and gray. Or letters "A" through "G," for example.

Reward yourself when you learn a specific set of facts. Give yourself a new outfit or some other extravagance that will serve as a genuine reward. The item is of no importance— the degree of motivation is.

How Effective Is Repetition?

Many people see learning as a grim process that consists of nothing but grinding mental effort; one must endlessly repeat what is to be learned.

While countless studies have established this fact, a little reflection will convince you. How well do you recall the details of your watch, which you look at many times a day? How many features of a dollar bill can you describe?

The fact is, people living in our complex society would be hopelessly confused if they couldn't filter out most of the messages that are constantly hurtling at them to allow them to absorb the few that are of immediate urgency.

Repetition has very little effect unless it is integrated with emotional involvement, motivation, or something bizarre. And the repetition itself cancels out an essential requirement for effective registration of the material on our long-term memories. As soon as it's seen to be repetitious, any item of information loses all power to impress itself on the memory by being unusual or outstanding.

MEMORY SYSTEMS

Memory systems go back a long way, which makes it all the more amazing that so few people today use them to enlarge their abilities and incomes. Volumes of information are available on various memory systems through your local library or bookstore.

Have Some Fun

Practice these skills with different lists until you've gained complete confidence in your ability to commit lists to memory.

The key phrase is complete confidence. Make sure you've earned it, then have some fun amazing your friends by repeating lists of ten random words they write down and read to you.

Linking

One of my favorite ways to remember a list of items is to form an association—the more outlandish the better—between one item and the next. That explanation is probably too brief to be of much help, but space doesn't permit me to detail it. Anyway, it's given in full in a terrific book that everyone who is serious about staying on top should read: *The Memory Book* by Harry Lorayne and Jerry Lucas, published by Stein and Day. Ballantine Books has it out in paperback.

The Memory Book seems as if it were written especially for salespeople. You'll want it just for its Chapter Twelve, on memorizing style numbers, prices, and telephone numbers, or Chapter Ten, on long numbers. The authors demonstrate a slick way to quickly memorize numbers, no matter how long. Like 91852719521639092112, for example.

Putting Names and Faces Together

Several authors have written excellent books on memory training. Take the time to read them and improve all areas of your life.

ORGANIZE YOUR LIFE'S FORCES

Allow yourself time to daydream, to visualize yourself gaining in status or in personal accomplishments. Start visualizing and dreaming and identifying the things that turn your turbo on. You can't just sit down and write a goal that will excite you unless you've first studied what you want in depth.

Many people never do this. Instead they plod along, content to pursue the goals inflicted on them by others—their spouse, TV advertising, what the guys down at the store think is great. Most people are slow to get around to deciding exactly what they really want.

Perhaps you're not sitting there craving material things— the latest technologically marvelous stereo, boat, auto, or home. Maybe you're thinking more of self-improvement, of acquiring the qualities possessed by someone you know, or by some famous person, living or dead.

In my seminars and both my books I have a lot to say about the vast importance of having goals that pull you forward, instead of relying on your ordinary needs to drive you. I'm not alone in believing that goals are vital: practically every modern thinker or speaker on the subject of success extols the benefits of setting goals. So let's review the basic rules of putting the power of goals to work for you.

1. Write down your goals. Unwritten goals are wishes that do nothing; written goals are active contracts you've made with yourself.

2. Review your goals regularly. Otherwise they'll fade from your memory and amount to zero.

3. Keep your goals with you. If you keep the cards you've written your goals on with you, you can review and revise them in spare moments. The whole idea is to make them a living, vital part of your life and a powerful influence on your daily decisions.

4. Make sure your goals are realistic. Goals you don't believe you can achieve are worse than useless because they blind you to goals you could achieve. And they discourage your belief in the whole goal-setting and achieving process.

Let me tell you about the second goal I wrote down, as a long-term goal when I was 21 years old. This is how vivid I want goal setting to become.

I was sitting in an airplane. It was my first flight. I was flying from California to Arizona. I'd never been in a plane before. You might remember your first flight. I was sitting there scared to death. We were taking off and I looked out the window to the right and on the runway next to our plane, this beautiful little plane took off.

I asked the man next to me, "What is that cute little plane?" He said, "That's a jet—a corporate jet." I said, "Boy, that's cute." I took out my goal-setting device right then and there and wrote it down: Jet—10-year goal.

Now the surprising thing about a goal that's in writing is if you concentrate on it every day it will become real. I will never forget the day that the jet arrived. It was ten years to the day later. I had just finished a program in Baton Rouge, Louisiana, and I stood there on that runway and that little plane came out and I thought, "This is it. Ten years and I've arrived."

When I got on the plane, the pilot welcomed me aboard. I said, this is it. I've arrived.

And do you know what happened? After a while it's just another thing. A fun toy. A big toy.

I'll never forget the first time we landed to refuel. The pilot came back and handed me the receipt—for $882. I said, "Is this for the month?" It wasn't. That long-term goal turned out to be a $30,000 per month goal, which turned out to be unrealistic for me. Even though I was earning enough to afford

PROPOSAL and AGREEMENT

Binding Contract of Commitment with the
"Person in the Mirror"

_____ 19 ___

Name _____

The undersigned proposes to furnish all materials and perform all labor necessary to complete the following goal:

_____

_____

_____

_____

_____

_____

_____

    I hereby swear to start today to reach out and do more with my life and achieve the greatness that I know lies within me, which is waiting to be brought out.

    From this day forward I will not be denied any longer. This is a day in my life that I finally get the guts to do what I know must be done and quit taking the easy way out, I will pay the price that is necessary to reach this goal because I know the pain of not fulfilling myself is greater than the pain of doing any job no matter how hard.

    I understand that my life's plan is going to be reached by reaching one goal at a time, each being but one step toward my greater future. I understand that each contract I fulfill always puts me one step closer to what I want out of life, and I will not have to settle for what others give me or just earn a living. I have a power to change my life.

_____
Signature of Commitment

As I OK this contract, I understand that my future is in my hands only and I can look to no one else for its fulfillment.

ACCEPTANCE

    I, as agent for the face in the mirror, upon the completion of this goal congratulate you for proving once again that you can do anything that you want and be anything that you want. You can also get anything that you want as long as you know what it is.

    You have taken one more step toward being the person you dream of. You may take great pride in knowing that you have the backbone to plan and reach a goal.

    You are now one step closer to your major goal. As you know, major goals are just a string of successful small goals that lead you to the top.

_____
Agent for the "Face in the Mirror"

Date Goal Fulfilled _____ 19 ____

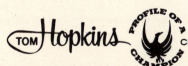

TOM Hopkins — PROFILE OF A CHAMPION — CHAMPIONS UNLIMITED

P.O. BOX 1969 • 7531 EAST 2ND STREET, SCOTTSDALE, ARIZONA 85252
© 1977 Tom Hopkins Champions Unlimited Inc.

TERMS and CONDITIONS

1. Use this contract with yourself for any goal, no matter how small or large. A goal, no matter how small, should be treated with great respect because it builds your character and self image.

2. Must be filled out in full and dated with starting and completion dates.

3. Your goal should be very descriptive and explicit. It should paint a very clear picture of what is wanted and when.

4. All of your contracts that have not been completed, should be read in front of the mirror every day with great conviction, so as to imbed your goals into your subconscious mind.

5. When a goal is reached, sign as agent for ''The Face in the Mirror'' and then write in large red letters on the face of the contract, ''This contract fulfilled''. Save all of these contracts and keep them in order by date completed, so as to see a growth pattern. You will be able to draw great strength from this string of successes that you have accomplished, no matter how small they may seem at first.

6. Remember, you can be as great as anyone, but you must have a plan. Each of these goals, no matter how small, will become a part of that plan and help you to turn your beautiful dreams into a fantastic, rewarding life.

7. Do not make conflicting goals, such as:
   I will spend more time at home and I will double my sales. These goals may not work together and may cause frustration in your life.

8. Your goals should be something you want bad enough to turn you on and light your soul on fire and make you move and act with enthusiasm.

9. What you are doing here is deadly serious. You cannot reach a place that you want to go if you do not know how to get there. It is the same way with life. Each one of these goals become a stopping point or starting point on the road map of your life. They will become the blueprint for your every success. If you don't have a blueprint, how are you going to build your life?

   Please, take these extremely seriously no matter how small each goal. Reward yourself and congratulate yourself for starting the habit of planning your life. You will reap unbelievable rewards.

10-100 If you want your life to change, you have to change or you are going to stay just about the same as you are. So set some goals that turn you on and get your life into gear. You can do it — You can change and become or do anything you want. *Just want!*

the expenses, I always thought of the plane as an extravagance. It was out of my comfort zone for me to have that plane. It just wasn't a part of my reality. That's why I only had it for two months.

You see, one thing you have to realize about long-term goals is that there are times when you must change your goals. Some people are so afraid of a long-term goal, though, that they'll set no goals. That's the sad part of it.

5. Act on your goals. Nothing happens unless you make it happen.

6. Give yourself rewards for achieving a goal. Your drive to achieve will wither and die if you don't feed it some benefits at least once in a while.

7. Plan how you'll make your goals happen. If you don't plan in detail how your goals will be achieved, how can you make them happen?

8. Resolve conflicts between goals immediately. People often set up goals that are in direct conflict with each other: Spend more time with the kids; spend more time planning and preparing for sales work. When you discover such a conflict, it alerts you to the necessity of making hard choices and scheduling most effectively.

9. Make your goals relevant to your family. Unless you involve your family in them, your goals will conflict with the aims of your loved ones. This is certain to increase tension within your family and make the achievement of your purposes more difficult. Don't leave them out; instead, get them on your side: "If I win this sales contest, we'll all go to Disneyland."

10. Preserve the inspiration of your goals by keeping them up to date. Your life is dynamic; your desires and capabilities are under constant change. New information may at any time make some or all of your present goals obsolete. When things change for you, change your goals. They're not carved on Mount Rushmore.

11. Recap your goals annually. At the end of the year, go over every goal you set the previous year and see how much you've really accomplished. This is a great motivator with which to launch a whole new, even more productive, year.

CHAPTER FIFTEEN

WHEN YOU'VE ACHIEVED SUCCESS IN SALES, DON'T ASSUME YOU KNOW IT ALL

It takes determination not to learn something new every day, although many people let their learning processes drift on Lake Indifference. If we do that, what we learn is not likely to be anything that will help us reach the top or stay there. More likely it will consist of such items as a new way to needle the guy next to us, recognition that our favorite socks have worn out, and what's on TV tonight.

WHEN DID YOU STOP LEARNING?

When did you stop learning things that will help you get to the top and stay there? I'm not talking about a haphazard program of perusing the *Wall Street Journal* for a few minutes every morning and occasionally reading a business book. No, by learning I mean scheduling periods of time every week that you spend studying and practicing, learning new skills and acquiring new knowledge that will develop your skills and increase your effective knowledge so that you can get more done, make more money, and prepare for your next step up life's ladder.

It may be that the last time you did this was in a school of some kind—high school, college, or a company-sponsored training program—when you were more or less compelled to study. If this is the case, a better question is, when are you going to take intelligent control of your own training program?

In reality, you have always been in control of your own training program. Even as a small child, how much you learned had more to do with your attitude than with your teacher's ability and methods. Certainly as an adult, only your own drive and initiative can keep you developing your skills and knowledge in ways that will keep you moving forward rapidly. In fact, the top producers we've talked with attribute their tremendous success to the knowledge they gained after they thought they knew it all.

Devoting part of your time to self-training allows you to increase your capabilities instead of merely growing older. It's one of the few ways you can get a favorable exchange from the passage of time.

When you look at your options, you have two basic choices.

Self-Training

Self-training involves considerably more than the solitary study of books, audio cassettes, computerized self-training programs, and videotapes. It includes seminars, lectures, and short evening courses.

At my seminars, I enjoy asking people in the audience about their hobbies. They will often go on and on about how much satisfaction a particular hobby gives them, how they read everything they can get their hands on about it, and how they will stretch their budgets to invest in the latest gadget related to that hobby. My next question is why not treat selling—the career that brings in the money to allow them to enjoy everything in life—like a hobby? The greatest salespeople in the world are always seeing the pluses and minuses of every selling situation. I don't just mean the ones in which they are the salesperson. When they are buyers of anything from groceries to banking services to automobiles, they are watching the salespeople and learning from them.

If you feel good after consummating the transaction with

a salesperson, take a moment to reflect upon what he said or did that made you feel that way. The real pros will make notes about it.

Read every selling magazine, newsletter, and book you can get your hands on. The realization of just one idea that increases your sales abilities will more than make up for the investment in dollars and time you put into finding it.

Watch your children carefully when they try to "sell" you on something they want. Watch them with other children. They are very perceptive and often very persuasive.

Make selling your hobby. Think about it as a fun and interesting aspect of your life and you will begin learning and increasing your sales income at a tremendously accelerated speed.

A Return to Formal Education

No matter what your age, you have the option of returning to the organized educational system for additional training, assuming that you can cope with the financial burdens this entails. However, don't fall into the trap of thinking that education doesn't amount to anything unless it's obtained at a college or university. Only if your goal is to become a professional in law, accounting, medicine, or one of the other traditional fields is this true. In the selling field, the best training is what works best for you, regardless of where you get it. When you're out in the field selling, a diploma hanging on your wall back at the office doesn't solve your problems. The information you learned to earn that diploma does.

In selling, people skills are all-important. You won't find them taught in many schools today—they're simply too hard to test. There are some schools, however, that have realized the importance of directing their educational efforts toward job skills required to become successful in today's marketplace. This includes skills vital to the success of those choosing sales and management careers. In fact, my book *How to Master the Art of Selling* is being used as a classroom text for salesmanship courses in several colleges around the country.

If you cannot find such courses in your area, you can learn about such things on your own.

Some people have a third option when they consider how they'll improve their skills and continue their training.

Company-Sponsored Training

These range from a casual afternoon's tour of the plant to a highly structured four-year course of intense study. Probably the company-sponsored training you'll be offered will fall somewhere in between. Company-sponsored training tends to be of high quality, and it's almost always accurately targeted on solving the problems you'll be encountering in the field selling for that particular company. In other words, it's excellent.

When company-sponsored training fails to help individuals improve, it's usually because the salespeople who need it most give it the least attention. Typically, the most enthusiastic students come from the top third of the sales force, the least enthusiastic from the bottom third.

Another astonishing reaction that's commonly encountered by some company trainers is the attitude that management is indicating a lack of confidence in salespeople by instituting a training program for them. On the contrary, management's decision to invest in training reflects their confidence that helping their salespeople do better will be good for them and for the company. One of the most self-defeating attitudes a salesperson can adopt is to resent company-sponsored training and to fail to take an energetic and enthusiastic part in it.

15 GREAT SKILLS YOU CAN ACQUIRE ON YOUR OWN

If we could reduce life's complications by a factor of about 10 million, I could give you an answer that would fit your most pressing needs today. Even if I could, your most pressing needs will soon change. As I suggested earlier, you must recognize that you are in charge of your own training and act on that fact.

Build on your strengths and correct your weaknesses. If you can't decide what to work on first, your sales manager or a salesperson friend may be willing and able to point out the strong points you can build on and the weak areas you most need to shore up.

In your search for the best areas in which to improve your knowledge and skills, consider the following:

1. Negotiation. Are you a trained negotiator? If not, why not? As a salesperson, you're uniquely positioned to benefit greatly from studying this vital skill in seminars, books, and on tapes.

2. Thinking about people. Would it help you sell if you could think about people clearly and influence them more? You can improve your abilities along these lines by working with the following books: *Influence: How and Why People Agree to Things*, by Robert B. Cialdini, Ph.D. (William Morrow and Company, Inc. New York, 1984); *Coping With Difficult People*, by Robert M. Bramson, Ph.D. (Anchor Press, Garden City, New York, 1981); and *How to Win Friends and Influence People*, by Dale Carnegie (Pocket Books, New York, 1936).

3. Become more creative. I doubt that people are born either creative or not creative. Everything points to creativity being a learned quality, not a genetic gift. See *Conceptual Blockbusting: A Guide to Better Ideas*, by James L. Adams (W. W. Norton & Company, Inc., 1980); and *DeBono's Thinking Course*, by Edward DeBono (Facts On File Publications, 1985).

4. A second language. Would being fluent in a second language help you sell? In many parts of the country, people who speak only Spanish have become a large part of the buying public. Other languages are important in many places and trades. You can invest in low-cost language courses on cassette tape and play them while you drive from one call to another to speed your progress.

5. Persuasion. Have you ever studied the techniques of persuasion? A greater knowledge of this fascinating subject may be exactly what you need to boost your production.

6. Product knowledge. You can't know too much about your product or service, and it's one area where you have to be an expert or your prospects don't have much reason to spend time with you.

7. Voice. Do you have the most pleasant speaking voice that you're capable of having? If not, voice training can be of enormous help. Check the yellow pages for voice trainers.

8. Public speaking. Public speaking is a terrific way to build confidence. Your library has a number of fine books on the subject, and your local branch of Toastmasters meets nearby to give you frequent practice.

9. Memory. As we have already discussed, an active memory is one of a salesperson's greatest assets, and it's easily improved. Great gains can quickly be made in one's ability to quickly recall customers' names and many things about them, prices, model numbers, and a host of other details. See *Total Recall: How to Boost Your Memory Power*, by Joan Minninger, Ph.D. (Pocket Books, New York, 1986); *The Memory Book*, by Harry Lorayne and Jerry Lucas (Ballantine Books, New York, 1975), and *Don't Forget: Easy Exercises for a Better Memory*, by Danielle C. Lapp (McGraw-Hill, New York, 1987).

10. Speedreading. In field sales—and certainly in sales management—people need to read a great deal in order to keep up with new developments in their industry, and to know where the best prospects are.

If you could do better by being able to read a lot faster, take the Evelyn Wood Dynamic Reading Course, available in many major cities. People who come in reading at about 300 words a minute routinely get into four-figure speeds with the Evelyn Wood techniques. Comprehension and retention are also improved.

11. Mathematics. Even today, when people often pay more for a sandwich than for an adequate calculator, every salesperson needs a confident quick command of ordinary calculation. Some sales fields demand a knowledge of more advanced mathematical procedures. Look ahead. If you can envision a situation in which you'll need more math, consider starting to improve your command of math right away.

12. Computers. If you're still dodging computers, your problems with trying to keep up using the old methods are going to increase. Today salespeople are using computers to speed many of their routine tasks. They're using them to route themselves more efficiently, to keep in touch with their customers more often, to knock out paperwork faster, to plan better schedules.

If you travel, a few minutes a night on a laptop computer can allow you to capture more details about the customers you've seen that day than you'd ever do manually. In fact, the ways that a personal computer can increase a salesperson's productivity are too numerous, and are expanding too rapidly, to be covered adequately here. If you haven't joined the computer age, get with it!

13. Touch typing. It's absurdly easy to learn to touch type today because computer programs that speed the process are readily available. If you can use a laptop in your work, a few minutes of practice a day will have you touch typing in a few weeks.

14. Delegation. As your sales increase, your need to delegate grows until you either become skilled at it or your growth stops. Read *Don't Do, Delegate!*, by James M. Jenks and John M. Kelly (Ballantine Books, New York, 1986); and *Running Things: The Art of Making Things Happen*, by Philip B. Crosby (New American Library, New York, 1989).

15. Reach for peak performance. You may be surprised to learn that peak performance is a learnable skill. See *Peak Performers: The New Heroes of American Business*, by Charles Garfield, Ph.D. (William Morrow, New York, 1986).

HOW SELF-TRAINING COMPARES TO FORMAL EDUCATION

Many people feel that there is a tremendous difference between formal education and the training you undertake on your own. In formal education at schools and colleges, courses of study are laid out and tests are given regularly with the avowed purpose of keeping the pressure on you to learn. The purpose of higher formal education is to turn out highly trained professionals in every field that needs them.

The reality of higher education often misses this goal. For example, some of our greatest writers graduated from medical school and immediately turned away from that trade. Without ever practicing medicine, they began a difficult struggle to make a success of their desire to write. In the same way, many of the nation's top executives hold degrees in almost every field except the ones their companies operate in. Someone with a degree in metallurgy will become the president of an insurance company, an electrical engineer the president of an information service, a chemist the driving force in a clothing manufacturing company.

A college education often influences a person to work in the kinds of highly structured environments that large organizations create. Furthermore, when people's formal education ends at the high school level, they seem to be somewhat better prepared emotionally for the rough and tumble of outside sales, and are more likely to take the risk of starting their own companies.

Many companies have studied the relationship between formal education and sales performance. Often they've discovered that high school grads outsell college grads by a wide margin—not in every firm, not in every line of selling, but often enough to bring into question whether the traditional four-year college curriculum turns out superior salespeople.

On the other hand, many people whose formal education ended in their late teens don't get around to much self-training until they reach middle age—if they ever do. This can be a great obstacle to success.

My life turned around when I attended a sales seminar in my early twenties that was conducted by J. Douglas Edwards. Years later I asked him to write the introduction to my first book, *How to Master the Art of Selling*.

No one has ever made a stronger case for self-training than Doug did in that introduction. The Watson he mentioned is Thomas J. Watson, the driving force behind IBM's spectacular early growth. Doug wrote:

> Watson's finest contribution to the profession of selling was his concept that no one should ever be out of training. This is a very profound idea. You don't have to go to school today to continue your training, to keep on learning. There are books, cassettes, lectures, seminars, magazines, videotapes—the list of training and learning sources goes on and on. If you stop training and learning you start sinking. Nobody can float; you're either rising or sinking. It's been this way for a thousand years. The only difference is that you can rise, or sink, a whole lot faster now.

CONQUER THE CHALLENGING SKILL OF DELEGATION

Should you hire people to do things that have to be done, but that you don't have to do yourself? Heavy hitters of the permanent type build up support teams. This allows them to concentrate on what they do best (usually the part of the work they like best) without letting the paperwork or other details suffer.

When you're first starting to get into the big time, you might feel uncomfortable about hiring help. It takes time to train people to do things your way. Delegation is not entirely a plus; some loss of efficiency and a changed way of doing things has to be accepted in order to gain the ability to handle more business.

Delegation is usually put off as long as you can do it all yourself by working longer and longer hours. Time passes and you get tired. Then one of two things happens:

> (a) You hire help for routine tasks, and concentrate on the vital things that only you can do; or,
> (b) You begin letting details slide, get a reputation for

poor follow-through that dries up your referrals, and fade out of the ranks of the heavy hitters. This problem doesn't go away by being ignored. When your sales production reaches the heavy-hitter level, either you put (a) into effect or (b) sneaks up and hits you in the back.

CHAPTER SIXTEEN

POOR TIME MANAGEMENT: A CAREER KILLER

For most people who get into selling, the sales job is the first job in which they've had no one telling them specifically what to do. There are no teachers, parents, supervisors, or foremen keeping them on a schedule. They must plan their own time. Too many people in selling careers fail simply because they haven't mastered the ability to control their time. They have a strong desire to retain the freedom offered in a selling career, but they don't have the strength to master their time effectively. Managing your time in selling is an awesome responsibility. If you are willing to accept that responsibility, you must also create a burning desire within yourself to master time management techniques. You must develop a tremendous pride in your ability to manage time in order to do it well.

To determine whether or not you're handling your time well, ask yourself this question: "Based on my overall production, which is a reflection of my ability to properly manage my time, would I buy stock in me?" If your answer is no, you need to learn to control your time and temper your freedom or you'll find yourself becoming a "job jumper," possibly jumping right out of sales entirely.

Most people see the major problem as the fact that there are only twenty-four hours in a day; we need thirty or forty. But, since the number of hours in a day isn't likely to change, we have to make hard choices about what we'll do with our daily allotment of twenty-four measly hours.

HOW TO GRAB CONTROL OF YOUR TIME

Most of us like the idea of controlling our time. We have the feeling that if we could just somehow manage to get on top of things once, we'd be okay from then on.

But it doesn't work that way. Running your job instead of letting your job run you is a skill, not an accident. Things will always happen to shove you temporarily out of control—a change in the market, a vacation, or a family problem. But if you're skilled at grabbing control of your time, you can quickly recover from these commonplace events.

Many people have a pile of paper on their desks that represents things they haven't gotten around to finishing. Buried in the pile are notes about important projects they must complete, memos they need to read, notes for memos they have to write, forms they need to fill out, magazines they should read, and all sorts of other stuff.

HANDLING PAPERWORK FAST

Here are some tips on handling paperwork fast:

1. If it has to be done sometime, do it now. The quickest way you can handle any paper is to finalize it the first time you see it. The ideal is to "touch paper once."

2. If it doesn't have to be done, trash it now. Don't make pets of paper you don't need; the longer the stuff hangs around the more overwhelming and discouraging the sheer mass of it becomes.

3. Develop a double standard of accuracy for paperwork. If big numbers are involved, give it your best grade of accuracy. If big numbers are not involved, give it your fast estimate grade of attention.

A champion realizes that he or she must operate like an independent company. The nature of the sales profession is that you are really in business for yourself. In fact, many salespeople have more freedom than most small business owners enjoy.

Because we in sales have so much latitude to do things when, where, and how we want, many of us don't discipline ourselves. You can earn twice as much money in half the time if you'll just discipline yourself to charge into your job, get on top of it, and then stay on top.

Your company may supply you with a highly organized file system. These systems can be great, but if you have to pay the price for using them by spending a lot of time on paperwork, they're not worth it. Remember, the simpler the better.

To most salespeople, paperwork is troublesome and messy, but unless they get it done and keep organized, no money comes to them.

Ask sales managers about paperwork. They'll tell you that although the top third of their sales force generates several times the volume that the bottom third does, they have more problems with the paperwork done by the bottom third.

Why? Because the bottom people have bad attitudes about paperwork, while those in the top third are too busy to answer avoidable questions about their paperwork. So they do it right the first time. In other words, they've overcome this time waster we call paperwork: They do it efficiently.

The first rule for the fast handling of paperwork is to be clear. Learn to print quickly and clearly or else type your orders and specifications.

Champions don't risk enraging their customers with costly delays or mistakes caused by carelessly written orders. They double-check everything relating to orders for accuracy and clarity.

Taming the Task Beast in Six Quick Steps

It will go fast if you'll keep in mind that you'll need to repeat these steps in abbreviated form every day in order to stay on top of the flood of paperwork coming at you.

1. Concentrate. Clear everything off your desk except the pile of paperwork you haven't handled yet.

2. Sort. Go through that pile carefully but quickly, and separate it into three piles: Urgent, Not Urgent, and Maybe.

Urgent: Put the items you're sure must be dealt with right away in the U pile.

Not Urgent: Stack material relating to things you don't have to cope with today in the Non-U pile.

Maybe. Heap all the stuff you can't instantly decide is U or Non-U in the M pile.

3. Discard. As you sort, trash everything you don't have to do anything about. Don't put this stuff aside for future reference. You're on a drive to get on top of the paperwork, so be ruthless; get rid of everything you can the easy way.

4. Analyze. Once you've made a quick split of your stack of undone paperwork into the three piles, analyze what you've done. Which pile did most of the stuff fall in?

If the U pile is the highest, go through it again. On this pass, however, look at each piece of paper from the standpoint of what will really happen if you ignore it until tomorrow.

Will you get fired? Will you lose a large order? Will the nation's economy collapse? In other words, get some perspective on what's really urgent and what isn't.

After the second pass, there's a good chance that your remaining U pile will be very small compared to the vast heap of material you began with. Ideally, by this time it will consist of a dozen or fewer items.

Make a third pass through your urgent material. This time, review each item thoroughly enough to establish whether: (a) you can dispose of the matter now with the information you have on hand or, (b) you have to get input from other people.

If you must get information from other people before you can complete an item, make a quick guess as to how long that will take. This consideration may change a moderately urgent item into a highly urgent one.

If the Non-Urgent pile is the highest, it's a very good

sign. It means you're really getting a boost from this approach. Set the Non-U pile aside and concentrate on knocking out all the urgent items before you look at this pile again.

If the Maybe pile is the highest, your resistance to making decisions could possibly be the chief reason why you're overwhelmed with paperwork.

Are you stressed out? Mentally or physically tired? Sick? Emotionally upset?

If you answered yes to any of those questions, your problem isn't paperwork; it's whatever made you say yes. You'll probably have to solve—or at least get a good handle on—that personal problem before you can make any headway against your career problems.

If you can answer no to all those questions, go back through your Maybe pile and put every item in either the Urgent or the Non-Urgent pile.

5. Isolate the single most important project. Divide the items remaining in your U pile into A (most urgent), B (less urgent), or C (I'm not sure). Then go through the C's and force them into either A or B.

Why bother with this two-step process?

Don't—unless it saves you time. The two-step allows you to delay deciding about doubtful items until, by reviewing all the other candidates for urgent handling, you've had a chance to see what you're up against more clearly. Most people find the two-step quicker than trying to put everything into A or B piles straight off.

Take the remaining urgent items and again divide them into A, B, and C; then reassign all the doubtful C's to either A or B. Continue narrowing your urgent items down in this way until you have isolated the single Most Important Task (MIT) for you to work on now.

6. Clear for action and start firing. Take everything off your desk that's not needed to complete the MIT. Then push your MIT as far forward as you can push it.

You'll get distracted from time to time by phone calls. And people will come to your desk. Handle interruptions as quickly as possible; you're okay as long as you don't start working on something else of your own free will.

Make a note of each new demand on your time on a To Do sheet or a master list of some sort. Many successful people use 3 × 5 cards for these notes. The cards can be handled easily and can be discarded as soon as the item is completed. Then, put the item on your pile of things to do, and get back to work on your original MIT.

THE SIMPLE WAY TO GET THINGS DONE

Over the years, I've noticed that successful people— those who lead companies, build estates, and fulfill their potential—don't spend much more time working than many unsuccessful people do. The difference is that the successful people have the ability to get more productivity out of each hour.

How do they do it? Their method is amazingly simple. In fact, it's so simple that many people just won't believe it works and won't give it a thorough trial. Now, I've given this method to thousands of people who have tried it and come back and told me that it works. And they still can't believe how simple it is.

The whole idea centers on not trying to do too much. It's an established fact that the average person can't successfully handle more than six things on his mind at any given time. But why try to keep those things on your mind?

It's far more effective for several reasons to write them down. Writing them down forces you to compress these matters into a few words, that is, to summarize them.

Even more important, it forces you to think about six items in terms of doing something about them instead of simply worrying about them. On their list of things to do tomorrow, nobody is going to list "Worry about . . ." It's obvious to even the most worry-prone that you won't make more money, improve your health, get that promotion, or achieve some other goal by reminding yourself to worry about something.

There's a third reason for writing down what you should do tomorrow. When you've summarized each item into an action, you can rank them in order of importance, route yourself, or otherwise decide what order is best for doing each of them. In other words, writing those six things down plans your tomorrow. When your day is at least loosely planned, you will accomplish a great deal more than if you simply show up at work and start swatting at whatever bees and wasps buzz around your head.

And here's a fourth reason. As you think about and write down which six items you should do tomorrow, you'll automatically tend to list the most important things and steer clear of trivia. In using this method, you'll also notice that you'll sleep better. By having your next day planned, you won't worry about what's going to happen. Your subconscious will work on the events of the day while you sleep, thus allowing you deeper relaxation and a better night's sleep.

It's one of the most powerful habits you can form: At the end of every day, write down the six most important things you must do tomorrow. That's simple enough, isn't it? But it won't have much effect on your life unless you make it a firm habit that you always do.

There are several reasons that this simple method works. It makes you focus on tomorrow before tomorrow gets here and finds you too busy keeping up to plan ahead. When you focus on the six most important things the night before, you're making tremendously important decisions about your future.

You're taking command of that future and not letting it run you haphazardly. Not many people—fewer than one in a hundred—want success badly enough to plan their tomorrows each and every night. You can put yourself into the top 1 percent of all success-seekers by adopting this system today.

The first time you do this, you'll need to jot down as many things as you can think of. Ask yourself, "What should I have done today that I didn't do?" Go on to, "What are the most important things I can do tomorrow?" Don't let it bother you if your list is impossibly long. Keep revising your list until you have it down to six really important things.

Then, rank those six items in order of priority or best time to do them. Some things can only be handled at certain hours of the day. Write those six items down and put them in your time planner. Handle them in their order of priority and you'll have a tremendous amount of satisfaction at the end of tomorrow when they're all checked off your list. Then, tomorrow evening you can sit down and clearly line up the six most important things for the next day.

Sometimes you won't be able to complete all six of the tasks you scheduled. Don't let that bother you; instead, learn from it. You may have listed something that you couldn't complete because working on it revealed additional complications.

Allow yourself some room on this list too. Don't start with six things that take three hours each to complete. Know your limitations. I can help you become successful, but after all, you're still only human. Don't give yourself twelve hours of work to accomplish in an eight-hour workday. By planning these six things the night before, you can figure about how much time each task should take and be able to have a smoothly flowing day.

The other reason for planning your day in the evening instead of first thing in the morning is that your mind will work on the tasks you face while you sleep rather than keeping you up nights. Have you ever experienced this? As you lie in bed the night before an important business meeting, you're thinking, "Tomorrow I've got to make this presentation. I'm going to tell them . . . and show them . . ." and so on. You don't get a good night's sleep and the presentation the next day goes poorly.

If you have planned your presentation the night before, when you're finally in front of that client, powerful words just flow out of your mouth. You handle the presentation just right and all goes well. Have you ever been in this situation and said something so effective that it almost stopped you? You may have wondered where it came from.

It came from your subconscious mind, from a response your mind kicked out to the stimulus you gave it. You gave your mind the stimulus when you were lying in bed the night before, mentally preparing yourself for the meeting. To gain this tremendous help, I recommend that you review your list of things to do tomorrow just before going to bed.

Your subconscious mind is there for you to use in any way you like. Take advantage of it. It'll often amaze you with what you really know and are capable of achieving.

Pull out your planner right now and go to your section for tomorrow. Allow yourself to put only six items in the slots for tomorrow.

But don't make it complicated. If you're not using a planner of some sort, I highly recommend that you get one as soon as possible. If nothing else, invest in a small notebook that you can carry with you at all times and write down everything you need to know or do.

So, if you want more from life, you have to use all of the resources available to you. Use this simple system for three weeks. I mean, fully commit to it every day for twenty-one days. If you'll do that, you'll learn—as I did—that this simple system, used with an efficient planning book or system, can help you achieve a tremendous amount of success.

AREAS TO PLAN

Let me give you some things that should appear in your planner in order for you to make the most effective use of your time:

1. Your scheduled appointments. Write them down first and foremost in your planner. If you don't write them down, you're going to miss some of them.

You might think you'll never miss an appointment, but when you get into a busy period—as you certainly will once you start planning your time properly—it can easily happen. Not because you're careless; it happens because as you move into higher levels of production you also move into higher levels of concentration. You'll miss an appointment because you're concentrating with unaccustomed intensity on another opportunity.

2. Research. Today's world is changing faster than ever before. For this reason you need to set aside time at least once each week for learning what's new in the market.

The only way you can truly benefit your clients is to be an expert in your field. Before a new product line, or an old product with a new development, becomes available, you must sit down and research it. Analyze its benefits so that you can explain them competently to your prospects.

3. Family. Start writing down all important family events—birthdays, anniversaries, school events your children are active in, and so on. The majority of salespeople take care of their clients well but forget that their families need them just as much.

If family times are written in your time planner, you won't forget them, thus increasing the quality of life you have with your loved ones. You'll be showing them that their needs are as important to you as those of your biggest client. If you promise your children or spouse that you'll do something with them, write it down and be there so that you don't lose them while you're climbing the ladder to success.

4. Physical Health. Write down the physical program that's going to keep you in shape. And, by the way, true champions—in sports, in sales, in any aspect of life—are highly concerned with their physical well-being. Why make a lot of money if you're not going to be healthy enough to enjoy it?

I'm not suggesting that you become a physical fitness fanatic; just don't let your health take a dive because maintaining it rates zero when you allocate your time and determination. You need balance between your mental and physical sides, between your acquisitive and maintenance drives, between your health-building activities and your health-weakening appetites.

5. Prospecting. Write it down. If you don't write down the hour or the times you'll do it, it'll always be the tail-end thing you never get around to doing.

Let's face it: in sales you're in the people business, and this means you must constantly meet new people. Why? Because any business that has new people calling constantly wanting to buy the product (I don't know of any such business) doesn't need a sales force; all they'd need would be a few order clerks. In any normal kind of selling business, you prospect or peter out. There's no middle ground.

6. Play. The top people in sales are the hardest working, but guess what? They're also the hardest playing. Playing is good if you've earned it.

The problem with some salespeople is that they play without earning it. By doing that, they're playing with a feeling of guilt. Plan your schedule to reward yourself on a regular basis with play time after effective work. Then, you won't have the guilt problem.

7. Company activities. By setting aside time for company activities, whether it be for sales meetings, luncheons, or company parties, you'll be mentally prepared for them when their time comes.

Do you have a weekly company meeting? Sales pros never miss a weekly meeting. You might be sitting there thinking that I don't know what your weekly meetings are like. They're so boring you'd rather skip them.

Think this through. Someday if you're in management you'll realize how difficult it is to have an exciting meeting planned every week. And to what extent are your meetings boring because you and the people you influence don't participate enthusiastically?

You should be a mature human being by now and understand that growing companies must believe in organization and structure. Supporting that view is called being part of the team.

Companies exist to perform activities that individuals can't do by themselves. Taking a job with a company declares to the world that you have chosen to devote your efforts to accomplishing objectives that demand greater resources than you possess as an individual. If you then avoid the meetings the company stages to provide communication among its staff, you stand in the way of the company's progress.

Managers will remember. When passing out benefits— for example, territory changes, choice assignments and leads—they are likely to favor the salespeople who demonstrate their team spirit by attending meetings enthusiastically.

If you look on participating enthusiastically in meetings as brown-nosing, you have a serious problem with your attitude. That problem will prevent you from achieving very much while working with a company. Your attitude problem is unlikely to have a great effect on the company's future, but it will have a negative, and perhaps a disastrous, effect on your own future with any firm you work for.

I suggest not only that you be on time for the meetings but that you bite your tongue on running down the company or the meetings it stages. Participate. Get involved. Be enthusiastic. Make suggestions.

Prove that you are a part of the team or you'll soon find yourself looking for another team. In business, as in war, there's a heavy compulsion to feel, "If you're not with me, you're against me." Don't be surprised if your manager marches to that drum.

Let me bring up one other point here. Never run down the competition when you're with a client. It destroys your professionalism. I've heard many salespeople try to slide it in by saying, "I really can't, as a professional, run down our competition, but . . ." And that word "but" gets them in trouble every time.

8. Education. Plan time to attend seminars, to take classes, and to read books that interest you. Constantly make yourself grow with new ideas and concepts. Don't miss any educational opportunity that comes your way.

9. Spiritual needs. While you're meeting all your other opportunities and obligations, plan time for practicing your religious beliefs. Doing so instills purpose and emotional security in your life as nothing else can.

TIME ALLOCATION

Now that you have the areas in which to plan, let me suggest approximate time allocations for the most effective sales work.

Prospecting

Spend only 5 percent of your prospecting time getting ready to prospect and 95 percent actually on the phone or in the field. Some beginners spend half their time getting ready; a few spend all their time getting ready. Prepare and practice your lines the night before.

There's no substitute for on-the-job training, and the only way you can get that in prospecting is by dialing a number and talking to a potential client. When you're new, spend 75 percent of your overall working time prospecting (that's six hours out of an eight-hour day).

Do that and you'll soon be in the top group in your company's sales force. You'll have the old-timers on the force walking around muttering, "Who is this person? How can a rank beginner come in here and outsell me in a few months' time?"

Preparing for Appointments

You should be so well organized that you need spend only 8 percent of your time getting ready to make top-quality presentations or demonstrations.

Presenting

When you're new, between 5 and 10 percent of your time should be spent actually in front of customers. Don't hang around—get in and get out. Your customers will have more respect for you if you move things along.

However, don't let yourself fall into the trap of taking shortcuts. You must perform each presentation as if it's the most important one you'll ever give. Don't leave anything out. You may have given the same presentation a thousand times, but you must give your best with a tremendous amount of enthusiasm every time.

As you become more organized and experienced, you'll be working more with referrals. This means you'll be able to spend more time actually selling. The elite of our profession have secretarial, clerical, and technical help for the express purpose of allowing them to spend nearly all their time planning and presenting.

Merchandising and Servicing

Five percent. Keep in mind that these starting percentages will change as your sales operation matures. Your initial prospecting will develop leads, then sales, then referrals. You'll start making money—and you'll prospect less because you'll be working with referrals more.

I MUST DO

I'd like to pass a great gift on you to—twelve words of wisdom given to me when I was twenty-one that have made all the difference in my career. First, let me tell you how I came into possession of this remarkable gem of wisdom.

After I started doing pretty well in sales—doing well but not breaking any records—I thought, why not get a few ideas from someone who is more successful than I am? That makes sense, doesn't it?

At a seminar I heard a man give a brief speech, although his speech didn't interest me as much as his introduction did. This man, the president of a gigantic corporation, earned a salary of $400,000 a year—that's about $2 million in today's dollars. I decided I could learn something of enormous value from this man.

It took me two months to get the appointment for lunch. But I was persistent and finally obtained it.

Incidentally, I heartily recommend to anyone not doing as well as they'd like—in sales or in life in general—that they take out to lunch a person they consider to be successful and learn from them. Don't fritter your lunch breaks away on people from the office who can't help you. Don't let lunchtime become a time waster for you; use that valuable time to move forward.

Sitting at lunch with the corporation president, I said, "Sir, I only have an hour with you. I'm here for a very sincere reason. I want you to tell me how you've become so successful."

He smiled and started talking about various things. After about twenty minutes I think he realized how sincere I really was.

"Please tell me what I have to do to make it," I said.

"Tom, I have lived by a saying all of my life, and it has made all the difference. If you live by this saying, you'll be a success too," he said.

Now, that's pretty heavy, but it was exactly what I had wanted to hear. I looked around nervously. I didn't have anything to write on. I wasn't really prepared to take notes.

I grabbed a napkin and my pen and said, "Give it to me . . . give it to me."

"If I give it to you, there'll be days you'll hate me for it," he replied.

"I don't care, just give it to me," I said.

"Tom, if you will live by these twelve words you will be a tremendous success," the man said. "It will be hard, sometimes you'll flinch, but if you really live by them you can't miss."

I couldn't keep all of my impatience out of my voice. "What are those twelve words?" I begged.

"I must do the most productive thing possible at every given moment," he said quietly.

I sat back, feeling shocked at the simplicity of it. For a minute or two I didn't say anything while I studied this revelation. It seemed so basic. Yet as I turned it over in my mind the enormous power of the concept began to fill me with excitement. That moment is etched in my memory because I have spent my life since living those words.

What is the most productive thing for you? Think about it.

Is sitting in the office with other salespeople productive? Usually not.

Is spending time on avoidable personal calls during working hours productive? No.

Is sitting on a beach in Hawaii soaking up the sun productive? Yes, if you've earned it by doing the most productive thing possible with your working time.

Enjoying a vacation is productive for two reasons: replenishment and proof that goal setting really works. If you don't recharge your batteries, some day they won't start your engine. If you don't actually reward yourself for achieving production goals, you'll lose faith in yourself and your goals. And your loved ones will lose faith in your motives for working so hard.

Let me also tell you, as the gentleman who gave me those twelve words did, that there'll be days when you'll hate me for inflicting them on you. But I also know that there'll soon be stretches of time when you'll bless me for giving them to you—if you live by them.

Start doing the most productive thing possible at every given moment and you'll not only enjoy a high income, you'll also become a finer, happier person. Please realize that the most productive thing at every given moment isn't always something aimed directly at making money.

The most productive thing you can do during many given moments is to be with your loved ones, relaxing, playing, re-energizing yourself. Rest and recreation are essential to the productive rhythm of your mind and body.

FILES TO KEEP

I like to use inexpensive 3 × 5 card files. How much more simple can it be? With the system I use, you only need four different categories.

1. The Client-Buyer File
Break this file into three sections: hot, medium, and cold.

Hot
The people in your hot file have the need, are qualified to buy and are sincerely interested in making a decision soon. When buyers are truly interested, they'll make a decision

within seven days. That doesn't mean they'll all purchase your product within seven days, but they'll make a decision on a product within seven days. A champion tries to work with between three and five highly motivated buyers at all times.

Some salespeople have a large stack of leads and don't call any of them. Average salespeople have rubber bands around their pack of prospect cards. When their attitude is down, what doesn't come off? The rubber bands.

Then, after a couple of weeks, they start feeling good again, so they start calling their best leads. Guess what? Those hot buyers didn't wait; they've already bought.

If you're the call-too-late salesperson, what will this disappointment do to your enthusiasm? Put it in another nose-dive? Or will it make you perk up your pace and keep in touch with all your buyers as frequently as possible? Keep feeding them bits of information. Keep demonstrating your professionalism and the service your company offers. Keep in touch so that you'll be able to keep on closing sales.

Medium

The medium file is for people who are apparently qualified, have the need, but are not yet highly motivated. Perhaps they're waiting for some future event to heat their medium needs up to a hot need. Learn what it is and try to make them heat up faster.

Cold

The third section, the cold file, is for all the leads you get from any source that you don't immediately classify as hot or medium. These are people who were just looking, who walked in, or who called in from ads or signs and seem to have a mild or future need for what you sell.

Keep in mind that few people call on ads, or come in when they see a store or sign, unless they have a definite interest in the product or service that's offered. Very few people spend their days wandering around looking at products and discussing services they have no need for and couldn't buy if they did.

The average salesperson is too quick to dismiss these people as being unworthy of any effort at all. If you do that, who will they go to when they truly have a need? Your competition. Don't let that happen to you. Treat every prospect with the same attention and respect because eventually, they'll all need your products and services.

Champions go through their client-buyer files every three days, spotting the best opportunities that day for adding heat. Every time one of their hot buyers gets happily involved, they find a medium prospect to put on the front burner.

And, all year long, they keep in touch with everyone in the cold section. Depending upon the itch cycle for what they're selling and the individuals involved, they'll be in touch once every ninety days, once a month, once a week— in any case, often enough to make sure that when their buyers' needs for their product or service shift into the do-it-now mode, they'll be the first person their buyers will think of calling.

Most people want everything that's new—but the average salesperson isn't organized to take advantage of this fact. On the other hand, champions know exactly what to do when their companies come up with something new.

First they work through their medium file, telling everyone about the new product or concept, knowing that it will turn at least some of those mediums into hots. When they've completed that run-through, they work on their cold files to turn some of them into mediums.

2. The Itch Cycle File
The next data base you need to maintain is the Itch Cycle File. Fill out a card on each client who has purchased from you and file it according to when they'll start to itch for something new. You must know the itch cycle for each product you sell. For example, people itch for a new car approximately every three years. When the time comes for them to start itching, you'll already be in contact with them—ready to scratch that itch. This system will keep supplying you with a fistful of hot buyers every month.

3. The Referral File

You also need to keep a referral file. This is where you put the names you gather from buyers. Contact each referral as quickly as you can and classify them as hot, medium, or cold prospects.

4. Tax Files

You'll also need to keep records of expenses, income tax deductions, mileage, and so on for income tax time. Get one idea firmly fixed in your mind: Thinking about taxes as a one-time-a-year event is a serious waste of time and cash—your time and your cash.

Keep constant track of your expenses and deductions, because unless you form this habit, you'll wind up spending several very stressful days in April trying to put together tax records out of thin air instead of working at your job. And the expenses you've forgotten or for which you've lost receipts will boom up your tax liability.

Some time planners provide you with cards just for this purpose on a weekly basis. These cards will help you develop the habit of keeping the necessary information and receipts. Whether you have a professional prepare your tax returns or do it yourself, you still have to accumulate the details; in either case your job will be enormously easier if you've done so in an organized fashion all year long.

The average new salesperson thinks he doesn't have time to keep records. He thinks he should wait until his sales have reached a certain volume. Believe me, even if you are not the highest producer for your company, you need this information. Why take the chance of losing hundreds of dollars of receipts and information for deductible expenses? Tax competence is part of sales competence. Operate like a company because you are a company unto yourself.

One last word about this paperwork. Don't fight the paperwork your company requires of you if you want to grow with them. Business lives and breathes with paper, and people who can't push their share of it along can't rise far. By having your paperwork and other resources organized you can perform with maximum effectiveness.

MULTIPLYING TIME

Staying on top doesn't mean trying to make time stand still; it doesn't require that you fight to keep things exactly as they are now. On the contrary, staying on top means that you have mastered two essential arts of living: You can cope with unavoidable change, and you can make swift, effective transitions from your working mentality to the other roles you play—spouse, parent, lover, companion, friend, relative, fitness buff, hobbyist.

There are several feasible ways to multiply time to help you achieve what you want. In fact it's done all the time. Here are some of those ways:

Delegate

Many tasks that need to be done take up time that you could use more productively in some other way. Be alert for these situations and pay someone else to do everything you can avoid doing yourself. If your closing ratio is high and you feel you spend too much time on paperwork, take some time to determine if it's economically feasible for you to hire someone to do the paperwork for you.

Do Two Things at Once

Listen to motivational tapes while you exercise. Listen to motivational tapes while you drive a car. Get a car phone.

I recommend that the tapes be motivational and/or sales related, especially early in your career. Later, you might want to try some other educational material. It won't matter so much once you've reached the top, because whatever you learn increases your self-confidence and self-image.

Make Effective Use of Waiting Time

The next time you wait for the attendants to wipe down your car at the car wash, look around. How many other customers are sitting there with glazed eyes, doing nothing and hating every second they have to wait?

You can get organized to productively use that time—

and the time you spend waiting anywhere for anything—very easily.

Load a small case with things you can productively do with waiting time: review your customer card files, educate yourself about a new product, send thank-you notes to customers, and catch up with other paperwork. You could also do personal things such as paying bills or writing letters.

KEEP YOUR SPIRITS AFLOAT

One of the greatest time-saving skills you can acquire is that of keeping your spirits soaring, or at least floating. When you're depressed, it isn't only your enthusiasm that's down; your effectiveness is down too.

You're more likely to find reasons not to do the important things that make money. Why? Because doing those things could also lead to rejection; when you're down the only thing that's up is your sensitivity toward rejection. In other words, if your spirits are sinking, your sales performance will too.

Keeping your spirits up has two sides: avoiding negative influences and intensifying positive inputs.

Deflate the Negatives

Almost every office has at least one person with whom you feel drained after even the briefest conversation; they just seem to draw all the life out of your body. If some people affect you that way, go beyond steering clear of them. Do whatever it takes to avoid getting trapped by them for any length of time. Your positive attitude is a precious asset that only you can protect; don't allow anyone to steal it from you.

Inflate the Positives

Organize your family or the people you're with so that you all get going on an upswing every morning. Some people lose a lot of their days before they ever get out of the house in the morning. You could do worse than to play a motivational tape every morning at breakfast, not only for yourself but also for your spouse and kids. It works for a lot of people; why not for you?

Daydreaming

This can be a very positive thing. Unfortunately, it's usually the opposite—people daydream about the most awful things happening to them. They daydream about losing their job, their health, their loved ones.

It's just as easy to daydream about positive things—and a whole lot more fun once you wean yourself away from the habit of depending on worry to keep your mind occupied.

Instead of daydreaming disaster, picture yourself doing and having wonderful things. Maintain that positive image. It will help you enormously by allowing you to quickly shrug off discouragement and spring back from disappointments.

CHAPTER SEVENTEEN

PROBLEMS WITH EARLY FINANCIAL SUCCESS

Salespeople because of their initial enthusiasm sometimes get off to a fast start and make a lot of money during their first few months in selling. But these fast-starters don't necessarily understand what caused their success. The fact is, few fast-starters think deeply about the whys of their success; it's too easy to assume they're just naturally terrific at selling.

I can't blame them. For my first six months in sales I made, on the average, $42 a month. So I'm impressed with anyone who gets off to a fast start in today's demanding sales climate.

Even fewer fast-starters keep much in the way of records. In other words, they're not jotting down what they're doing day by day in any sort of diary or log. Fast-starters feel as if they're riding the crest of a wave; there's no time to look around to see how they're achieving all these great feats.

They're hitting a cycle. They don't have to deliver anything yet. They have no disappointed customers coming after them. There are no service problems or unfulfilled promises.

Suddenly they're not doing so well—and they don't know any more about why they're slipping than they did about why they took off so fast. Only now their problems are multiplied because the self-confidence that quick success thrust upon them has abruptly vanished. They're left with a host of negative feelings they don't know how to deal with.

WHAT HAPPENED?

Instead of working with eager enthusiasm and infectious confidence and goodwill, the fallen fast-starters suddenly discover that they hate to face customers. Even though their sales have dropped like a stone, they begin hanging around the office "catching up on the paperwork." But instead of orders, now they're turning in noncommissionable excuses.

In this situation, the tendency is to look for quick fixes and scapegoats rather than search for the real causes of the sales decline. The disgruntled fast-starters blame their companies for not developing and pricing products that beat the competition. And they blame their sales managers—when they're not avoiding them.

The sales managers, who have come to expect high performance from the fallen fast-starters, keep the pressure on. Tension grows in an atmosphere that's thick with mutual recriminations and disappointment.

Many of the disillusioned fast-starters quit in disgust. Starting over elsewhere seems more exciting than staying and building on the customer base and product knowledge they've already acquired.

Staying on top demands that we confront the real problems that are pushing us off the peak. Otherwise, we can spend all our years desperately climbing one slippery cliff after another instead of sitting on the peaks and enjoying the warm sunshine of success.

Let's look at the most common causes of sales declines.

Not Keeping Records

Professionals keep a diary or log showing how many sales calls they make, how much time they spend prospecting, how many hours a day they spend in front of people who can buy what they sell. They know exactly how many prospecting calls they have to make to find one buyer. When their sales start slipping, they can analyze the records made when they were doing great. This allows them to see exactly where their sales efforts are falling behind. Once they know the precise part of the sales chain they've allowed to snap, they know exactly what they must do to repair the damage.

Losing the Presentations' Good Stuff

In their first flush of enthusiasm, fast-starters create a terrific presentation. But as the months roll on, their presentations often lose the sharp edge that made sales—in any of a thousand ways.

To prevent this, top professionals tape some of their sales interviews for two reasons: to study what could be done or said better, and to find out exactly what worked in the past so that they can resume doing it if they've somehow slipped.

Carry a small tape recorder and record a few of your presentations. Ask permission, of course. Some of your customers won't mind; others will clam up. And some will love it. You have to know your customers. Beware that you don't use a very large recorder. Nothing takes a customer's attention from the purpose of your meeting faster than a professional recorder sticking in his face. You can buy tape recorders so small that they'll fit in your pocket. If a customer agrees to have you tape your conversation with him, but seems nervous, the smaller recorder allows you to get what you want without intimidating him.

Financial Conditions

Let's say that when you make your fast start the economy is coming out of a recession. This means that lots of buyers are making purchases they've been postponing for months or even years. While this condition lasts, you can have some very good months. Once almost everybody catches up, it's not so easy anymore.

If you raise your overhead to meet your artificially high income during this prosperous period, any cutback can hurt. Be keenly aware of the difference between living higher by paying cash for extra goodies, and buying them on credit. During a period of reduced commissions you'll adjust easily if you're on a cash basis. It's different if you have taken on higher obligations. In this case the pressure can easily hurt you out of all proportion to the amount of money involved. This happens when that pressure makes you come across to your customers as money-hungry and noncaring.

Maybe you're selling cars, and the car industry is enjoying low interest rates for a few months. As a result you're making money hand over fist. Then the interest rates are shoved back to normal and buyers start staying away in droves.

What's the solution if you're facing a sales decline of this kind?

Work smarter and harder. Make twice as many prospecting calls. Give better service. Work through your old customer lists and develop your referrals.

Cycles

Have you taken the time to look at what kind of cycles your industry goes through? Are you prepared financially for the lows in the cycle? You won't be if you've built up a huge overhead during the upturns of the market that you won't be able to carry during the downswings.

There are all kinds of places where you can find the facts and figures about your industry's cycles. Your trade associations and publications are the places to start looking. Don't fail to make yourself an expert on your industry's cyclical pattern. Few things you can learn will help you more.

For example, if you're in any field that depends on real estate, whether resales or new construction, it's vital to know at all times where the economy is on the real estate cycle. Many lines of business move in lockstep with the real estate cycle, sometimes with a characteristic time lag, such as home furnishings and appliances. If you're making a career in one of these peripheral fields, it's also vital to understand what time lag, if any, stands between your industry's sales and movements in the real estate cycle.

When was the last real estate downturn? Are we on an up cycle right now? Is this a good time to go into debt? Or is now a dangerous time to add debt because it looks like we could have a downturn soon? What you do in these situations, unfortunately, can hurt your attitude. And if your attitude goes, you're out of business.

Getting into Too Much Debt Too Soon

The entire economy is highly cyclical. If you go heavily into debt at the wrong time and can't carry the debt when things turn down, it gets pretty depressing for your financial future. Instead of being able to work harder in the downturn to keep yourself successful, you're so busy trying to cover debt and coping with problems and worries that you're not effective.

WHO DECIDES HOW MUCH DEBT YOU'LL TAKE ON?

One sales management philosophy is to urge—and sometimes pressure—their salespeople to get into as much debt as possible. The idea is that this makes the salespeople work harder.

You may be told that management would like it if you drove a fancier car to enhance the company's image. This is fine for some salespeople because of the prestige. The fact that they have to make the payment may be good for their selling.

But for other salespeople the thought of a $500 car payment changes their whole attitude. That payment is on their minds every moment they're with a customer, and it makes them come across as being hard, money-hungry, and totally disinterested in what's best for the customer. As a result, they suddenly plunge into a sales slump.

I have an acquaintance who is a top salesperson in his company, earning a rather large income. On a recent visit with him, I noticed a new van in his garage. When I asked him why he bought it he said, "I had a day open up." I asked him what he meant by that and he went on with, "I work best when I have a bill due each working day of the month. That's my motivation. If I don't close enough sales today, I can't pay for the van this month. Tomorrow, I work for half the house payment and so on. If I have a day without a bill, I'm not motivated to work."

You have to understand your own personality. If you feel more comfortable with $500 a month in the bank than with $500 a month due on a car, you need to know that about yourself and not just let people—your sales manager or anyone else—talk you into buying the new luxury car you don't need. You have to really know yourself before you assume higher debt.

There are two kinds of salespeople in relation to debt. The people at one extreme aren't effective unless they feel totally secure. They've got to have money in the bank, no worries about their job, and only a small amount owed on bills.

Then there's the other extreme, salespeople who are never self-motivated unless they're carrying a heavy load of debt. These people, if they start getting comfortable financially, simultaneously start slowing down. By backing off their activity, they hit a plateau of effort and income. Thus they don't achieve the outstanding income they're easily capable of reaching because they literally can't cope with being financially comfortable.

These two types of people look, walk, talk, and act the same. Yet they are motivated by debt in opposite ways. If you find this hard to understand and relate to yourself, consider your upbringing.

Perhaps you were raised in a family situation of, let's say, scarcity. Little money was available as you grew up. Your parents lived on a strict budget. They, like so many Americans, lived from paycheck to paycheck. As a result, your parents may have instilled fears and insecurities in you—scars of scarcity—that remain part of your personality for your entire life.

Many people raised in extreme scarcity have a real problem if they don't have a financially secure base. Often they cope with this discomfort by choosing careers that offer more security than money. If they go into sales work, maximizing

272 ▲ TOM HOPKINS' GUIDE TO GREATNESS IN SALES

their security remains their major goal, even if they pursue it unconsciously.

They also have a problem if they suddenly start making a lot more money than they're used to. Floods of money rushing down on people who are emotionally unprepared for it can really mess them up. It can create ego and self-image problems because they're used to scarcity. Having been taught and raised by parents who had adopted scarcity as a life-style, they find sudden abundance and financial security strange and therefore worrisome.

On the other hand, you may have been fortunate enough to be raised under circumstances in which wealth or a high financial standard was the norm. As a result, you may only function well if you're under the stress of obtaining the abundance you're used to. You need that pressure. It's nothing unusual for you.

You may need to be deep in debt to be motivated. Some salespeople coming from a background of abundance are so petrified of scarcity that they can be immobilized if they don't feel sure they can achieve financial abundance.

So analyze yourself. Ask yourself these questions:

"Were my parents able to cope with financial insecurity?" If not, did they teach you similar feelings?

"Was I raised in abundant circumstances to the point where I expect abundance and fear not having it?"

"Can I function well with little money in the bank, or do I need lots of it?"

Neither makeup is right or wrong. You are what you are, and you'll be far happier and successful if you understand who you are and where you came from and decide where you're going. Debt can play a tremendous part in your success or failure, but it's all determined by you in the way you handle debt and financial growth.

THE EFFECT ON FAMILY

How will added debt affect my family? With more debt to pay, it's likely you'll be putting in longer hours. The extra time probably has to come out of the hours you formerly spent with your family.

If you're a salesperson, everything you do affects your attitude. If you're married and aren't able to devote enough time to your family and you feel guilty about it, that's going to affect your selling.

Whether you're a salesperson or a sales manager, it's vital to realize that anyone's sales performance ultimately depends on how well his career and personal life meshes. Family pressures have ruined as many salespeople as have poor sales.

More and more you'll find yourself staying late at the office. "And now I've got to work this weekend." How's that going to affect your selling attitude?

On top of all these negatives, if you take a large share of your family's disposable income for a $500-a-month car payment, how will your spouse feel?

You need to be sensitive about these things and avoid making emotional decisions, or yielding to management or peer pressure to boost your debt load. You're in a business in which your emotions can govern how well you're going to do. If you feel bad, unfortunately you're probably going to sell bad. If you have a bad day on a nine-to-five desk job, you will still be paid. You can, in essence, hide in the office, and bury yourself in paperwork. You will be forgiven by coworkers for having a bad day. In selling, staying in the office means less income, and customers are not quick to forgive bad attitudes. So as a salesperson you need to do whatever you can to keep your emotional stability on a level plane.

Over the years I've seen hundreds of salespeople going up and down emotionally. Almost always, their selling performance—and their incomes—follow their emotions closely.

Selling is great there, awful here. It would be far more productive for the most volatile salespeople to replace their occasional spurts and catastrophic dives with a steady pace. Those who perform consistently earn far more over a year's time than do salespeople whose production follows their emotional peaks and valleys. The consistently high sales performers run themselves more like a business. They control any leanings they might have toward excessive emotional reactions. By steadying out their performances they make their personal lives more enjoyable, their families' lives more enjoyable, and their relations with their customers more enjoyable too.

HARDER THAN MAKING MONEY

Keeping money is harder than making money. Even very powerful and wealthy people fail to do so over long periods of time. Had the Medici family in Florence, Italy been able to keep their enormous 16th-century fortune together, and keep it working at 5 percent interest, they could own the world today.

Hundreds of sports and entertainment figures in Europe and America have earned large incomes in their careers and died penniless.

Keeping some of the money you make doesn't happen without careful planning and the exercise of considerable discipline and intelligence. You can't start too soon. Divert some of the money that flows through your fingers into income-producing investments that will be there after your earning power has peaked.

YOUR VITAL NEED FOR AN EMERGENCY FUND

An emergency fund is a sum equal to six months of your present income set aside in a savings account. This money you don't touch for any reason unless you lose your job.

Some people don't accomplish anything unless they're driven by a compelling need for quick money. To such personalities, emergency funds are sure disasters because they'll do nothing until they've spent their emergency fund's last nickel.

If you're not that type, however, an emergency fund can be a source of great power to a salesperson. In compensation discussions, knowing that you're not able to pay your immediate bills if you have to walk away from your job allows you to negotiate from a position of strength. In price negotiations with customers, an emergency fund also provides great strength. An emergency fund can significantly reduce the stress you're under in your daily routine.

Once you have an emergency fund built up, you're in a position to consider setting a financial independence goal.

SETTING A FINANCIAL-INDEPENDENCE GOAL

What your goal should be depends on what you want to have and do. To some people, the goal of financial independence is simply to live in a style that pleases them. The more adventurous want to have enough money to conquer a specific challenge: float over the Himalayas in a balloon, explore a cave no one has been in before, win an ocean race.

Others crave to be remembered long after they're gone, and accomplish this purpose by funding an activity that will outlast them. James Smithson, who never visited the United States, left a bequest that established the Smithsonian Institution in Washington, D.C. Today Smithson is known to millions; when he died in Scotland nearly two centuries ago it's doubtful if ten thousand people knew of his existence.

My definition of financial independence is to be able to live in a style I feel is comfortable, and to do it entirely off the income generated by my net worth. Your definition of financial independence may be quite different.

What's important is to have your definition firmly in mind. Until you know exactly what you mean by financial independence, it's not a real concept that you can set a goal on.

For example, let's say that financial independence to you means living in comfort off your net worth, and $2,000 a month coming in will satisfy your concept of comfort. Different cycles of the economy will provide returns on investments ranging from 8 percent to 12 percent, so we'll use 10 percent as an average. If your goal is $2,000 a month, it takes an investment fund of $240,000 earning 10 percent to bring in the $24,000 annual income you need to be able to live on that level without working.

Desired Monthly Income	Annual Income	Investment Fund Required	Average Rate of Return
$2,000	$24,000	$240,000	10 percent
3,000	36,000	$360,000	10 percent
4,000	48,000	$480,000	10 percent
10,000	120,000	$1,200,000	10 percent

Let's say you feel you need $240,000 when you retire. How do you go about accumulating it? There are just five simple steps:

1. Figure out how much time you have to do it; deduct your present age from the age at which you want to retire. For example, let's say you're 25 now and you want to retire when you're 50. Your time frame (the number of years you have to accumulate your retirement funds) is 25 years (50 − 25 = 25).

2. Decide on the interest rate you feel confident your investments will earn over a period of years. I recommend using the more conservative 8 percent column (see table on page 277). If your funds earn more, great. The chances are that your level of expectations will rise between now and when you retire.

3. Divide the amount you need by the amount you find on the following table opposite the number of years you have to accumulate your fund. (For example, you've determined that you will need $240,000 in 25 years. The table shows that $1,000 a year saved at 8 percent compound interest will give

you $73,613 in that time. Divide $240,000 by $73,613; the answer is 3.26.

Now multiply $1,000 by 3.26 to get your answer; the amount you must save for 25 years at 8 percent to accumulate $240,000 is $3,260 a year.

4. Divide that amount by 365 to figure out the amount you must save each day. In this case it comes to just $8.93, or $268 a month.

5. Do it. Put an amount equal to that given in step 4 aside every day, and at the end of the month pop that sum in the bank.

SAVINGS TABLE .

The effect of depositing $1,000 each year for the period given at various rates of compound interest.

Interest Rate				Years Saved
8%	10%	12%	14%	
1,080	1,100	1,120	1,140	1
5,975	6,250	6,542	6,845	5
14,647	16,173	17,882	19,793	10
27,387	32,152	37,866	44,719	15
46,107	57,887	73,086	92,713	20
73,613	99,332	135,311	185,121	25
114,028	166,081	244,543	363,044	30
173,412	273,579	437,321	705,620	35

Select an investment fund goal that inspires you and then work your plan to achieve it. An essential part of the plan must be the commitment of a set dollar amount or a set percentage of your earnings to savings every month.

After you've accumulated investment capital through savings, you're in a position to take advantage of investment opportunities that offer greater returns than 10 percent. But, without investment capital, those opportunities are closed to you. The key element is to begin accumulating a given amount each month.

When you begin making investments outside of federally insured savings accounts, be aware that seeking a higher rate of return automatically involves accepting a higher degree of risk. Keep the remark that Will Rogers made firmly in mind. Rogers said, "I'm not so much concerned with the return on my investment as I am of the return of my investment."

THE REAL CHALLENGE OF BUILDING FINANCIAL SECURITY

The real challenge in building personal financial security is not only in making money; it's in keeping part of it for the rest of your life.

Most salespeople lack the discipline to put aside a significant part of their monthly earnings to build their investment funds. As a result, they lose the most dependable wealth-building power known to mankind: compounding the returns on investment.

How many twenty-year-olds realize that if they put $1,000 in the bank at 8 percent interest and leave it there until they're sixty, they'll have $21,724? Compound interest—interest paid on interest already earned—is a wondrous thing.

Sure, inflation will eat up some of that interest growth, but by no means all of it. And, while that sum is accumulating, it's also providing the emotional security that helps its owner make better career decisions.

Let's consider the average earnings of salespeople in the United States. Average annual earnings in a recent year were:

Entry-level salespeople:	$25,000
Middle-third salespeople:	$37,000
Top-third salespeople:	$63,000

By putting away 10 percent of gross earnings before taxes, even a trainee can have a rapidly growing investment fund. Let's assume a $2,500 annual savings. At 10 percent interest that program will have accumulated $144,716 in 20 years.

However, when top-third salespeople begin saving 10 percent of their incomes, in 20 years their annual savings of $6,300 will grow to $364,685 at 10 percent interest. It's worth noting that only $126,000 of that amount represents what they put in; $238,685 is compound interest their savings have earned. As I said, compound interest is a wondrous thing.

CHAPTER EIGHTEEN

THE INEVITABLE SALES SLUMP

WHAT IS A SLUMP?

A slump is a sudden decline in productivity, which shows up rather quickly in your personal bottom line. If you keep charts and graphs of your activity, you'll be able to see a slump coming before it strikes a devastating blow. In many cases, you'll be able to change your course of action to lessen its overall effect.

Jump starting a sales slump—that is, finding a way to give your sales a big boost fast—is a four-step process. Take it one step at a time and you'll get quicker results than if you charge off into the sunset before you know what you're doing. Here are the four steps:

1. Acknowledge the fact that you're in a slump.

Sometimes this is the hardest part. Denial is a common reaction to unpleasant developments; many people react this way when they discover a health problem. Instead of admitting that something is seriously wrong and seeing a doctor, they do nothing and hope the problem will go away by itself.

But, like serious health problems, sales slumps won't go away unless they're treated properly. When your sales are down sharply, admit to yourself that you're in a slump. Then resolve to take vigorous action that will allow you to work your way back into heavy production.

2. Figure out exactly why you're slumping.

If you've been keeping accurate records of your activity, you'll quickly be able to determine if the slump is self-induced or not. If you find yourself making fewer calls, you need some self-motivation. If you are finding it harder to close sales, you may need additional sales training. If customers are just not buying, it may be your product or the marketplace.

Until you know precisely what disease has infected your sales performance, you can't inject the only antibiotic that will cure you. No one gets over pneumonia by taking quinine for malaria. Don't automatically assume it's you, either. Take the time to investigate the market if you don't know it inside out already. Maybe there's a new product out there that's taking some of your market share. Look at the other salespeople around you. Are they slumping too? If their sales are down too, chances are the problem is not all you. If they're selling about normal, you will have to take an in-depth look at what you are or aren't doing properly.

3. Plan how you'll counteract your selling problem.

This means scheduling precisely—and completely—how you'll jump start your selling recovery. For example, let's say that your analysis of why you're slumping reveals that you've fallen out of the habit of prospecting heavily enough to sustain a high level of sales. To cure this problem precisely, schedule a specific number of prospecting calls every day.

However, making this work calls for a complete solution. This might require you to develop an effective new source of good prospects to call; it might require you to improve your prospecting skills with study and practice; it might demand that you set exciting goals for yourself and motivate yourself as you've never done before.

4. Do it.

Study, analysis, and planning are vital, but what actually brings you out of a slump is working your plan. If you were making forty calls a day when you were at the peak on your charts and graphs, do it again. Get on the phone or out in the field and start doing what has to be done to make the sales you need as soon as you've sketched out your plan. Don't wait for morning. Don't stall until Monday, next month, the new quarter, the first of the year. Start rebuilding this minute. The time to jump start your slump is now. Perhaps all you will need is something as simple as an adjustment to your presentation or an increase in prospecting. But, whatever you decide it is, you must act upon it immediately.

WHAT MORGAN SAID

Between 1895 and 1912, J. P. Morgan dominated America's financial affairs; no one before or since has ever matched his enormous influence. One day Morgan was approached by a man hoping to get a profitable tip on the stock market.

"What do you predict the market will do in the next few months?" the man said.

Morgan growled, "The market will fluctuate."

Your sales will fluctuate too. Part of the ups will come from your skill and determination, part from favorable market conditions. In the same way, part of the downs will come from favorable market conditions, part from your lack of skill, energy, and determination in adjusting to and overcoming the marketplace's changed conditions.

As a professional salesperson, you must accept that sometimes the market will be up and sometimes down in your industry. You can't control that any more than you can control the movement of the planets.

You can control your attitude, however. You can also adapt your thinking to the new market conditions and change the way you operate. By learning how to do that, you will learn how to make a better than average income in all phases of the economy in general and in your industry's cycles in particular.

THE TWO GREAT SLUMP MISTAKES

It's a great mistake to blame your slump entirely on a down market. Why? Because that makes it okay for you to whittle on a stick until the market turns up again.

It's an equally great mistake to blame yourself for all of a sales slump—unless you're almost the only salesperson in your company having one. Even if that's the case, it's far better to think in terms of taking responsibility for the slump instead of blaming yourself.

The difference between blaming yourself and taking responsibility is greater than you might think. Blaming yourself sets you up for all sorts of negative have-to responses likely to make your prospects feel you're only out to get their money.

Taking responsibility leads you toward more positive want-to responses. This means you're more likely to operate in ways that show your customers that you really care about them and their problems.

So now we've isolated two kinds of sales slumps: (a) the kind mostly kicked off by tougher competition or a drop in demand for what you're selling, and (b) the personal kind, where your sales are down but just about everybody else's are normal.

The two kinds of slumps have another distinguishing feature. The first is caused by outside forces beyond your control, the second by internal emotions and attitudes that are completely under your control—if you choose to exercise control instead of allowing your feelings to control you.

Many salespeople react the same way to both kinds of slumps. Some do this by spending their days and nights blaming themselves in long, agonizing bouts of negative thinking that leave them in no shape to sell anybody anything. Others do it by blaming the market, the product, the company, their boss, their territory—anything or anyone else—instead of assuming responsibility themselves for increasing sales.

The two kinds of slumps should be treated differently. If the market is down, change tactics. If the market is okay but your sales performance is down, go back to the fundamentals. Let's take a closer look at these options.

TACTICS

Look on the bright side of a down market. A down market gives you the chance to work with the smaller accounts you couldn't cover during boom times. A down market also gives you a fine opportunity to work with people and departments you don't ordinarily call on at your larger accounts.

Think creatively instead of reacting negatively. How can you help train your customers' people to operate more profitably? How can you help your regular buyers save money? What can you do to help your heaviest consumers increase their sales even more? Working in greater depth with your clients, prospects, and purchasers can put you in a solid position to score big when economic conditions improve. Psyche yourself up to be a bright spot in their day when calling on customers in a down market. Times may be bad, but your enthusiasm and positive attitude will carry you farther than the salesperson who agrees with all the gloom and doom being presented in the news.

Investigate whether there are untapped sources of business and types of potential buyers in your territory. Use your imagination. Risk a few cold calls—you have nothing to lose except the slump you're fighting to get rid of.

Have you been relying entirely on personal calls in the field to unearth new prospects? If so, try spending more time on phone prospecting. In a down market you have to dig deeper faster for more and better prospects. It may be time to readjust your goals and reallocate the percentage of time you spend on each area of sales.

Consider a prospecting campaign through the mails. Keep it simple and inexpensive; address postcards or letters by hand and be sure to follow up by phone.

FUNDAMENTALS

When your sales skid during a good market, it usually means you're somehow not swinging the bat right. Often your problem is almost identical to that of a major league baseball player suffering a batting slump. Just like you, his income is threatened by the slump, his sense of self-worth is wavering, and he's probably trying too hard. The relaxed confidence it takes to bat well (sell well) seems impossible to achieve. The slump's pressure can send both of you looking for the wrong kinds of relief in bad places.

What's the right thing to do?

Go back to the fundamentals.

To the batting cage and the training ground for the ball player. In sales, going back to the fundamentals means reviewing your basic selling skills and techniques, perhaps deepening your product knowledge and updating or perfecting your presentation in the process.

You may need to prospect more. Your goal should be to see more people every day who need what you sell and are capable of buying it.

Records

Review your records and compare what you were doing when you were selling well to how you're spending your time today. Lately, have you been prospecting as much as you did then? Have you been spending less time servicing your customers than previously? Are you getting fewer referrals these days? If so, why?

The answers to those questions, or others that you can devise for yourself to fit your exact circumstances, will point directly at the cause of your slump. Knowing the cause identifies the cure. I found I was always better after a slump than I was before it began because of the learning experience. Unfortunately, slumping is a costly course to take.

The Opportunity

Look on a sales slump as an opportunity to rebuild and increase your selling skills. When things are going well you have little incentive or time to improve; when things are tough you have the need and pressure to improve. Don't let it slip by. The new skills you acquire and perfect during a slump will send you soaring to greater heights than ever during the next up market.

The Chance

Adversity gives you the chance to demonstrate that you have what it takes to be outstanding. It's no great thing to do well in boom times; what marks the truly effective self-starter is outperforming the pack in tough times.

THE LUMPS AND BUMPS THAT MAKE FOR SLUMPS

In previous chapters we discussed stress and burnout, two closely related conditions that often lead directly to sales slumps. Unfortunately, a sales slump almost always intensifies a salesperson's stress and burnout symptoms. The added strain tends to make the person's sales slump even further, and that redoubles the stress. If this dangerous downward spiral isn't reversed, serious consequences can follow.

Beating a sales slump seems to call for greater effort; yet putting forth greater effort can be a dangerous response from highly stressed, burned out salespeople. In these cases, smarter effort directed toward realistic new goals can be more helpful.

I recommend that you take my burnout test in Chapter Twelve once every month. If your numbers are on the increase, it's likely you're headed for some sort of slump. By recognizing this early warning sign, you can take action immediately to lessen the burnout effect on your productivity.

Snowballing

In a sales career more than in most kinds of work, you're usually snowballing down if you're not climbing up. That is, when things are going right they build a positive momentum that makes more right things happen. This takes place more often in sales work than in routine jobs because success in the selling game depends heavily on having the confidence, determination, and energy to keep hitting.

Unfortunately it often works the same way when things start going wrong: the negatives build their own momentum into a devastating downward spiral. Simple changes in your operating methods can switch your snowballing from positive to negative.

For example, getting a different car that doesn't have a cassette player could undermine your motivation.

How? A busy day in the field generally puts you through a series of emotional ups and downs that chip away at your determination and confidence. One of the best ways to keep yourself hitting on all eight cylinders all day long is by playing inspirational and motivational tapes while you drive from one call to another. There's no better way to ensure that you'll recover from a hard knock quickly. But if you switch cars and start driving one that only has a radio, what happens?

Driving between calls, you listen to music and the news. The news is always bad because the media moguls know that's what keeps people listening. So instead of a push up from a motivational tape you get a push down from hearing about the latest poison in the food we eat, another drop of the dollar, or a terrorist bombing. Then, between commercials, you listen to music that does nothing to increase your motivation.

That adds up to maybe two hours a day of down-push replacing your former two daily hours of up-pull. Keep it up over several months and this minor change can put you into a sales slump all by itself.

You have to know what's good for you psychologically, what's good for your physical and mental health. How much doom and gloom about stuff you can't do anything about can you put up with before it starts tearing you down?

Now let's take up some of the other causes and then talk about cures.

Lack of Proper Management

The lack of proper management can cause slumps, but you can't use that as an excuse for poor performance if you want to stay in sales. The fact is, the odds are against your having a top-notch sales manager throughout your sales career. Even if you do, what are the chances that your top-notch manager will have enough time to work with you as much as you want? They're very rare.

In other words, for most of your selling life, you'll have to rely primarily on your own resources. And sometimes you'll have to rely entirely on yourself. But isn't that what you wanted when you went into sales? To be independent, to make your own schedule, to call your own shots?

Anyway, you're not a windup toy; you can't depend on someone else to get you going every day, every week, or even every month. Face it: Windup toys cost money, they don't make money. You have to take it on yourself to figure out what gets you down and how you can avoid those bad things, and also what gets you up and how you can bring more of those good things into your performance and lifestyle.

Putting it another way, digging out of slumps and staying on top demands that you carry on a determined, ongoing effort to discover how to motivate yourself by learning how to get more mileage out of what motivates you the most.

Dodging Problems

Not being able to confront problems—whether they are personal, economic, or in the product or service you're selling—is one of the most difficult kinds of sales slump to deal with. If you have this problem, the first success-barrier you have to beat down is obvious: you have to face the fact that you are dodging problems so much that it's hurting your sales performance. You may need professional help to reach that conclusion before you can even begin to solve the underlying problems you've been dodging.

If you suspect that this is the explanation for your less-than-satisfactory sales performance, check it out. I've included a list of all the qualities a strong salesperson needs and the things such a person must do. Rate yourself from 0 to 10 on your performance in each of the areas on my list. Then study the items on which you placed your lowest numbers. Chances are that any problems you've been dodging lie in those fields.

The Qualities of Strong Salespeople

_____	1. They are well-organized.
_____	2. They use a time planning device.
_____	3. They schedule and spend time each day prospecting.
_____	4. They fill out paperwork properly and on time.
_____	5. They return phone calls promptly.
_____	6. They maintain a positive attitude by avoiding gossip, jealousy, and negative thinking.
_____	7. They attend all company functions.
_____	8. They invest monthly in their minds.
_____	9. They have performance goals established and keep records of their sales figures and performance.
_____	10. They send thank-you notes every day.
_____	11. They have written down their life's goals.
_____	12. They make time to keep themselves and their relationships healthy.

Don't stop here. Work out a plan to improve your performance in each of your low-scoring areas.

Whether or not you actually do anything effective to improve your performance in those low-scoring areas will tell the tale. If the main barrier standing between you and greater sales performance is your habit of dodging problems, you aren't likely to do anything about the low-scoring areas you've discovered. More probably you'll ignore this whole section.

However, your habit of dodging problems will continue to block progress until you conquer it. If you won't move forward on your own, don't stagnate; get professional help.

Salespeople by definition are professional problem solvers. If you can't solve your own problems, you'll never master the ability to solve the problems of others and become a top salesperson.

Family

Another name for this cause of sales slumps is guilt. Your spouse can make you feel guilty because you're putting in so many hours. And it isn't always the spouse who does this. Sometimes you lay the guilt on yourself without any help from your spouse or anyone else except the people who gave you your value system when you were a child.

Regardless of who it comes from, guilt of this kind can reach the point where your subconscious mind starts searching for ways to ease the strain. If you give yourself a guilt hit for not spending enough time with the kids and your spouse, you can easily talk yourself out of working effectively. You can spend your time on the job worrying about the family, and when you're with the family you're worrying about the work you're not getting done. At all costs, avoid this kind of reciprocal destructive behavior.

You promise your boy that you'll show up for his Little League game, and then something comes up that makes keeping your promise very tough. You can sit there thinking, "Why don't I get into something where I won't have to work these kinds of hours?" The next thing you know, you're not working those kinds of hours. It can work on you subconsciously, eating away at your productive thrust.

What's the solution?

Recognize that you have to mesh making a living with having happiness.

Recognize that doing this will always pose problems no matter what field you're in.

Recognize that the key element will always be how well you manage your time, how well you balance your career's demands against your family's needs.

The salespeople who get in the most trouble in this direction are the ones who always put their jobs before their families. No matter how keenly someone in their family wants them to attend an activity, any hint that the job needs that time will win out. When that happens, this message gets through to the family: "You're not important to me." Generally the situation heats up slowly, until suddenly it breaks out into a gigantic crisis that can send the compulsive worker into an emotional tailspin. In sales that spells slump.

Other Problems at Home

To some degree, everybody has problems at home or in their personal lives; very few people consider their personal situation to be absolutely perfect. Yet most of us manage to shut our personal involvements and problems off—or at least turn their volume down—while we're working.

However, some salespeople have such severe personal problems or are so undisciplined (the two things often go together) that they fail at the necessary task of separating their private lives from their careers. In other words they take their personal problems to work with them.

For many people, work is merely an irritating interruption to their almost total concentration on their personal concerns. Can such a person be effective in sales? Not likely. It's far more likely that not only will they be ineffective themselves, they will also drag down the people around them.

If you want to reach the top, or stay on top, you must draw a line between your individual difficulties and concerns on the one hand, and your career responsibilities and opportunities on the other. This doesn't mean that you can't respond to a major personal emergency; certainly you do that. However, your standard routine must be to handle your personal affairs on your own time in such a way that you're free to devote your working hours wholeheartedly to your career. In no other way can you achieve your full potential.

Other People in the Office

The attitude of the other people in your office can drag you down. Nearly every office has a Joe Negative—sometimes she's Jo Negative. Every negative development, or even possibility, throws Jo or Joe Negative into high gear. You hear an exhaustive analysis of how bad things are going to get before you can make your own judgment.

One good thing about the J. Negatives of the world: They soon acquire such a reputation for crying wolf that most people ignore them. Yet their constant harping on defeat, disaster, and doom has a way of getting to you.

The best way to handle the J. Negatives is to consciously ignore them. If they insist on getting their message to you, I suggest you simply tell them, "I don't have time to be bothered with that, I have work to get done," and you're off to a good start. If one of them comes up to you croaking his usual downside line after that, don't dodge the problem. Look him straight in the eye without smiling and say, "I'm not interested."

Chances are that will work the first time, and from then on you won't have to listen to all the bad news J. Negative can dream up. You'll be able to concentrate on building the enthusiasm that makes for high sales.

Sacrifice

Sacrifice can cause slumps. Let's say you're working hard to provide everything for your family. Maybe you're supporting your parents and putting your kid brother through college. There's nothing left over—time or money—for you. And one day you ask yourself, "Why am I doing all this?"

You'd better know exactly why you're working so hard. You'd better get some satisfaction and happiness out of it for yourself. Otherwise, one of these days you'll go into a slump that, because so many people are involved, can be emotionally devastating when the whole bunch go down the drain together. That's why I keep going back to the value of goals. By having your goals in writing so that you can sit back and take a long look at each of them, you'll be able to see whether or not your life will be in balance. If it's not in balance, it'll be ten times more difficult to achieve those goals. By having balance and knowing where you're going, you'll eliminate the feeling that you're making sacrifices.

Other Personal Problems

Under this heading I'm going to cover a whole flock of personal problems without getting too specific about them. All sorts of addictions, obsessions, and negative habits, of thought or action, can prevent people from achieving what they desire in life. One of the worst of these personal problems is a feeling that success is more trouble than it's worth.

Most of these personal problems stem from a lack of clearly defined and ardently desired personal goals that are attainable. Without goals to inspire them to want to put forth greater effort, few people operate under enough self-discipline to accomplish much.

Playing the "Busy Game"

Salespeople who play the "busy game" spend their time getting organized instead of seeing people. Their paperwork is always on time and usually it's perfect in every detail—but they just aren't doing any new business.

A simple change can solve this problem quickly: Make your calls before you touch your paperwork. Then, after you've put in a good day in the field, do your paperwork in the time that's left.

ECONOMIC CONDITIONS THAT CALL FOR ADJUSTMENT

You can't control the swings that your industry or the economy go through. However, you can control how vulnerable you let yourself become to the alternating cycles of recession and expansion. How? By refusing to take on more debt during an up period so that your income in a down period will be enough to meet your payments. In good times, pay cash for what you want; in bad times, borrow only what you can repay with current income.

Recession

In the 1970s the Northeastern states were going through a painful adjustment. Century-old companies were closing plants and in some cases going bankrupt. Suddenly, vast numbers of formerly well-paid workers were jobless nonspenders. Thousands of salespeople and other professionals who had never worked directly for the troubled industries soon saw their incomes almost vanish in a ripple effect.

Many of the Northeasterners saw opportunity in the Texas oil boom and moved there. But booms have a way of busting. When the oil glut drove the price of crude through the floor, the energy boom collapsed. The people hit worst were the recent arrivals from the Northeast because they hadn't had time to pay off homes and otherwise get set to withstand another recession.

If you want to get away from a regional recession where you live, don't jump at the first place you hear is booming. Before you make your decision, also consider moving where the economy has been holding steady or gradually improving.

Increased Competition or Obsolescence of Your Product Line

If increased competition or product obsolescence is the primary reason why your sales are down sharply, just about everybody else in the company will be hurting too. This means that management must take the lead in solving the problem. Are they moving aggressively to strengthen the company's competitive position?

Sometimes problems with the product are so severe that you start avoiding prospects and customers. If you sell for a service organization, you can have the same problem with the company's policies. Your career and future are at stake too; you have the right to know what's being done and when the countermeasures will take effect.

Sometimes management's attitude is that the product's problems will go away by themselves if they're ignored. In this case, it might be wise to protect yourself by investigating other employment opportunities.

SLUMP CURES

Records

After a bad month, you need to work harder. But unless you kept good records when things were going well—a daily log of how you spend your time—you'll have a tough time seeing where you've been going wrong. Very few people do keep these helpful records. They don't seem to realize the value of keeping a journal when things are good. Take the time to write down what you are doing, how you feel, and some brief notes on the other areas of your life as well. Keep your old sales quota records or ratios. Save your planner sheets. You have to have something to compare today's activities with. Keep these records so you can prove to yourself what works and what doesn't.

The longer you keep these records, the more valuable they become. Leads you followed up on and cold calls you made two years ago are probably the mainstay of your last year's sales success.

Do you know that your follow-ups and colds calls last year put a solid foundation under this year's sales? The easiest way and probably the only way to be sure is to keep good records.

Goals That Work Wonders

When I talk about goals, I mean clearly defined and ardently desired personal goals that are believable because they are attainable. Not easy, attainable. What is an attainable goal? It's something you can achieve with sustained effort and driving determination—something that will call on you to stretch your abilities without breaking your resolution.

When you have a set of balanced personal goals in all the

major areas of your life, they perform another vital function. They simplify decision making, so that it's enormously easier to keep on track. By reflecting on your set of balanced goals, temptations and opportunities that conflict with them are more easily avoided.

But keep in mind that to be effective, goals must be written down. If you only think about them, they're almost certain to remain wishes.

THE MOTHER OF EFFECTIVENESS

The mother of effectiveness is self-discipline. Without self-discipline, we don't do the things we know we must do in order to succeed; without self-discipline we always do the trivialities first, often spending all our time doing the least important things while the vital opportunities slide out of reach. Without self-discipline we substitute the dubious pleasures of avoidance for the real satisfactions of getting the job done right.

Self-discipline by definition comes from within. All I can tell you is what worked for me: I cultivated a burning desire to succeed. A burning desire to succeed caused me to define specific goals that inspired me to greater effort. In the pursuit of those goals I kept my credo constantly in mind: **I must do the most productive thing possible at every given moment**.

INDEX